J. William Fulbright

J. William Fulbright

Advice and Dissent

Eugene Brown

University of Iowa Press Iowa City

University of Iowa Press, Iowa City 52242
© 1985 by The University of Iowa. All rights reserved
Printed in the United States of America

Library of Congress Cataloging in Publication Data

Brown, Eugene, 1943–
  J. William Fulbright: advice and dissent

  Bibliography: p.
  Includes index.
  1. Fulbright, J. William (James William), 1905–   .
2. Legislators—United States—Biography.   3. United
States.   Congress—Biography.   4. United States—
Foreign relations—1945–   . I. Title.
E748.F88B76   1985   973.9′092′4 [B]   84–16134
ISBN 0–87745–130–3

To Diane, Karen, and Jennifer

Acknowledgments

ONE OF THE PLEASURES of seeing this work come into print is to acknowledge some of the people whose help and encouragement have meant so much to me. I'm especially grateful to Professors Edwin Rutkowski, Walter Filley, James Young, and Charles Forcey of the State University of New York at Binghamton for their aid and support.

My research in Washington was greatly facilitated by Dr. Michael Prucker, now on the staff of Congresswoman Barbara Kennelly. During a professional detour in Florida, Lori Schirard typed and commented on portions of the draft, and librarians Genevieve McMillen and Ruth Hansell procured hefty amounts of inter-library loan material for me. In Pennsylvania, Susan Karli graciously offered to type the final manuscript.

I wish also to thank two scholars, Professor Forest Grieves, now at the University of Montana, and Distinguished Teaching Professor Edward Weisband at SUNY-Binghamton, whose example and encouragement have shaped my academic life.

Finally, I record my deep love and thanks to my family.

Contents

Introduction

IN A LESS TROUBLED time he might have attracted little notice. His quiet diligence and determinedly uncharismatic manner would likely have yielded a bland, if untainted, public career. Inclined by upbringing and temperament toward scholarly solitude and earnest oratory, there is little about the man—either in the public facts of his early life or in his private manner today—that hints of polarizing dissent, public acrimony, and media celebrity. Improbably but indelibly, however, it is as a leader of foreign policy dissent that J. William Fulbright is remembered.

This study of Fulbright's public career has two main goals. First, it seeks to uncover elements of continuity and change in Fulbright's views on American foreign policy. Secondly, it tries to discern the evolving relationship between his ideas, on the one hand, and the nation's policies and outlook on the other. But beyond these immediate, formal goals lie other, more serendipitous reasons for taking a retrospective look at Fulbright's thirty-odd years of public life, not the least of which is the opportunity it affords us to take the measure of a genuinely interesting man. Urbane and bookish, a former Rhodes scholar and university president, Fulbright fits few of our ordinary notions about what politicians are like. By turns witty and caustic, innovative and tradition-bound, profound and banal, Fulbright has often seemed a figure of paradox. Surely the root paradox is that of the contemplative man of ideas caught up in

1

the turbulent routines of public life. It is, indeed, this fusion of intellect and influence in Fulbright's life that continues most to spark the interest of students of politics. Thoughtful people must sometimes despair over the apparently limited power of ideas to shape political tides, but before surrendering to the gloom of our deepest doubts, we might profit from a reconsideration of Fulbright's labors. He is, one remembers, the author of the international exchange program that bears his name, the man who stood with courage against McCarthy's coarse onslaughts, who urged the nation to discard its foreign policy myths and grasp changing global realities, who fought for the restoration of congressional power in foreign policymaking, and who helped lead the Congress and, eventually, the nation to repudiate its tragic course in Southeast Asia.

This study was born of a long-standing admiration for Fulbright's efforts to bring reason and clarity into the nation's foreign policy. Those of us whose political outlooks were irreparably altered by the charms and terrors of the 1960s retain, likely as not, a distinct memory of Fulbright as a leading opponent of the Vietnam War and, more generally, an articulate critic of American foreign policy. So firmly fixed is his position as foreign policy critic that the principal published account of his career bears the declaratory title *Fulbright the Dissenter*.[1] Virtually everything written about the man has taken his famed dissent as its point of departure, implying more than demonstrating that Fulbright has proceeded from a world view that lies outside the bounds of conventional postwar American thought.

A typical academic treatment claims that "his dissent . . . amounts to offering a new universe of discourse."[2] Another has Fulbright striving to "introduce novel opinions into the public debate of great international questions."[3] To Harvard's Daniel Yergin, he was "the famous dissenter."[4] His name became "synonomous with dissent throughout the world,"[5] his biographers wrote, while another writer insisted that "dissent is a way of life with him."[6] To *Newsweek*, he was "the great dissenter" of the day,[7] while *Time* preferred the more pejorative label of "gadfly."[8] A "Cassandra," huffed Henry Fairlie,[9] "a thinker and prophet," claimed the *Nation*.[10] Eric Sevareid styled him as "the leading American critic of America in the world,"[11] a view seconded by the *New York Times* ("the most outspoken Congressional critic of American foreign policy of this generation"),[12] and scholar Kenneth Grundy called him "the most celebrated congressional critic of this nation's foreign policies."[13] To Stanley Karnow he was "a philosopher and commentator who would rather be right than popular."[14] Another writer likened him to "a risen Pythagoras" who "has tried to entice every American head of state since Franklin D. Roosevelt into a brotherhood for the moral improvement of mankind."[15] All agree on one thing: Fulbright was different, "a nonclassifiable enigma," in the words of Russell Baker.[16] Whether viewed positively as "a thoughtful critic"[17] or negatively as an "iconoclast,"[18] Fulbright is remembered as a thinker untethered by orthodoxy.

Yet it is when one looks into this familiar, received image of Fulbright-as-dissenter that an interesting thing occurs. The ringing dissent so well fixed in one's memory has a way of thinning into ephemera when seen again from the detached observation post afforded by the simple passage of time. The point entails a good bit more than the sometimes-strained efforts of dissertation writers to find novelty where it is least expected.

We are arguing that one of the major public figures of the postwar period has been widely and seriously misunderstood. It is the thesis of this study that Fulbright's underlying beliefs about America's proper international role and interest were, in the main, strikingly similar to the dominant, mainline views long held by both the nation's governing elite and the mass public. His fame as a foreign policy critic has severely obscured the highly conservative nature of his dissent, which has typically dealt with matters of means and style rather than fundamental ends.

To so argue is emphatically not to demean the thrust of Fulbright's long labors; it is to insist that the lasting effect of those labors is bound to be limited by, among others things, the sharply circumscribed character of his critique. The burden of the argument is not that Fulbright was a less significant figure than has previously been supposed, but rather that his significance has largely been misunderstood.

In stressing the essential conventionality of the nation's leading foreign policy "dissenter" of the postwar era, we open the door to a fuller understanding of our national self. Our exaggerated memory of Fulbright's dissent allows us the comforting notion that, whatever its substantive defects may have been, American foreign policy has at least had the virtue of having undergone the fundamental, penetrating scrutiny of broad public debate. To a polity steeped in essentially procedural notions of democracy, it is reassuring to believe that our policy is the product of rational choice made after reasoned consideration of alternative courses. Inflated images of Fulbright's dissent and confusion as to the purpose his dissent was meant to serve have surely fed that flattering belief. In offering a long overdue corrective to the nation's chronic incomprehension of a major public figure, this study must at the least prompt concern about the depth and quality of what has passed for foreign policy debate in this country.

The study stands atop several assumptions which, in the name of clarity, ought to be brought from hiding. First, as distinct from a large and generally worthy body of scholarship which emphasizes the impersonal demands placed on its members by the ineluctable workings of the international system,[19] our study proceeds from the contrary view which holds that in their external dealings states can—indeed must—continually make choices from a shifting array of policy options.[20] Necessity—that sternest of taskmasters—only episodically reveals its raw demands. Inherently, the diplomatic calculus of nations must proceed, however haltingly or blindly, from existential choices made amid chronic uncertainty.

Secondly, we note that the choices made by nations are only sometimes the product of randomness and caprice. More typically, they are structured according to the beliefs and perceptions of the nation's decision makers.[21] While it may perhaps be taken as axiomatic that foreign policy is fashioned so as to serve the national interest, it is quite a different matter to hold that the national interest is at all times a self-articulate standard capable of drawing to itself a working domestic consensus. In the course of giving flesh-and-blood substance to the ghostly concept of the national interest, statesmen proceed from a conceptual repertoire legitimized by the domestic political process.[22]

In this study, we speak of foreign policy premises. By this, we mean to call attention to the values, assumptions, and logic that guide the process of defining the nation's international role. It is useful to distinguish between two kinds of foreign policy premises. The first we will call philosophical premises. This involves one's most basic sense of where the nation ought to fit into the broader global system. Should the nation define its role narrowly or should it attempt to guide the broader evolution of the international order? Should the nation work to uphold the essential features of the existing system, or seek their transformation? Should the nation seek to foster a congenial international environment by promoting its domestic values abroad, or confine itself to the narrower goal of securing its physical safety? It is little help to reply that these issues should be resolved in a way that best promotes the national interest since some will see that interest advanced by a broadly-defined international role while others will insist with equal conviction that that same national interest requires a more modest sense of our place in the sun.

As the political process elevates to official status the bearers of one or another set of philosophical premises, a second kind of foreign policy premises comes into play. We will refer to these as operational premises, by which we mean those assumptions made about the appropriate tools and actions required to attain the national sense of self, defined by our philosophical premises. What forms of power will best enhance the nation's agreed position? How functional is military coercion? Which nonmilitary tools are likely to achieve desired results? Taken together, the philosophical and operational premises adopted by its decision makers give to a nation's foreign policy a degree of order and coherence.

As a member of the legislative branch, Fulbright could not hope to define directly the nation's foreign policy premises, but sought instead to influence both the executive policymakers and, more broadly, the nation as a whole. His thirty-two years in Congress spanned the flood tide of American power. From World War II to the fall of Saigon, successive administrations, backed with rare exception by public approval or acquiescence, shared an exceedingly expansive sense of the nation's international role and interest. Nurtured by dreams of an "American century" and galvanized by Cold War tensions, postwar America and its leaders acquired an imperial sense of self which equated the national interest with the maintenance of a receptive international environment. Sharing for the most part the expansive philosophical premises of the day, Fulbright seldom looked beneath operational questions to examine critically the nation's consensual insistence on its own global primacy. It was as a self-conscious conservator of America's global sway that he denounced unilateralism, militarism, and a fervently crusading style, arguing instead that the nation's preeminent position could best be preserved by restraint and cooperative action.

We emphasize Fulbright's evolving outlook and opinions over the minutae of his role in the policy-making process because that was the emphasis of his own effort. Aloof from legislative routine, he authored relatively little legislation but sought instead to affect the broader climate of opinion through a steady stream of public commentary, and it is in this role that he is best remembered. As one contemporary account noted, "his national reputation is based mainly on his neatly-turned, tightly reasoned Senate speeches. He works them over laboriously, then rapidly mumbles through them in a near whisper across the Senate's mostly vacant desks. . . . Next day, however, because of his eminent position, his words often get front-page newspaper play and are attentively read the world over."[23] Walter Lippmann surely had it right when he wrote that Fulbright "is not listened to on the floor of Congress until he has been heard around the world."[24] But while being heard around the world, he was frequently misunderstood at home.

Our argument unfolds in stages. Early chapters narrate the contours of Fulbright's life up to 1964, including his entry into public life and his rise to the chair of the Senate Foreign Relations Committee in 1959. The remainder of the book covers the tumultuous decade from the mid-1960s through the mid-1970s, during which Fulbright's name became indelibly linked with dissent and controversy over the uses of American power.

1 *The Shaping*

of Fulbright's Views

IF ONE WERE seeking some singular, overriding characteristic of Fulbright's early life that seems to foreshadow his later conduct,
particularly his bold outspokenness, one surely would ponder the un-
commonly tranquil, nurturing security that so surrounded and graced
his formative years. Though he would later refer to his life through ado-
lescence as "a very parochial experience,"[1] it is by no means clear that his
was the constricting, narrowing kind of experience ordinarily suggested
by the pejorative "parochial." Rather, he seems to have absorbed from
his stable, affectionate environment an abiding sense of self that would
later stand him in good stead. Journalist Tristram Coffin quotes a long-
time Fulbright friend who emphasizes that the future senator came
from "the most important family in town. Never had to worry about
money. Tremendous support from the family . . . . I'm sure this is
why he could stand up to Joe McCarthy without flinching or challenge
the President of the United States."[2]

Where other, less confident politicians of his generation often took
their policy bearings from the shifting tides of safe orthodoxy, Fulbright
would follow an inner compass, once its direction was clear to him, with
sturdy resolve. To say this is by no means to attribute to Fulbright a
world view which in any fundamental way put him at odds with the
dominant outlook of America in his time. His was not—save, perhaps,

7

for a brief period early in his public career—the relentless iconoclasm of the alienated. Fulbright's personality was too well-integrated, his life too pleasant, for him to sustain the negative energy of the malcontent. Rather, what his upbringing gave him was, precisely, the courage of his convictions.

Born in 1905, Fulbright grew up in the university town of Fayetteville, Arkansas. One of six children, he was doted over by an energetic mother and became the favorite son of a successful, hard-driving father. "My father was extremely influential in causing me to do whatever I did," Fulbright later recounted. "We hit it off very well. I don't know why. He didn't get along with my older brother and perhaps I was compensating or vice versa. I don't understand all those psychological inspirations. But my father and I got along very well."[3]

The father, Jay Fulbright, had begun as a farmer in Missouri. Through an uncanny business acumen and sheer hard work he managed to parlay his originally modest means into substantial wealth. After moving his growing family to Fayetteville in 1906, the senior Fulbright began a string of business ventures that would in time include a lumber company, the local newspaper, a bank, a Coca-Cola franchise, a grocery store, a hotel, and an ice company.[4] As leading citizens of their community, the Fulbrights could bask in the comfort of affluence and social prominence.

Young Bill Fulbright elected to stay at home and attend the University of Arkansas, despite the fact that its reputation was undistinguished. During his last semester at Arkansas, Fulbright was encouraged by college officials to apply for a Rhodes scholarship. At that time, each state was allocated one scholarship two out of every three years. In the 1920s, few Arkansas students even bothered to apply. Fulbright's selection in December 1924 opened an experience that, by his own estimation, would permanently change his life.[5]

Arriving at Oxford in the fall of 1925, Fulbright soon displayed his flair for outdoor sports. In place of American football, he reveled in lacrosse, rugby, and tennis. Off the playing field, however, he quickly became aware of his academic deficiencies. He would later realize that he "never became intellectually curious until I got to Oxford."[6] By his own account,

> I was ashamed of my ignorance and lack of knowledge of literature and other things, and I began to read just to learn. I never had thought much of that at home—or of reading just to learn. Before, I had studied because it was the thing to do. I was conforming to what was expected of me. I had a minimum of intellectual curiosity from within.[7]

Fulbright read history and political science during his three years at

Oxford. His tutor was the late R. B. McCallum, a distinguished historian and later master of Pembroke College. What an opportunity for an earnest young American just discovering the life of the mind! Fulbright came under the spell of McCallum's contagious passion for international relations.

An ardent admirer of Woodrow Wilson, McCallum imparted to his pupil an abiding insistence that the international system offers its members existential opportunity for moral choice even while imposing constraints on the range of permissive action. Fulbright learned to doubt determinism of all kinds, stressing instead the real if limited possibilities of consciously-planned political action aimed at lessening the stark terrors of competitive state sovereignty. His outlook embraced a sometimes-heady architectonic insistence that man can subordinate will to reason and thus prove master of his secular fate. A rational world design consciously erected through deliberate political action seemed to Fulbright an altogether attainable ideal. He thus absorbed the philosophical idealism so ubiquitous in Anglo-American international thought in the smoldering aftermath of World War I.[8]

Yet alongside his belief in the possibility of rational choice in world affairs was a kind of Burkean caution, more instinctive than cognitive, against the sheer improbability of drastic, transforming drives. History, he came to feel, teaches nothing so much as the practical limits of reason in shaping human tides. In his view, the reformer's tidy dreams too often become, when yanked out of the gentle climes of academe and injected into the play of power, the slogans of demagogues and the chiliastic nostrums of the great mass for whom rational reflection is at best an episodic thing.

There is thus, for Fulbright, a gap between the possible and the probable in world affairs. He never entirely lost his Wilsonian faith in the possibility of collective, rational self-mastery, but neither would he be able to shake, except for a brief time during World War II, his gloomy doubts about the actual liklihood of man rising to claim the promise of the mind in place of the centuries-old cycle of brutality and war.[9]

As Fulbright's outlook was taking shape at Oxford, he soon hit upon a theme that he would sound throughout the rest of his life: the great need for a democratic society to recruit its political leaders from the select ranks of talent and intellect. Leadership, he came to feel, is one of the crucial variables in the overall well-being of a society. Only by following the lead of its most able, best prepared citizens can a nation fulfill its true potential. In 1940, years after he had left Oxford, Fulbright delivered a speech which reveals how fully he had retained, despite changing times and circumstances, the ideas first acquired during his university days:

9

Lesser people have often wondered how England, a tiny, frost-bitten island, came to dominate the greatest empire the world has ever seen. The envious seem to think that it was accidental, but such accidents do not happen. Being small, it was perhaps easier for England to organize her manpower and resources, but to my mind the real secret of her success is in the fact that her best brains, her outstanding talent, was always induced to enter politics and to direct the coordination of her every power for the benefit of the country. For centuries the English have honored their politicians above all other citizens, and have supported them, regardless of their personal idiosyncrasies.[10]

In Fulbright's view, the task of the true leader in world affairs is to strive to lessen the gap between the world as one finds it and the world we can picture in our best visions.[11] A leadership which simply codifies into policy the prejudices of the masses will be doomed to the sterile repetition of the discredited, strife-torn past. Alternately, the overly-ambitious reformer risks outrunning the pace of mass adaptation, with the result that his cherished visions become easy targets of derision by those to whom reform is inherently suspect. To lead, then, is both to accept and ameliorate a certain tension between one's own policy goals—based, ideally, on reason and learning—and the views of the mass public—based, all too often, on ignorance and prejudice. It is not enough that leaders assert the primacy of elite, educated opinion in the realm of foreign affairs. While this is often necessary, the true leader will also strive unceasingly to educate the public, thus narrowing the potentially dangerous gap between the leaders and the led.

Fulbright's firm convictions on the need for independent leadership in foreign affairs do not carry over into domestic affairs. Many commentators have remarked with dismay on the sharp contrast between Fulbright's progressive views on global issues and his retrograde stance on civil rights.[12] Fulbright himself has addressed the question directly. In a speech delivered early in his public career, he drew a sharp distinction between domestic questions on which the public holds strong views, the violation of which would surely spell political defeat, and world issues on which the leader might rightly claim superior understanding and thus must be prepared to take unpopular stands.[13] He used the question of isolationism as an example of an issue on which a true leader must be willing to risk his career: "regardless of how strongly opposed my constituents may prove to be to the creation of, and participation in, an ever stronger United Nations organization, I would follow such a policy in that field unless it becomes clearly hopeless."[14]

By the time he finished his studies at Oxford in 1928, Fulbright had acquired most of the essential features of a worldview that would guide him the rest of his life. Already, at age 23, his interest in world affairs was well formed, as were his clear views on the necessity for independent, rational leadership in the field of foreign policy. Considerably less clear was Fulbright's sense of how his own life would relate to these abstract notions.

With no concrete goals in mind, Fulbright left Oxford in June, 1928 and set out on a long, leisurely tour of the continent. Settling in Vienna late that summer, he was exposed to a cultural richness undreamed of back in Arkansas. "What I saw was a civilized society," he would later recall, and he began sampling its fruits with an unbridled joy that comes through vividly as he recounts the period more than fifty years later.[15] Opera, literature, art, cafe conversations—these were the delectable fruits of Viennese life, and Fulbright reveled in their sophisticated pleasures.

The half year he spent basking in Vienna's cultural glories gave him, once and for all, a deep sense of the primacy of a nation's domestic goals. For the rest of his life he would remind all who would listen that it is in the excellence of its domestic life that a nation finds greatness. Foreign policy can, at best, protect the peace which civilized life requires. Preoccupation with foreign affairs and an overemphasis on military might distract from the truly civilized undertakings in fields like education, the arts, and advancing the social and material well-being of the population as a whole.[16]

While in Vienna, Fulbright became friendly with the veteran journalist, M. W. Fodor. A scholarly man with an inveterate curiosity, Fodor offered young Fulbright the opportunity to meet the leading Austrian political figures of the day. In the spring of 1929 he accompanied Fodor on a swing through the Balkans. Daily contact with diplomats and governmental leaders in this cauldron of ancient hatreds left a deep impression on Fulbright. He was absorbed by the thought of how apparently limited is the capacity of leaders to transcend the elemental, centuries-old divisions among peoples and forge through reason a basis for lasting peace.[17]

Upon his return home, Fulbright enrolled in law school at George Washington University. After graduating second in a class of 135, he worked briefly in the anti-trust section of the Justice Department, where he was one of the government's attorneys in the famous Schecter case involving the constitutionality of the National Recovery Act. Notwithstanding his experience in Washington during the 1930s, Fulbright had little sense of personal involvement with the heady reform currents of the New Deal.[18]

11

Following a one-year stint as a law professor at George Washington University, Fulbright returned home to Fayetteville in 1936. For the next three years he lived a life he now regards as idyllic. He taught part-time at the University of Arkansas Law School. The rest of his time centered on his 110-acre farm where he found welcome tranquility for solitary study, indulged his love of rustic outdoor pleasures, and enjoyed his growing family.[19]

In September, 1939, Fulbright was tapped by the University of Arkansas Board of Trustees to become the school's president. At thirty-four, he was the nation's youngest university president. During the next two years he attracted national attention by his articulate commentaries on a few favored themes: "the role of education and the university, the art of the politician and the legislator, the call for greatness and the American potential, the rejection of the cliche and the questioning of myths, the hopes for peace and the pleas for new approaches to old problems, the challenges and the imperfections of democracy" as his biographers put it.[20]

Touched by the pervasive poverty of most Arkansans, Fulbright came to see his native state as analogous to a colony, owned and exploited by Eastern capitalists. As he put it to an audience in 1940:

> The finest land, the oil, the aluminum, the bauxite, and whatever minerals we had—all the cream of this accrued to somebody out of the state. All we got out of it were a few jobs at a dollar and a half a day.[21]

Federal aid to the poor states, he argued, offered hope of ending the inherited cycle of poverty and external control. In later years his support of American foreign aid to the nations of the developing world would be grounded in his mental model of Arkansas first articulated during his days as a university president.

Besides outside economic aid, he felt that education offered the brightest hope of alleviating the poverty and enhancing the opportunities of a backward area. Again, he felt that the federal government should do more to equalize educational opportunities throughout the nation. His abiding faith in the promise of education would surface years later in the celebrated exchange program that bears his name. Even today Fulbright insists with vehemence that "we still neglect education."[22] Something of the depth of his passionate belief in the promise of education is indicated in a revealing line from a speech he gave in 1939: "Man is not naturally a cooperative animal, and only education can persuade him that progress, in fact, a decent existence, is possible only by intelligent organization and cooperation which is the essence of government."[23]

By 1940, Fulbright's speeches dealt increasingly with foreign affairs. His public remarks revealed a clearly militant interventionist stance. In uncharacteristically harsh tones, he assailed the then-credible isolationists who felt that America should avoid foreign entanglements. In a speech prepared for delivery at the University of Missouri in the summer of 1940, Fulbright planned to launch a bare-knuckled assault on his adversaries. "The weasling, timid, and fearful policy of the isolationist senators is one of the greatest dangers to our true interests," ran one passage.[24] In fact, the speech was never delivered. Fearful of offending the state's isolationist Senator Champ Clark, University of Missouri officials cancelled Fulbright's invitation.

Within a year, Fulbright would again find himself caught in a political riptide. The 1940 election saw the defeat of Arkansas Governor Carl Bailey, who had been vigorously supported by the Fulbright family. Homer Adkins, the new governor, set out to put his personal stamp on the state university. Once Adkins had appointed a majority of the Board of Trustees, Fulbright's fate was sealed. On June 9, 1941—graduation day—Fulbright was fired from his post, thus becoming the nation's youngest former university president.[25]

2 *Public Service,*

1942–1959

Wartime Congressman

ARKANSAS' HOT AND DUSTY summer of 1942 found Fulbright still smarting from his dismissal as president of the university and, at age thirty-six, somewhat adrift. Certainly his prospects were by no means bleak: his family's wealth and position in Fayetteville assured him a life of ease and security, but having viewed the world from Oxford, law school, and the presidency of a university, his sights had been raised considerably.

By coincidence, Clyde Ellis, the local congressman and a friend and former student of Fulbright's, decided that summer to abandon his safe House seat to enter the upcoming senatorial race. It was Ellis who apparently first suggested that Fulbright run for Congress.[1] In Fulbright's telling, the very thought of entering politics left him somewhat nonplussed: "I'd have never dreamed of it," he recalled. "I hadn't even been in three of the (3rd Congressional District's) 10 counties in all my life."[2]

With his family's blessing—and financial backing—Fulbright entered the primary race. He soon learned that in the tempestuous world of electoral politics, what might normally be regarded as assets in one's life could prove to be liabilities with the voters. As his biographers put it:

> In the Ozarks, that year, babies still were born in log cabins and fiddlers still called the square dance sets in many a remote village; and, in the Ozarks,

14

education and money were still highly suspicious commodities. Bill Ful-bright, everyone knew, had both.[3]

Adjusting quickly to the demands of campaigning, Fulbright fought to overcome his aloof formality and present himself, as the title of a magazine article later put it, as "just a boy from the Ozarks."[4] Observers then as now have often insisted on viewing Fulbright as an impractical, idealistic visionary; those who bother to look back to this, his maiden venture in politics, will see the limits of that characterization. Noble ora-torical pronouncements aside, Fulbright soon showed a substantial streak of pragmatic realism. Four years later, in a well-known speech delivered at the University of Chicago, he would look back on his first political campaign and draw these conclusions:

> The ability to compromise and reconcile the differences among people is of the essence of (politics) . . . . There are no absolutes in politics and one learns this quickly in a campaign among the voters.[5]

While few would find in these words the stuff of cynicism, neither do they conjure up visions of millennial rapture.

When the primary votes were counted, Fulbright had won by the big-gest margin in the 3rd District in thirty years.[6] In the still-solid South, victory in the Democratic primary was tantamount to election to office; with the ritual of a general election that fall, J. William Fulbright gained formal entry to the 78th Congress.

Wartime Washington was a place of austerity and purpose. The huge influx of government workers was one more reminder, along with ration coupons and victory gardens, that the fight against Hitler and Hirohito required an all-out effort, one that could be organized only by the na-tional government. For their part, ordinary Americans were setting aside their customary antipathy toward government and its odious product—controls—and taking up the government's cause as their own.

Fulbright took office in January 1943 and grappled with the elaborate mores of congressional life that had gradually built up in more tranquil times. He did get his first choice in committee assignments, foreign af-fairs, but chafed nonetheless at the sharp restrictions placed on junior members.

So, too, apparently, did another member of Fulbright's "freshman class": Clare Booth Luce of Connecticut. Sleek and willful, she had come to know success as others know tedium, variously as a Broadway play-wright, wife of *Time-Life* baron Henry Luce, and now as an acid-tongued proponent of right-wing republicanism. Shunning tradition, she delivered her maiden address barely a month after the 78th Congress was sworn in. To a packed and delighted gallery, she gave free play to her well-nurtured gift for malevolent wit. Liberal internationalist notions she ridiculed as so much "globaloney": America's postwar role, she suggested, must rest on a hard-headed grasp of nationalist self-interest and unilateralism.[7]

On February 16, Fulbright stepped up to the House podium for his own maiden address.[8] With barely-concealed sarcasm, he set out to rebut Mrs. Luce and, by implication, her fellow unilateralists. Alternately coy and acerbic, Fulbright conceded the "sparkling beauty and suavity of manner of the honorable lady from Connecticut."[9] Globaloney, he said, is "a wonderful word which convulsed the gallery and will certainly live for many seasons in the folklore of Broadway. There is no denying it, our honorable colleague is a wit."[10] But despite Mrs. Luce's evident charms, Fulbright professed himself "not as susceptible to her logic and persuasion . . . as some of my colleagues appear to have been."[11] Arguing that "the narrow, imperialistic policy of grab, advocated by the honorable lady, carries within itself the seeds of its own destruction," Fulbright urged the Congress to begin "a thorough study of all proposals for postwar international organizations designed to prevent war."[12] At the heart of his argument lay the hopeful belief that "the only substantial benefit this nation can realize from this war is the assurance of a peaceful world, based upon a world-wide system of collective security."[13]

To this point, his very first rhetorical outing as a member of Congress seems to lend some credence to the familiar if caricaturized view of Fulbright as archetypal international idealist. Largely lost to public notice however, due in part to the media's focus on the personal styles and atmospherics of the Luce-Fulbright exchange,[14] was as bald a statement as Fulbright would ever make of his own abiding, deeper purpose: "I do not propose that we undertake some sentimental and idealistic enterprise," he said. "I believe our own selfish interests—in fact, our very survival as a great nation—is dependent upon an intelligent and practical system of collective security."[15] Fulbright's call for a collective security system was thus explicitly grounded in his self-concious analysis of America's own "selfish interests."

Two decades later, in a celebrated work, Professor Inis Claude would demonstrate convincingly the sheer improbability of collective security schemes, concluding that "from Wilson's day to our own, advocates of collective security have entertained unrealistic hopes or expectations concerning the transformation of the foreign policies of states; states are not prepared to do . . . the things that an operative system of collective security would require them to do."[16] As a purely practical proposal to enhance the nation's security, then, Fulbright's maiden address may indeed be found wanting. There should be no mistaking, however, the eminently practical purpose animating Fulbright's words and deeds as his congressional career got under way.

Here at the start of a public career that would span three decades, we can recognize certain characteristics that later became widely known as distinctively Fulbright's: a style somewhat arch and professorial with a distinct undercurrent of personal antipathy toward those of opposing views; in substance, an abiding preoccupation with world order and an acute concern about America's concept of its own role and self-interest in forging that order.

Heartened by the good notices his first speech had won,[17] Fulbright was eager to try his hand at legislative craftsmanship. In April 1943, he introduced the measure that, in a matter of months, would win him national fame. House Resolution 200, soon known simply as "the Fulbright Resolution," consisted of a spare assertion that:

> . . . the House of Representatives hereby expresses itself as favoring the creation of appropriate international machinery with power adequate to establish and to maintain a just and lasting peace, among the nations of the world, and as favoring participation of the United States therein through its constitutional processes.[18]

In this, his initial foray into policymaking, Fulbright evidenced a clear belief that the contemporary tragedy of war could lead men consciously to transform the very nature of the international system.[19] Rational self-mastery was at hand, he believed, and could be had by a voluntaristic act of will. As he put the matter to a New York gathering, where he shared the podium with such academic heavyweights as James T. Shotwell and Ralph Barton Perry, once we "rid ourselves of our isolationists' dream," we then can grasp the exciting prospect of turning "this barren, ghastly tragedy into a tremendous opportunity to create the world of the future."[20]

At this point in his life, Fulbright regarded the centuries-old state system as an anachronism, and a deadly one at that. As one writer put it, "for realists, like Dean Acheson, sovereignty was the original fact of the international system. For Fulbright, sovereignty was the original sin of international politics."[21] With the universal crisis of World War II an object lesson in the perils of competitive state sovereignty, Fulbright believed a unique opportunity was near when the peoples of the world could come to see the need for a thoroughgoing structural transformation of the world political system.

Fulbright's vision was one of radical change, consciously planned. His public comments during the war show that he did not contemplate

17

another mere confederation along the lines of the ill-fated League of Nations. Instead, a functioning world government, with the authority and power to control even the war-making potential of nations, was Fulbright's clearly sought goal.[22] On May 10, 1943, he delivered an address at Constitution Hall in Washington; in it, he gave his most fully-developed treatment of the intended purpose of his brief resolution. Emphasizing that "to do nothing, as we did in 1920, will be a decision in favor of international anarchy," he proceeded to sketch a postwar global organizatioṇ whose powers must include "the supervision, not merely of existing force, but of the productive capacity of heavy armaments, of chemical processes, or of any techniques essential to the production of instruments of aggressive war."[23]

If global transformation was the goal, Fulbright was equally insistent that it was America who must seize the moment and lead others away from the degenerate terrors of anarchy. Leadership—that was what America owed the world, and it could fulfill its mission only by casting off its instinctive isolationism. It is worth quoting Fulbright at some length in order to capture fully the thrust of his argument on this key point. Here is how he put the matter before his House colleagues in September 1943:

> It is brains and leadership that we must supply, and not merely gifts of bread, and milk, and money, and oil. It is not contemplated that we . . . are to give our goods to others, that we are to raise the standards of living of the peoples of the world, or even to give them a free and democratic government. If we can contribute leadership and our fair share of the force found necessary to make an international system of control effective, that is all the world can or should expect.[24]

The sharply limited character of Fulbright's alleged utopianism is unmistakable. American leadership in securing the peace which will maintain American leadership—this theme was clearly central to Fulbright's vision of the postwar order.

The final link in Fulbright's wartime chain of reasoning concerns the policymaking role of Congress, especially the House. Here his views are equally vivid. In his May 10 speech he argued strongly that "in the field of foreign relations the proper function of the legislative power is to express the broad fundamental policy of the nation."[25] Within the legislature, he asserted on another occasion, "since the House of Representatives is at all times more nearly reflective of the will of the people than any other body, it should play an important part in the formulation of fundamental policy."[26]

Fulbright's single House term thus found him bouyant in his hopes for the future. Politics, which to him meant reason yoked to power, offered the means by which man could consciously plan his fate. And he had no doubt that America was uniquely qualified to lead a global mission of redemptive activism.

Clearly, though, some formidable obstacles would have to be overcome before the young congressman's idea could become national policy. Fulbright's ultimate success was due in large part to his skill in dealing with three potentially crippling liabilities: the nation's residual isolationism, his lack of seniority in the Congress, and inter-branch wrangling between the House and Senate. In dealing with these challenges, Fulbright employed a strategy that mixed forceful public rhetoric with self-effacing coalition building behind the scenes.

First, opposition grounded in the nation's lingering, visceral isolationism had to be blunted. Ohio's Senator Taft, one of the isolationists' principal publicists, had taken to denouncing the Fulbright plan in shrill terms. "About the only policy which it definitely excludes," he charged on one occasion, "is one which reserves freedom of action to the United States in the future."[27] To Fulbright, it seemed clear that the isolationist position had suffered serious domestic erosion as a result of the war. Though still an estimable force, its sway over American thought was by 1943 but a shadow of its prewar strength. He thus decided to meet the issue head-on. In a running public commentary during the summer and fall of 1943, Fulbright lambasted the isolationist outlook as hopelessly, dangerously retrograde and sought to equate opposition to his resolution with the doctrine he so thoroughly denounced. Typical of his rhetorical punch was the assertion to a gathering at Columbia University that the isolationists "appeal to our emotions, our prejudices and selfishness."[28] Though we lack suitable data to measure the actual impact of Fulbright's public anti-isolationist campaign, the inability of the isolationist forces to mobilize an effective opposition to his resolution suggests that their voice had been effectively neutralized.

Secondly, there was the fact that he was a still-youthful freshman in an institution whose tribal rites included seniority worship. Today's reader might well be jolted by the extraordinary informal constraints the congressional culture has placed on its junior members until quite recently.[29] Fulbright's response to these restrictive norms was to adopt a low profile in formal House proceedings while engaging in quiet, behind the scenes efforts to recruit support from key House leaders. Crucial help was provided by Congressman Sol Bloom, the dapper chairman of the House Foreign Affairs Committee. Under Bloom's prodding, sentiment within the committee gradually coalesced around the Fulbright measure. By mid-June, the committee's fourteen Democrats and eleven Republicans closed ranks to produce a unanimous endorsement of the Fulbright measure.[30] When the full House took up the committee's recommendation, its astounding 360–29 endorsement did indeed constitute, as the *New York Times* put it, "a display of unity unsurpassed in Congress since the declaration of war on the Axis."[31]

Finally, there was the matter of inter-branch rivalry within the Congress. Georgia's Senator Walter F. George, surveying events from the lofty chair of the Senate Foreign Relations Committee, let it be known that he considered the House's iniative in postwar international planning to be a clear offense against Senate prerogatives.[32] Clearly, the Senate's traditional pride of place in foreign affairs would have to be assuaged. This Fulbright sought to do by both avoiding any public comment that might be construed as pressuring the Senate to yield its independence and by working quietly behind the scenes to promote his views on the Senate side. It soon became clear that the question was not whether the Senate would adopt a resolution of its own, but rather how closely its work would be patterned after the House-backed Fulbright measure. One proposal, sponsored by Senators Ball, Burton, Hatch, and Hill, drew fire because of its excessive complexity.[33] Another, crafted by Vandenberg of Michigan, followed generally along the lines of the Fulbright model.[34] A third measure evolved from a special subcommittee within the Foreign Relations Committee chaired by Senator Connolly. Its language was strikingly similar to the House-passed Fulbright version.[35] With the none-too-subtle support of President Roosevelt,[36] it was the Connolly measure that won easy Senate approval in early November.[37]

Of the dozens of proposed resolutions before the Congress concerning postwar organization, then, it was Fulbright's that had carried the day. Its successful passage signalled that the way was clear for the U. S. Congress to accept American participation in the United Nations. The contrast with the American rejection of the League of Nations was widely noted, and Fulbright was duly praised as a forward-looking internationalist. The resulting national acclaim would transform the quiet, reflective congressman, in the words of his biographers, into:

> . . . that American phenomenon, the instant celebrity, subjected to all of the pleasures and annoyances of fame in America: his telephone rang constantly; his fan mail increased 100 percent; his company was sought by the noted and by those on the make.[38]

Fulbright's quick rise to prominence meant that he would henceforth be counted among the relatively small circle that comprises the nation's foreign policy elite. Along with his new stature came the assurance that

his views would be routinely heard, if not always heeded, in the policy-making process. An attentive, sometimes doting, media would ensure a broad dissemination of his views among the interested public, which in turn lent added weight to those views in Washington's play of power.

The young lawmaker from Arkansas had barely begun his personal rise in the Capitol firmament when the nation was forced to confront the jarring realities of Soviet-American tension in the aftermath of World War II. Fulbright's—and the nation's—hopes for a stable and progressive postwar order were based in part on the expectation that Allied unity would survive beyond the immediate task of defeating the Axis powers. Between 1945 and 1947, however, American officials and, eventually, the public came to see in Soviet actions a pattern of hostility toward the West that would negate realistic hopes for continued big-power unity. In the wake of its disillusionment the nation would take on a growing array of foreign involvements in its capacity as leader of the western bloc. At home, mounting suspicion of the Soviet adversary issued in a tide of anti-communism whose demand for uniformity would sharply alter the domestic political climate.

Onset Of The Cold War

In his memoirs, President Truman recalls how in the early months of his presidency he became aware, particularly through the counsel of Averell Harriman, of a growing need to reassess Soviet intentions. As early as April 1945, Harriman urged the President to project a firmer verbal posture in order to disabuse Stalin of the notion that America's desire for cooperation would render it indifferent to the unilateral assertion of hegemony along Russia's frontiers.[39] Tough talk, he argued, would help rather than hinder Soviet-American dealings; Stalin's need for American assistance would prevent an open break, thus giving the United States a unique opportunity to moderate Soviet ambitions.

By early 1946 Truman had come to doubt whether words alone would counter what he regarded as growing Soviet truculence. Stalin's refusal to carry out his Yalta pledge to allow free elections in Eastern Europe, his failure to withdraw Russian troops from Iran, and his behavior at Potsdam all convinced Truman that the recent ally could well turn into a serious adversary. In January he concluded that "unless Russia is faced with an iron fist and strong language another war is in the making. Only one language do they understand—'how many divisions have you?' "[40]

At this point, however, Truman was reluctant to take his growing concern to the public. The nation's deep urge to demobilize and turn back to domestic concerns was unmistakably strong; such a public mood would render suspect any new call to arms and sacrifice in the absence of compelling evidence that Soviet actions posed a clear threat to America's own security.[41]

In this context, George Kennan's analysis of Soviet behavior contained in his famed eight-thousand-word telegram of February 1946 played a catalytic role in giving coherence to official thinking and—later—public attitudes. The "long cable" was prepared by the then *chargé d'affaires* in Moscow in response to a State Department request. In it, Kennan developed the thesis that the Kremlin leaders embrace Marxist ideology as a way to rationalize their own autocratic rule. In the name of Marxism, they insist on viewing the world as irreconcilably divided into competing blocs. The capitalist bloc, they believe, must ultimately collapse from inherent internal contradictions. While awaiting the millenium, however, Russia must act to weaken the capitalist bloc and strengthen the socialist bloc. In Kennan's view, Moscow's rulers believe that permanent peace cannot be achieved between the two sides; hence, Soviet power must be amassed and applied wherever Western weaknesses become apparent.[42]

Kennan's missive was widely circulated within the government. Its lucid analysis struck a broadly responsive chord, providing American officials, in John Lewis Gaddis' view, with "the intellectual framework they would employ in thinking about communism and Soviet foreign policy for the next two decades."[43]

The inchoate division of the globe into hostile camps, each presided over by a military superpower, was hastened by the galvanic events of early 1947. In February the British notified the State Department of their impending cessation of aid to faction-ridden Greece. Without outside assistance, Truman felt, Greece could succumb to Communist guerrillas and be brought under Soviet domination.[44] This, plus Soviet pressure on Turkey over control of the straits leading to the Black Sea, was read in Washington as a stark geopolitical challenge to the West. Truman was now convinced that the nation must meet that challenge or face an emboldened Stalin at some other point of Western vulnerability. The line must be drawn, he felt, and to do that the nation must be aroused from its postwar slumber.

Accordingly, on February 27 congressional leaders were brought to the White House in the administration's opening bid for support of the bold action it now believed to be necessary. Following a somewhat lackluster presentation by Secretary of State Marshall, Dean Acheson proceeded to paint a vivid picture of bipolar global division unparalleled since the epic struggle between Carthage and Rome. Faced with a stark world-wide ideological offensive—rather than a credible Soviet defensiveness of limited scope—the nation had no choice but to join the fray, Acheson argued. In a duel of this type, seemingly local conflicts take on global significance, since a gain for one side must invariably be a loss for the other.[45]

Acheson's bravura performance won over the bipartisan assembly. Arthur Vandenberg, the Republican chairman of the Senate Foreign Relations Committee, turned to Truman and declared: "Mr. President, if you will say that to the Congress and the country, I will support you and I believe that most of its members will do the same."[46]

The stage was thus set for the unveiling of what became known as the Truman Doctrine. On March 12, 1947, Truman addressed the Congress and, by radio, the nation. Although aid for Greece and Turkey was the immediate goal, Truman located those crisis points in a wider ideological struggle between the United States and the Soviet Union:

> At the present moment in world history nearly every nation must choose between alternative ways of life. The choice is too often not a free one.
>
> One way of life is based upon the will of the majority, and is distinguished by free institutions, representative government, free elections, guaranties of individual liberty, freedom of speech and religion, and freedom from political oppression.
>
> The second way of life is based upon the will of a minority forcibly imposed upon the majority. It relies upon terror and oppression, a controlled press and radio, fixed elections, and the suppression of personal freedoms.
>
> I believe that it must be the policy of the United States to support free people who are resisting attempted subjugation by armed minorities or by outside pressures.[47]

Truman's rhetoric—aimed primarily to rally the Congress and the public—had its intended effect. Following their president's cue, Americans were coming to view the rising East-West tension in terms of ideological conflict.[48]

George Kennan's celebrated anaylsis of Soviet motives became available to interested readers outside the government with its publication in *Foreign Affairs* in 1947.[49] The Soviets' urge to fulfill the universal aspirations of their creed will draw them, he wrote, into "every nook and cranny available . . . in the basin of world power."[50] Their expansionist drive will stop "only when it meets with some unanswerable force."[51] The United States, Kennan concluded, must respond with a swift show of "unalterable counterforce" under the overall strategy of "firm and vigilant containment."[52]

Meanwhile, domestic polls were showing a swift drop in public sympathy for the erstwhile ally, and a corresponding rise in anti-Communist sentiment.[53] The fall of China in 1949 and the outbreak of the Korean War in 1950 further fueled the nation's mounting anxiety and seemed to confirm the image of a Manichaean struggle between the two ways of life that Truman had declaimed in his historic address.

Of those "present at the creation" of America's new postwar stance, few could have known that they were setting the nation on a course that it would follow for decades to come. At bottom the new course reflected the triumph of a new set of philosophical premises about America's place in the sun, premises that rejected, once and for all, perhaps, prewar attitudes. Towering, intact and exuberant, above the ashes of World War II, it is little wonder that postwar America acquired a decidedly expansive sense of its role in the global scheme of things. The repudiation of isolationism gave free play to that strand in the American character that itches for far-flung ventures, not in the name of upholding the inherited order by submitting to the impersonal discipline of balance-of-power politics, but rather in the name of remaking that order so as to create an international environment congenial to the nation's own values.[54] From the articulation of the Truman Doctrine onward, America would approach the outer world through a domestically-dominant set of philosophical premises which equated the nation's well-being with the attainment of a pro-American global order. Henceforth, foreign-policy debate would largely revolve around operational questions of how best to attain the universal vision Truman had given voice to on that unforgettable afternoon in March 1947.

Among the president's listeners that afternoon had been the junior senator from Arkansas. Clearly, Fulbright's cherished hopes for an effective United Nations were being swept away by the chilling global rupture. In the coming months, he would be forced to reassess his own assumptions about what man could attain by way of world order and about America's role in forging that order.

Fulbright In The Truman Years

Fulbright's election to the Senate in 1944 seemed of a piece with his earlier successes. At age thirty-nine, he had won a coveted spot in the national government, one that offered an ideal outlet for his evolving interests in world affairs.

In the immediate aftermath of World War II, Fulbright took full advantage of his rising fame to set before the nation his concept of an appropriate foreign policy for the years ahead. In two speeches widely noted late in 1945 he held aloft the hope of a new international order based on supra-national organization and law. This was, of course, the vision behind the so-called Fulbright Resolution of two years earlier. But what was new in the fall of 1945 was a sinking feeling on Fulbright's part that the nation under Truman's new and uncertain leadership was adrift in foreign affairs. The scrappy Missourian, Fulbright came to feel, lacked Roosevelt's commitment to international ideals and was allowing the nation to slide into a quarrel with the Soviet Union.

In the first of his two important speeches that fall, the young senator gave evidence of a new strain of pessimism, one that never entirely left him in later years. To an elite audience at the Foreign Policy Association, he offered the forlorn observation that:

> We have lost our bearings and are unsure of our future. . . . We have had an ugly but powerful demonstration at Belsen, Buchenwald, Dachau, and many other extermination camps, of what lies beneath that thin crust of civilization so laboriously acquired by man through countless centuries of struggle up from the jungle.[55]

The horrifying destructiveness of atomic weapons—first revealed at Hiroshima and Nagasake just two months before—lends added urgency to the quest for a rational political order, he argued.[56] Such an order will require change of the most fundamental kind:

> To me, it seems clear that the medieval political status under which the world operates is obsolete, and that it must be discarded just as we discarded the horse and buggy, not overnight, but by stages as we develop the appropriate machinery.[57]

In perhaps his bluntest statement of his most basic views on the subject, Fulbright declared flatly that

> the greatest obstacle . . . is the ancient and antiquated concept of sovereignty. The absolute sovereignty of nations is utterly inconsistent with the establishment among nations of any laws with sufficient force to give confidence in their effectiveness to the peoples of the earth.[58]

The new United Nations Organization he regarded as unfortunately mere "skeleton machinery, without life and vitality."[59] In a passage that greatly irritated the Truman administration, Fulbright suggested that the U.S. should give up its then-monopoly of atomic weaponry in order to strengthen the fledgling organization: arguing that our policy should be to nurture "the creation of a bona fide organization based on law, and with force and vitality in its system," he speculated that "the control of the atomic bomb, coupled with important strengthening of the organization's powers, could be that vitality."[60]

One month later, Fulbright stepped up his attack on the administration in a nationwide radio address broadcast by NBC. "I have come to the conclusion that our government has lost its bearings, that it is drifting about in a fog of indecision," he said.[61] Arguing that "there can be no lasting peace without law," Fulbright again made the case that "the principle of absolute national sovereignty is utterly inconsistent with the existence of binding rules of conduct."[62] Criticizing the administration for seeking bases in the Pacific while objecting to Russia's search for bases in the Mediterranean and Dardanelles, Fulbright decried the fact that "our actions and policies in foreign affairs seem to be improvised on the spur of the moment. We 'play by ear' without the slightest regard for the harmony of the composition."[63]

At the heart of his address was the assertion that

> . . . I cannot understand why our present government does not exert all its influence toward the creation of rules of conduct applicable to all peoples. The logical subject matter for a beginning is armaments, including the atomic bomb. The machinery to begin with may be created by relatively simple amendments to the Charter of the United Nations. The abolition of the veto provision, and the delegation of certain rulemaking powers to the United Nations Organization would go far toward the accomplishment of our purposes.[64]

In late 1945, then, Fulbright still believed ardently in the "rule of law" approach to international affairs. From this perspective, Truman's adherence to a traditional state-centric paradigm was seen as a retrograde tendency that must be criticized and rejected.

Within a matter of months, however, Fulbright would be forced by events to reexamine—and, eventually, refashion—these deeply held views. By early 1946 the intellectual certitude that had been so apparent in his speeches just months before was now noticeably absent. Journalist Tristam Coffin believes that "his faith in the United Nations, in the reasonableness of the Allies was smashed by torturing doubts as during March, April, and May, 1946 a strident Cold War psychology . . . sprang from the earth."[65] In his own reflections, Fulbright blames the onset of the Cold War for the loss of optimism, his as well as the nation's.[66]

In an important address delivered in May, Fulbright displayed the extent of his mounting disillusionment. Terming recent Russian actions in Iran, Manchuria, and the Balkans ". . . not consistent with a policy of security only," he asked rhetorically: "is it the purpose of Russia to dominate the world?"[67] Avoiding a clear-cut answer, the senator nevertheless voiced his belief that "crusading communism appears now to be on the march."[68] Nearly a year before the unveiling of the Truman Doctrine, Fulbright asserted that "it is highly important that all the world know that, while we do not seek war, yet we are willing and able to fight whenever we believe any power threatens the right and opportunity of men to live as free individuals under a government of their own choice."[69]

By September 1946, Fulbright's attitudes toward the Soviet Union had become more fully formed. Soviet expansionism, he now believed, was the overriding fact of international life, one that necessarily negated realistic hopes of attaining a world community based on law.[70] From this point onward Fulbright essentially shared in the nation's cold war consensus. As a matter of personal taste, he would eschew the florid, breast-beating professions of America's global destiny common to other political leaders of the day. Instead, as befit an Oxford man, his articulate vision of America's world role bore the guise of the tempered, reluctant discharge of global "responsibilities," not the least of which was held to be the responsibility to lead a resistant world to a new form of international community. That the stability and order presumed to follow from a transformed system of international organization and law would serve to protect against anarchic upset America's new-found global prominence was a nuance that had not escaped Fulbright's notice.

Nor was he unaware that his eloquent pleas for world community would likely bear little practical fruit in the short-term future. Sharing the Truman Administration's operational premises on the threat posed by Soviet belligerence to our broadly-defined global role, he became—in addition to architectonic thinker—a dedicated "cold warrior," committed to the acquisition of national power and the formation of an elaborate alliance system as necessary means of thwarting what he perceived as a dangerous, unilateral Soviet offensive.

It is worth recalling that there were, in fact, vigorous contemporary protests against the nation's emerging Cold War posture. Walter Lippmann, in a collection of articles published as *The Cold War*, criticized the rigidity of the containment doctrine, calling it a "strategic monstrosity."[71] Instead of an indiscriminate, over-militarized posture, he argued, greater weight should be placed on diplomatic solutions to what he saw as essentially political issues separating the two sides.

Others questioned the political universalism of the new policy. Voiced notably by Henry R. Wallace, a former vice-president who by 1946 was serving as Truman's secretary of commerce, the liberal-left critique questioned the universality of America's interests and stressed the dangers of an overly militarized response to what was seen as an essentially political contest. In his famous—some would say "notorious"— Madison Square Garden speech of September 1946, Wallace urged acceptance of existing global spheres of influence. Advocating a realistic grasp of the rightful limits of our global sway, Wallace urged the view that "we have no more business in the *political* affairs of Eastern Europe than Russia has in the *political* affairs of Latin America, Western Europe and the United States."[72] In an apparent swipe at hardening national attitudes, Wallace asserted that "we are reckoning with a force which cannot be handled successfully by a 'Get tough with Russia' policy. 'Getting tough' never bought anything real and lasting—whether for schoolyard bullies or businessmen or world powers. The tougher we get, the tougher the Russians will get."[73] Wallace's efforts got him fired from Truman's cabinet, but won him a niche in the sparse gallery of early dissenters against the nation's Cold War globalism.

Fulbright's contemporary position was a rather different matter. Temperamentally unsuited to the style of the hard-line crusader, he nonetheless envisioned a decidedly more expansive American role than did, say, the hapless Henry Wallace.[74] In announcing his support of the watershed Truman Doctrine, for example, Fulbright avoided the undifferentiated anti-communism that had marked both Truman's address and much of the enthusiastic response to it. Instead, his position was couched in a kind of economic *realpolitik*. Soviet expansion, he argued, threatened the Middle East, upon whose energy resources our allies were so dependent. The U.S. should be willing, he argued, to negotiate with the Soviets for "an equitable disposition of these [Middle East] resources, once we can be assured that she will not take over the political domination of the region."[75] So much for self-determination by weak nations! His stated fear that expanding Soviet power in Asia and Africa would leave us "shut off from the resources and markets of the greater world"[76] reveal Fulbright as perhaps a more thoughtful and analytical cold warrior than most, but a no-less determined one.

From the earliest days of the cold war Fulbright stressed the distinction between the specific threat of expanding Soviet power, which he took to be a serious danger requiring a firm American response, and the more general challenge posed by the ideology of communism, whose peril he thought was exaggerated by domestic right wingers. In the MacArthur dismissal hearings of 1951, for example, Fulbright noted bluntly that "I had not myself thought of our enemy as being communism, I thought of it as primarily being an imperialist Russia."[77]

It would not be until the middle of the 1960's that Fulbright's emphasis upon this distinction would prompt him to unfurl the banner of foreign policy dissent. Then, along with other spokesmen for the so-called limitationist critique, he would denounce as arrogant the global pretensions of a policy that equated American interests with the maintenance of the status quo and identified leftist revolution as the principal threat to the status quo. In the Forties and Fifties, however, the distinction between Soviet interests and the spread of communism was perhaps more conceptual than existential. In any case, its logic had not yet impelled Fulbright to deviate significantly from the national consensus forming around the premises of the Truman Doctrine.

During his first of what turned out to be thirty years in the Senate, Fulbright initiated the program that remains the most memorable part of his legacy: the international exchange program that bears his name. Since its inception, tens of thousands of American students have studied abroad while many more thousands of foreign students, many of them future leaders in their own countries, have been brought to the United States for advanced instruction. Scholars and prominent cultural and artistic figures have also shared in the unprecedented program of international exchange.[78]

One writer later noted that "it is difficult to name any other Federal program which is so much the creation of a single man."[79] So too is it difficult to imagine another postwar public figure who so thoroughly embodies the mix of qualities displayed in the creation and passage of the bill. The authors of a scholarly account of the exchange program have commented on the nation's deep-rooted "faith in the power of education to solve our problems."[80] So deeply does Fulbright share in this faith that it helps define the very nature of the man. But yoked to such frankly idealistic views has been a thoroughly practical appreciation of the requirements of political reality. In the case at hand, Fulbright's practical side produced an ingenious financing method which worked political magic by providing public funds without requiring an appropriation of public revenue.[81] In a similar vein, Fulbright's political stealth must be credited for securing approval of the measure by a Congress that was, at best, only half-conscious of what it was passing. Months of meticulous preparation, assiduous cultivation of a handful of key congressional leaders, and a studious effort to downplay the bill to the congressional rank and file, all contributed to its adoption with minimal debate and controversy.[82] Journalist Don Oberdorfer recounts that "a powerful Senator later informed Fulbright that he would have killed the bill instantly if he had grasped its contents. 'I don't want our impressionable American youths to be infected with foreign isms,' he explained."[83]

Thirty years after it was signed into law by President Truman, Fulbright reflected on the origins of the uniquely successful endeavor. In

29

the shadows of World War II, he recalled "it was my thought that if large numbers of people know and understand the people from nations other than their own, they might develop a capacity for empathy, a distaste for killing other men, and an inclination to peace."[84] Fulbright also feels that the exchange program complements his oft-voiced plea for the creation of genuine international community. In his words, "institutions don't mean a damn if you don't have people."[85] So broad has been the acclaim for the program, and so closely has Fulbright's name been linked to it, that Webster's Third International Dictionary added a new entry:

> ful-bright . . . n-s usu cap (after James William Fulbright b1905 U.S. senator): a grant awarded under the Fulbright Act that makes U.S. surplus property in foreign countries available to finance lectures or research abroad by American students and professors.

Fulbright In The Eisenhower Years

Fulbright's predilection for independence in thought and action seldom served him so well as during the sordid years of McCarthyism. For nearly five years—from the famous Wheeling, West Virginia, speech of February 1950 until the Senate vote of censure in December 1954—Republican Senator Joseph McCarthy of Wisconsin led much of the nation in a frenzied orgy of anti-communism. The spectacle of a man so lacking in grace, charm, or eloquence leading a mass movement of such genuine passion and force left an indelible mark across the times.[86] While many public officials were repelled by the coarseness of McCarthy's onslaught, few dared openly cross him for fear that they themselves might fall victim to the flood tide of hysteria. Amid this melange of unreason and timidity, Fulbright stood apart by virtue of his consistent refusal either to support McCarthy or to join the many who chose simply to remain silent.

Fulbright made little effort to conceal his intense dislike for McCarthy. He regarded McCarthy as a bully and a boor, "immune from the ordinary restraints of civilized people," as he would later say.[87] Their public encounters soon took on an adversarial tone colored by the unmistakable presence of personal antipathy. McCarthy particularly delighted in referring to "Senator Halfbright" whenever the opportunity arose, while Fulbright, for his part, seemed to find pleasure in presenting a calm and reasoned contrast to McCarthy's wild antics. "McCarthy was so objectionable it tended to drive me the other way," he recalls.[88]

During the summer of 1953 the two men squared off in a memorable verbal joust. The occasion was provided by Senate Appropriations Committee hearings on the old International Information Administration, forerunner of the U.S. Information Agency. At stake was the entire future of the Fulbright exchange program, whose funds were bound up with those of the IIA.[89] On the afternoon of July 24, television cameras captured the raw acrimony of the occasion as McCarthy unleashed the full force of his bluster in an effort to discredit the loyalty of the Fulbright scholars. Fulbright's measured, deliberate response so frustrated McCarthy that from then on he dropped the exchange program from his "list" of subversive activities.[90]

Walter Johnson and Francis J. Colligan, in their study of the exchange program, argue that Fulbright's performance on this occasion "represented the first successful resistance to McCarthy within the government since his premier appearance on the national scene."[91] Perhaps. But the strength of McCarthy and his movement was still awesome. The electoral successes of pro-McCarthy candidates in the 1952 elections, the defeat of his enemies such as Tydings of Maryland and Benton of Connecticut, and Eisenhower's refusal to criticize McCarthy in public all lent weight to the then-current folklore that McCarthy was politically indomitable. It is against this background that one must view the Senate vote of February 2, 1954, on the question of additional funds for McCarthy's vehicle, the Permanent Investigations Sub-committee. When the votes were tallied, only one senator had opposed McCarthy: Fulbright of Arkansas. His biographers later judged this to have been "the single most courageous act of his career."[92]

By the end of 1954 Fulbright found himself in the midst of a growing reaction against the Wisconsin senator, as lawmakers who earlier had struggled with their consciences—and won—now found that they could oppose McCarthy with less fear for their own careers. What had happened, of course, was the remarkable spectacle of the Army-McCarthy hearings. From April 22 to June 16, 1954, the nation watched with rapt attention as McCarthy and the grandfatherly Boston lawyer, Joseph Welch, dueled before the television cameras. Welch's definitive humbling of McCarthy ("Have you no sense of decency, sir, at long last? Have you left no sense of decency?")[93] marked a clear shift of fortune for the Senator and his followers as well. When it was over, McCarthy was, for all practical purposes, finished as a national force. The final Senate motion of censure served to seal McCarthy's political demise. Fulbright was personally active behind the scenes in drawing up the censure motion and lining up votes among his colleagues.[94] On December 1, 1954, by a vote of sixty-seven to twenty-two, the Senate formally censured McCarthy.

Throughout the whole tawdry era, men would later recall, Fulbright alone had never wavered in his opposition to McCarthy. While some, like Nixon, had lent McCarthy their support, and most, like Kennedy, had simply been silent, Fulbright had tenaciously fought in his calm and deliberate way against the tide of extremism and character assassination.

It is this memory, more than anything else, which best explains Fulbright's later standing in the eyes of the nation's liberal intellectuals. Their intense hatred of McCarthy became translated into a special regard and affection for Fulbright. In liberal circles the memory of his courage and independence took on near-mythical proportions. Fulbright-as-McCarthy's-Nemesis took its place in the liberal pantheon, and from this point on the Senator's foreign policy pronouncements would routinely receive a respectful hearing from a key segment of those domestically influential.

In winning the White House for his party in 1952, Dwight Eisenhower brought to a close a twenty-year period of Democratic dominance. The prominence of foreign-policy issues in that year's presidential campaign created the impression that a Republican victory would bring with it a significant redirection of the nation's foreign policy. Sincere doubts among thoughtful Republicans about the long-term viability of the Truman administration's containment policy coexisted in expedient if uneasy alliance with the shrill anti-Communist demagoguery of McCarthy and his fellow-travellers of the right. Taken together, the weight of Republican discontent seemed to foreshadow a fundamental rethinking of the foundations of the nation's foreign policy.

Upon taking office, Eisenhower lent weight to those expectations by setting in motion an elaborate, full-dress review of the nation's foreign policy premises.[95] Task forces were formed to examine and assess three contending approaches: containment, deterrence, and liberation. The first would essentially continue the main outlines of policy developed by the Truman administration. The second, deterrence, would look to nuclear weapons as the principal guarantor against Communist aggression. Liberation, the final option, would fulfill Secretary of State Dulles' call for a "political offensive" aimed at altering the status quo by toppling existing Communist regimes.[96]

In the end, Eisenhower's instinctive pragmatism combined with his strong desire to reduce government spending, including the defense budget, resulted in a set of premises that built upon rather than displaced the Truman approach. The liberation doctrine, though of great emotional appeal among domestic right wingers, struck Eisenhower as simply too dangerous, and so was rejected. He opted instead for continuing the broad policy of global containment but with greater reliance on the threat of nuclear retaliation as the principal policy tool for deterring Communist expansion. The shift away from primary reliance on ground troops, with its inherent risk of involvement in local, conventional wars, would result in substantial budget savings over the more rapid military build-up started under Truman.

What was saved in the budget, however, would be lost in policy nuance. The new stress on a "deterrent of massive retaliatory power," as Dulles termed the approach in unveiling it before the Council on Foreign Relations, gave American foreign policy a new rigidity.[97] As two analyists have recently noted, "in the event of local aggression the United States would rely on local forces, perhaps backed by American air and sea support, but if that was not sufficient or if the aggression was major, there remained only nuclear war."[98] Another commentator has said, admiringly, that "the policy was deliberately ambiguous, designed to make the enemy weigh the danger of a limited challenge turning into a nuclear holocaust."[99] A policy of deliberate ambiquity, however, entails enormous dangers of misperception and miscalculation. This, together with the lack of flexibility inherent in the new nuclear monism, would add to the tensions of the already tense 1950s.

Although sharing in the broad national consensus concerning overall foreign policy goals, Fulbright's penchant for independent and critical thought was often evident during the Eisenhower years. During the early years of Eisenhower's tenure, Fulbright's attention was largely given over to domestic matters; when he did turn to foreign issues, it was usually to reiterate the pervasive hawkishness of the day. During the spring of 1954, in fact, Fulbright was one of the few members of Congress to urge direct American intervention in Indochina if necessary in order to prevent a Communist victory there.[100]

As the 1950s wore on, however, Fulbright came to doubt the soundness of administration efforts to counter Communist power abroad. As his doubts grew, so did his public prominence as an outspoken critic of the direction of American foreign policy. His critique arose not because his concept of the appropriate ends of American power differed greatly from that held by Eisenhower or Dulles, though few grasped the point at the time. Rather, it reflected his growing mistrust of the administration's ability accurately to discern the course of contemporary events.[101] His critique arose from what he regarded as the administration's twin intellectual errors: the militarization of the concept of containment, and the tendency to equate Third World nationalism with communism. On both points, Fulbright differed from contemporary opinion largely in being well ahead of it. In little more than a decade, his line of reasoning would be at the heart of a potent political and intellectual uprising. The limitationist critique, as it came to be known, would ultimately triumph for a time—at least, in the early 1970s—over the more swashbuckling interventionism favored by cold war cultists. But surrounded by the nation's anxieties of the mid-1950s, Fulbright was cast in the rather lonely role of dissenter against the massive weight of the then current foreign policy consensus.

His remarks came to focus particularly on Eisenhower's secretary of state, John Foster Dulles. An illustrative episode occurred in late February 1956. On the 25th, Secretary Dulles appeared before the Senate Foreign Relations Committee for a general review of the world scene. Fulbright listened with shock and dismay as Dulles proceeded to characterize Soviet foreign policy as a complete failure. The Russians were now on the defensive, the secretary argued, and would have to completely revise their tactics. Two days later, Fulbright rose in the Senate to deliver an acid denunciation of Dulles' grasp of the tides of the day. The secretary of state, he charged, "midleads public opinion, feeds it pap, tells it that if it will suppress the proof of its own senses, it will see that Soviet triumphs are really defeats and Western defeats are really triumphs."[102]

The heart of his comments focused on Fulbright's belief that the main area of East-West competition was shifting to the developing areas of Latin America, Asia, Africa, and the Middle East. Here, amid the rising chorus of anticolonial and anti-Western sentiment, could be found the new locus of Communist opportunity, he argued. "Wherever one looks," he noted, "there is the Soviet Union, parading itself as the friend of the underdeveloped peoples."[103] Amid this new emphasis on the Third World, the United States suffers from a widely-shared caricature of it "which a good part of the world takes for reality. It accepts it, among other reasons, for reasons that can be laid directly at the door of the present Secretary of State. It believes that America can think of the fight for peace in no terms except that of military alliances and the shipment of arms."[104]

The themes he had raised—on the growing significance of the Third World, and the need for more flexible policy tools to secure support and access in the new arena—continued to dominate Fulbright's thinking in the late 1950s and shape his lively assaults on administration policy. Again and again he returned to his central critique: that American foreign policy had grown muscle-bound under the blunt doctrine of massive retaliation, and was less and less attuned to the revolutionary winds of change that were battering traditional structures throughout the Southern Hemisphere. In a Senate colloquy with Montana's Senator Mansfield, for example, Fulbright bluntly asserted that "the present administration is placing entirely too much emphasis upon purely military affairs, and too little on political and economic consideration" in the Third World.[105]

The autumn of 1956 brought with it the complex and dramatic crisis in the Middle East. When the dust had finally settled—following Egypt's nationalization of the Suez Canal, a joint invasion of Egypt by Israel, France, and Britain, and public American pressure on its allies to call off the invasion—it was clear that Western influence in the region had suffered a severe reversal. Eisenhower concluded that America must make its weight felt in the Middle East in order to counter a growing radical, pro-Soviet tide. Under what came to be known as the Eisenhower Doctrine, he turned to the Congress for backing of an expanded regional aid program and prior congressional commitment "to use armed forces to assist any nation or group of such nations requesting assistance against armed aggression from any nation controlled by international Communism."[106]

Taken together, these events deepened Fulbright's belief that America's diplomacy was weakened by what he increasingly regarded as the limited acuity of its leaders. His response was to escalate the verbal attacks on the administration that were now becoming his trademark. At a mid-December press conference, Fulbright unleashed a barrage of criticisms against the Eisenhower-Dulles stewardship, calling it "extremely awkward, maladroit, and unwise." Their diplomatic blunders, he said, were "weakening the west very seriously." Singled out for special rebuke was Secretary Dulles, whose "preoccupation with pacts" Fulbright scored as "misguided."[107]

In January, 1957, Dulles testified before joint hearings of the Foreign Relations and Armed Services committees on President Eisenhower's proposed resolution on Middle East defense. On the third day of the hearings Fulbright surprised Senate colleagues and administration officials by delivering, from prepared remarks, what the *Reporter's* William Harlan Hale called ". . . one of the most sweeping indictments of a policy and a cabinet official that have been heard in the Senate's precincts in our time."[108] Fulbright could not, he said, support the sought-for "blank check" when he could not feel confident about the men who would use it. He had no wish to grant such broad powers to "people who have disproved their foresight, their wisdom, and their effectiveness in the field of foreign affairs."[109] His policy differences with the secretary were matched by the contrasting styles the two men displayed. Fulbright, noted the *New York Times,* was "reading in a calm voice from a manuscript, while Mr. Dulles sat silent and rigid on the witness stand."[110] It is ironic, in light of his sponsorship of the ill-fated Gulf of Tonkin Resolution seven years later, that Fulbright in 1957 denounced the Mideast resolution as "a broad, unrestricted grant of power over our armed forces and over economic resources. It is blank check for the Administration to do as it pleases with our soldiers and with our money."[111]

Later that year Fulbright rose in the Senate to deliver a summary of a seven-month study of the Suez fiasco and related developments in the Middle East. The study was conducted by a special subcommittee of the committees on Armed Service and Foreign Relations which he had chaired. In his Senate remarks, he lambasted Dulles' decision to withdraw America's offer of aid to Egypt's President Nasser in the latter's ambitious Aswan Dam project. Fulbright charged that the secretary's actions had been hasty, intemperate, and shortsighted. Far from punishing Nasser from his alleged flirtation with the Soviets, the bizarre chain of events begun by Dulles, he argued, had actually enhanced the Soviet's position in the region.[112] Fulbright placed particular stress on a theme that would, a full decade later, lie at the heart of his "limitationist" critique of American foreign policy: the notion that Third World nationalism can, if properly understood and appreciated by the West, curb rather than aid the expansion of Soviet influence, thus diminishing the need for American interventionism. Our policy in the case at hand, he charged, "did not appreciate the significance to the United States of the vigor of the nationalist and neutralist drive in Egypt. I believe the Secretary of State confirmed nationalism and neutralism on the one hand with communism on the other."[113] Dulles failed to grasp "that Egyptian nationalism was a powerful force which could, if recognized for what it was and carefully handled, be directed toward political freedom instead of communism."[114]

These and other attacks on Dulles leadership led William Hale in 1957 to characterize Fulbright as "long Dulles's severest critic on the Hill and today his most implacable foe."[115] Certainly Fulbright's criticisms of administration foreign policy were not entirely separable from his evident disdain for the frosty secretary of state.[116] James Reston observed at the time that Fulbright and Dulles ". . . have established a relationship roughly equivalent to the chemical reaction of dogs and cats. When Mr. Dulles talks, Mr. Fulbright growls, and when the senator talks, the Secretary arches his back."[117]

Yet it would be a mistake to reduce Fulbright's criticism to personality factors alone. His comments reveal some genuine differences with the Eisenhower-Dulles approach, differences which, if not of a truly fundamental nature, nonetheless involved questions of the appropriate operational premises that would advance the nation's consensual philosophical premises. His widely-noted Senate speech of June 20, 1958, for example, contained the expected swipe at Eisenhower and his appointees ("a leadership that is at once aimless and feeble" marked by a "lack of taste for the hard work of the intellect that must precede meaningful action,")[118] and a ritual affirmation of the anti-Communist consensus ("I know that the Russian leaders are as inflexible in their determination that Communist totalitarianism shall one day dominate the world as they are flexible in the methods by which they pursue that objective.")[119] The heart of the address involved a thoughtful critique of the doctrine of deterrence, a set of assumptions which, then as now, lay at the heart of the nation's strategic defense policy. Deterrence, he argued, presupposes "a degree of technical and human perfection which nothing in the experience of mankind leads us to expect. It is, in short, irrational because of the very degree of rationality it requires."[120] Our overreliance on deterrence, he argued, was causing us to ignore more flexible political and military options in coping with a fluid environment. His conclusion was one that would become commonplace a full decade later: "the world is changing, but our policies are static."[121]

Later that year, as a torpid Washington August overtook the final days of the 85th Congress, Fulbright unloaded a double-barrelled broadside against the entire thrust of the Eisenhower-Dulles era. On August 6, the Senate heard his general dissection and critique of administration foreign policy. This speech was perhaps his sharpest attack yet on the administration. In it he charged that the nation had failed to develop a forward-looking foreign policy, one which went beyond mere crisis management to seize the initiative for the United States. This, in turn, reflected a failure of "the present leadership of the country which, when it is not weak and desultory, tends to be impetuous and arbitrary."[122] Fulbright seemed deliberately to avoid specificity; instead, he wished to use the immediate crisis in Lebanon to provoke a broad rethinking of administration policy. Such rethinking, he concluded, would reveal

> . . . the truth . . . that our foreign policy is inadequate, outmoded, and misdirected. It is based in part on a false conception of our real, long-term national interests and in part on an erroneous appraisal of the state of the world in which we live. . . . We should put off no longer a complete reconsideration and reorientation of our foreign policy.[123]

Here Fulbright was raising, though with little immediate effect, a theme to which he would frequently return in later years: that due to the intellectually-flawed vision of our leaders, the nation's global position is often weakened and its influence lessened. He specifically singled out for attack the administration's—and nation's—reflexive anti-communism as the principal obstacle to a clear-headed and effective diplomacy: "in the fear of the deviltry of communism, we have cast ourselves indiscriminately in the role of the defender of the status quo throughout the world."[124]

Two weeks later, in the final hours before adjournment, Fulbright rose in the Senate to deliver a general denunciation of the Eisenhower nineteen fifties. In dyspeptic tones, Fulbright ridiculed not only the nation's leaders and their policies, but also the American people themselves and the society they had created. As he saw it, America had become a nation of superficial materialism and anti-intellectualism marked by "its weakness for the easy way."[125] The 1950s, argued the senator, were a time

> . . . when the word 'egghead' became a word of abuse; when education was neglected; when intellectual excellence became a cause for suspicion; when the man in public life, or the writer, or the teacher, who dared articulate an original thought risked being accused of subversion. . . . this (has been) a period when the man of distinction was the man who had a station wagon, a second car plated with chrome, a swimming pool, a tax-free expense account, and a 21-inch color television set with a 36-inch star on its screen.[126]

Thus, on the eve of his elevation to the chair of the Senate Foreign Relations Committee, Fulbright had established himself as a major commentator on American politics and diplomacy, one who typically sought to look behind the events of the day in an attempt to discern the flow of deeper tides. In so doing, he had acquired also a growing reputation as a thinker of a decidedly critical bent who would not hesitate to voice his criticisms, often cast in sharp language. As his August 21 speech showed, his verbal barbs were sometimes flung in so sweeping a manner that they were more likely to provoke broadly defensive reactions than thoughtful reflection. Their very generality, in turn, left the senator open to the suspicion that his criticisms stemmed more from personal pique than from a carefully-formulated analysis.

In fact, his analysis was reasonably well thought out. Sharing fully the nation's broad sense of purpose, he doubted the practical efficacy of the Eisenhower-Dulles premises on operational questions. Evangelical anti-communism in the Dulles mode aroused his skepticism. Besides its purely aesthetic deficiencies, to Fulbright its great deficiency was its intellectual simplification and distortion. Never one to look kindly on allowing into foreign policy discourse the populist nostrums whose force in domestic politics he readily accepted as simply necessary, Fulbright went out of his way to debunk as hopelessly simplistic the crusading spirit typified by Secretary Dulles. His preferred crusade would appeal more to the head than the heart. It would value acute calculation of global reality more than the rousing rhetoric of righteousness. A crusading sobriety, perhaps, but no less for that a crusade.

3 *Public Service,*
1959–1963

Chairman of the Senate Committee
on Foreign Relations

JANUARY 1959, PROVED to be the precise mid-point of Fulbright's public career. Sixteen years earlier, at age thirty-seven, he had come to Washington as a jaunty House freshman. Sixteen years later, at age sixty-nine, he would wearily clean out his Senate desk after suffering a humiliating rejection by his fellow Arkansans. But this January found him serene in the maturity of his personal powers. At fifty-three he seemed confident and comfortable in the amiable niche afforded by his Senate role. Quietly bemused by his near-celebrity status, he plainly enjoyed the civil routines of solitary study and public discourse on his long-favorite subject of foreign affairs.

On January 30, ninety-one-year-old Theodore Green of Rhode Island relinquished his chairmanship of the prestigious Senate Committee on Foreign Relations.[1] Following the time-honored principle of seniority, his fellow Senators turned to J. William Fulbright as the new chairman.

He brought to his new role a style that would change remarkably little throughout thirty-two years of public life. In a contemporary profile, writer Beverly Smith noted that Fulbright

> . . . has in him a certain strain of individualism, of independence, of wry humor, which does not quite harmonize with the clublike camaraderie of the

Senate. He is more studious, more reflective, less gregarious than most of his colleagues. He spends much more time in reading which others devote to politicking and persuasion among their fellows.[2]

He is "hardly an organization man," said another writer, adding that "inevitably Fulbright's independence and insouciance have given rise to the legend that he is lazy."[3] The obligatory profile in the *New York Times* noted that "in a body not much given to introspection, Senator Fulbright's polished professional manner, Oxford education, and constitutional inability to be a blunt-handed clubby fellow have marked him as an intellectual." It added that "Mr. Fulbright is not unaware that his style is an impediment in an institution where important things get done over cigars, bourbon-and-branch-water, and Pullman-car jokes."[4]

The new chairman did not hestitate to voice his views on both the policy-making process and the substantive direction he would have the nation's foreign policy take. Though sharply critical of unilateral executive dominance, Fulbright emphasized the practical limits of the foreign policy role of the Congress.[5] In Sidney Hyman's characterization, the new chairman believed that "the functioning of the Senate, and of the Foreign Relations Committee in particular, is to try to be the conscience of the Executive—without in any way indulging the frivolous delusion of co-equality."[6]

It was, ironically, an academic who pointed out to the Congress that its active participation need not entirely be a "frivolous delusion." On April 15, 1959, Professor Hans J. Morgenthau appeared before the Foreign Relations Committee. Fulbright openly bemoaned the parochial outlook common among legislators. "Members of the legislative bodies are experts in domestic affairs . . . but in foreign policy I find a great reluctance to substitute the judgment of the State Department," he said. "I think it arises from the fact that we are, after all, primarily local political figures."[7] In response, Morgenthau took the position that

. . . the conduct of foreign policy is not a secret art like, let me say, nuclear physics, but something which anybody can understand who has sufficient common sense, say, to get himself elected to Congress. If you can do that, you ought to be able to judge the basic problems of foreign policy.[8]

Winning good notices in his early months as chairman,[9] Fulbright adopted a noticeably more fervent outlook when he turned to substantive matters of policy. As the recently published transcripts of the Foreign Relations Committee's executive sessions reveal, he was at this point altogether hawkish on military matters. In March of 1959, for example, he treated Secretary of State Herter to a tart monologue on the dangers of reducing American ground forces committed to the defense of Berlin. "It is very poor psychology for this country to continue to decrease its existing forces and to give the appearance that it relies completely on atomic war and there is no intermediate stage," he argued. "And it might lead them to believe we are really not serious."[10] This, indeed, was his underlying concern: that our foreign policy was not sufficiently activist and militant due to the leadership's lack of "seriousness." We must avoid, he lectured Herter,

> . . . conditions that invite excessive bluffing or temptations to make Khrushchev think we are really not determined. I can't understand how anybody would think a country is seriously concerned about it and still proceed to cut its armed forces. It is a lack of seriousness on our part, I suppose. That, coupled with the statement we can't afford it . . . leads the Russians to think that Americans are not serious about this matter and are not willing to spend the money to keep up an army. That is what disturbs me.[11]

His pronounced militance behind closed doors was matched by an emotional, hard-line stance in public. Early in 1960, for example, in an address before the Harvard Club of Washington, he engaged in florid histrionics to paint a dire picture of the world scene. Russia, he said, "rose from a second-rate under-developed country to loom menacingly over the world."[12] Elsewhere,

> . . . a colossal specter rises in the Far East. . . . China's millions are as the fingers of the hand manipulated by their determined and ruthless masters. . . . We may expect that within forseeable time the fingers will become a clenched fist prepared to smash all that stands in the path of China's domination of the Asian reaches.[13]

In berating the Eisenhower administration for allegedly neglecting the nation's defenses ("we have apparently believed we could not afford to spend enough to secure our liberties"), Fulbright called for nothing short of an all-out effort to counter the foe he had so dramatically portrayed: "Since we are now in deadly conflict with a prodigious antagonist, we can neglect nothing that might assure our security."[14]

Later that year, in the midst of the presidential campaign, Fulbright turned the volume of his rhetoric still higher. In an address to the American Bar Association, he depicted in stark terms "the lengthening shadow of the hammer and sickle."[15] Referring repeatedly to the "long term struggle," "the world wide struggle," the "threat to all of us," and "the pressure of expanding Communist influence," Fulbright moved to his principal argument: "the United States has been thrust into the center of world affairs."[16]

What has been "thrust" upon us cannot be declined. To Fulbright, the nation must grasp the rare opportunity afforded by its unwanted preeminence to "strengthen the mechanisms of world peace."[17] Defined in practice as increased multilateral cooperation with our allies, the American-designed "mechanisms of world peace" would have as their goal the protection and promotion of "the human values which are important to the West."[18]

Quite clearly, the new chairman of the Foreign Relations Committee contemplated an ambitious world role for America. His call was for nothing less than the creation of a pro-American global order, one conceived in the image of our domestic values and backed by the collective might of an American-dominated alliance. His operational premises differed from those on his political right in two ways. One involved his rhetorical stress on the possibility of attaining, in the long term, a measure of detente between the U. S. and its Communist adversaries. In pursuit of what he termed a "gradual adjustment," he urged a constant search for diplomatic common ground and, well before it was fashionable to do so, advocated direct negotiations with mainland China.[19] Secondly, his approach to the emerging nations of the so-called Third World was somewhat different from the conservative orthodoxy of the day. In place of the conventional anti-communist rationale for American aid, Fulbright was sensitive to the force of particularistic nationalism sweeping the Third World. One example of this position appears in the transcript of the Foreign Relations Committee's markup session on the Mutual Security Act of 1959. In proposing new language which would somewhat shift the rationale for our aid effort away from anti-communism and toward national development, Fulbright noted that "the purpose of this is simply to try to begin to emphasize the independence of these countries, their own prosperity and viability, if you like, rather than [being] purely defensive against communism."[20] His operational premises, then, were somewhat progressive by the standards of the day. Fundamentally, though, his philosophical premises were entirely orthodox. His capacious vision of America's rightful world role would prove to be of a piece with that of the incoming Kennedy administration.

The Foreign Policy Premises Of Camelot

John F. Kennedy's accession to the presidency produced a marked quickening of the pulse of American politics. In place of the middle-brow blandness of Eisenhower Republicanism, the new Kennedy team exuded vigor, youth, elegance, and intellectuality. That fabled team—the brilliant, flawed men David Halberstam has called "the best and the brightest"[21]—brought to Washington a buoyant, exhilarated sense of America's global destiny. Celebrating himself along with the moment, Arthur Schlesinger, Jr., wrote that "a new breed had come to town, and the New Frontiersmen carried a thrust of action and purpose wherever they went."[22] But if these articulate dandies of the New Frontier stood apart from the great mass of their countrymen, it was more by their self-conscious sophistication than by the substance of their beliefs. The heady mood of Georgetown had rippled out through the nation's anonymous suburbs and pastoral reaches. When Schlesinger recalls that "we thought for a moment that the world was plastic and the future unlimited,"[23] it is best seen as capturing the authentic hubris of an entire people rather than the distinctive ethos of a stylish elite.

To the knights-errant of Camelot, the global sway of American might was simply axiomatic, both as empirical description and as normative vision. Expressed most dramatically in the bracing rhetoric of the Kennedy inaugural, the new administration proceeded from a set of philosophical premises which equated the national interest with the global vindication of its values: "Let every nation know," Kennedy had said on that cold and brilliant day,

> whether it wishes us well or ill, that we shall pay any price, bear any burden, meet any hardship, support any friend, oppose any foe to assure the survival and the success of liberty.[24]

The vision Kennedy was holding aloft was hardly new in its sense of the nation's place in the sun. Kennedy, wrote historian Robert Divine, "sincerely believed in the cold war shibboleths that men like Dean Acheson and John Foster Dulles had been voicing for a decade and a half."[25] What was new was the generational zeal pledged to attaining the unquestioned goal of a pro-American global order:

> Let the word go forth from this time and place, to friend and foe alike, that the torch has been passed to a new generation of Americans, born in this century, tempered by war, disciplined by a hard and bitter peace, proud of our ancient heritage, and unwilling to witness or permit the slow undoing of those human rights to which this nation has always been committed, and to which we are committed today at home and around the world.[26]

Summoning his eager countrymen to "bear the burden of a long twilight struggle,"[27] Kennedy voiced the nation's instinctive sense of purpose, one that clearly transcended the quest for physical security.

It was at the level of operational premises that the Kennedy administration fulfilled its self-concept of innovation. It was Kennedy's belief that the Soviet-American duel would increasingly be waged in the steamy new nations of the Third World.[28] Thus, in addition to a buildup in the nation's strategic capabilities, Kennedy initiated a new emphasis on the coercive tools of counterinsurgency and the social and economic instruments of modernization.[29]

Behind the shield of American might, the new nations could follow the path of American know-how. The Kennedy premises thus equated the national interest with a global mission. The vigorous outward thrust of American power would generate much of the drama and excitement of Kennedy's brief reign. Not until it became mired in the cruel quagmire of Vietnam would the nation rethink the practical applications of its power.[30]

Fulbright In The Kennedy Years

Though hardly a New Frontiersman in terms of personal style, Fulbright was sympathetic to Kennedy's plea for a diplomacy of vigor. There was, in fact, considerable speculation that he would be named secretary of state.[31] Schlesinger recounts how at one point Kennedy's "thoughts were turning more and more to Fulbright. He liked Fulbright, the play of his civilized mind, the bite of his language and the direction of his thinking on foreign affairs."[32] In Schlesinger's telling, it was the senator's civil rights record, with its negative implications for U.S. prestige in the Third World, that led Kennedy to drop Fulbright from his list of prospective nominees.[33] Other accounts have drawn from interviews taped for the John F. Kennedy Library and have reached rather different conclusions regarding Kennedy's grounds for rejecting Fulbright. Of particular interest is former Secretary of State Acheson's account of his meeting with Kennedy shortly after the 1960 election. When Kennedy indicated that he might name Fulbright as his Secretary of State, Acheson objected strenuously. Fulbright, he said, is "not as solid and serious a man as you need for this position. I've always thought that he had some of the qualities of a dilettante. He likes to criticize—he likes to call for brave, bold new ideas and he doesn't have a great many brave, bold new ideas."[34] For whatever reason, no invitation to join the new administration was forthcoming.

From his position in the Senate, Fulbright supported the broad thrust of Kennedy's foreign policy. Of all the postwar presidents he worked with, Kennedy was his favorite, a fact reflected in his hesitancy to voice public criticism of the youthful leader. Even when Kennedy's policies failed, as, for example, in the Bay of Pigs disaster, Fulbright took pains to pronounce the underlying contemporary policy premises as "correct and unassailable."[35]

Repeatedly, in fact, Fulbright wondered aloud whether the nation was doing enough to facilitate the president's bold vision. The inadequacy of Congress in the field of foreign policy became a recurring theme. "For the existing requirements of American foreign policy we have hobbled the President by too niggardly a grant of power," he wrote.[36] Again, on another occasion, he argued that "we must contemplate the further enhancement of Presidential authority in foreign affairs."[37]

Enhanced formal authority would not be enough, however if the nation as a whole failed to respond to Kennedy's summons to a "long twilight struggle." Twice in April 1961, Fulbright took up Kennedy's cause, arguing that "in the President, we have an articulate and vigorous advocate of the national interest."[38] His plea was that the nation rally behind its "articulate and vigorous advocate" so as to match the enemy in the zeal of our commitment:

> In contrast to our tentative or even reluctant approach to power, the Russians boldly and aggressively grasp at every opportunity to expand their empire. . . . I am suggesting that, as the leader of a free, pluralistic society of nations, we recognize and accept the leadership, that we engage *all* our faculties in the contest.[39]

The day after he made those remarks, Fulbright delivered another public address in which he showered lavish praise on Kennedy, concluding that

> . . . I hope that by his speaking more frequently and in greater depth on foreign policy issues, and directly to the people, they may acquire that 'zest of action' so greatly needed if we are to win the contest of will which engages us today.[40]

Specifically, Fulbright advocated the strengthening of multilateral bonds under American leadership. Ever alert to signs of disunity among the western allies, he continually preached the advantages of institutionalizing American primacy by forging the bonds of international concert. If he criticized America's instinct to "go it alone," he himself would urge a course of unilateralism in the name of creating a less-than-universal concert under American leadership.

This line of reasoning was expressed most clearly in his much-noticed article written for the Fall, 1961, issue of *Foreign Affairs*. In it he surveyed the infirm condition of the United Nations. His principal argument was that

> it is clear that the United Nations, although it was designed to form just such a concert, has fallen far short of the hopes which attended its creation; we must look elsewhere for a system that can unify the forces of freedom effectively. [41]

It goes without saying, of course, that those "forces of freedom" would be dominated by the sole superpower in their midst.

It is on the subject of American policy in Southeast Asia that Fulbright's essential conformity with the orthodoxy of the day comes through most clearly and most disturbingly. To be sure, throughout the Kennedy years Fulbright's worldview did indeed embrace the essential ingredients of what would later come to be known as the limitationist outlook. That stance, which Fulbright himself would in the late 1960s develop into a cogent rationale against America's Vietnam policy, appears fully-formed in his April 1961 television appearance on "Meet the Press."

Fulbright's logic on that occasion was summarized by the columnist Arthur Krock: "When the conditions of combat logistics and terrain were very bad, he said, and the people and armed forces of a country showed little interest in preserving their independence, or whether they lost it to a foreign dictatorship, no military intervention by the United States should even be contemplated." [42] A prescient warning against an expanded American role in Vietnam? Hardly. Fulbright was referring to neighboring Laos, and he did indeed oppose escalating our involvement there. But he then went on to argue, in Krock's words, that, "in South Vietnam, Thailand and Burma these factors were in reverse. Therefore, if these governments, being expressions of the popular will, requested this United States aid as necessary to preserve their independence, he would favor it." [43] Within a week of his "Meet the Press" appearance, Fulbright let it be known that, as the *New York Times* put it, "the Kennedy Administration was considering the possibility of direct military intervention to counteract Communist threats in South Vietnam and Thailand." He stated flatly that he "would support the moves in South Vietnam and Thailand if they were considered necessary and if the nations concerned wished them." [44]

Despite the inchoate limitationist outlook that occupied a corner of his mind, then, Fulbright was altogether unable to link the facts concerning Vietnam to the logic of that outlook. It was this crucial intellectual lapse that reduced him to the role of lending encouragement to the fateful American buildup in Vietnam. Within three years this mind-set would lead him to serve as senate sponsor for the historic Gulf of Tonkin Resolution. Only when the tragic consequences of that resolution became all too clear would Fulbright rethink his own foreign policy premises and discover the broader applicability of the limitationist view.

If his public comments reveal an essential harmony with the Kennedy premises, his private dealings with the administration were less than satisfactory. On two critical occasions—the Bay of Pigs invasion in 1961 and the fabled 1962 missile crisis—Fulbright attempted to alter the operational premises on which commitments of American power were based. Both times he failed.

It was quite by accident that he had the opportunity even to try to influence the Bay of Pigs deliberations.[45] In late March 1961, Kennedy, upon learning that Fulbright and his wife would be spending the Easter holidays in south Florida, invited them to make the trip with him on Air Force One.

Washington had been rife with rumors of a pending American-backed invasion of Castro's Cuba. With the upcoming trip in mind, Fulbright, aided by Pat Holt of the Foreign Relations Committee staff, worked up a detailed memorandum urging that the U.S. steer clear of any such invasion.[46] If the invasion failed, the memorandum argued, the United States would be humiliated before the entire world. If it succeeded, we would inherit the responsibility for the social, economic, and political reconstruction of Cuba. Either outcome would be disproportionate to the actual threat posed by Castro: "the Castro regime is a thorn in the flesh; but it is not a dagger in the heart."[47]

Kennedy read the memo during the March 30 flight to Florida, but made little comment. Fulbright made the return trip with Kennedy on April 4. As the plane neared Washington Kennedy invited Fulbright to attend a meeting that afternoon at the State Department on the subject of his memo.

The meeting proved to be a final review of the planned invasion. In the words of Arthur Schlesinger, Jr., who was present,

> Fulbright, speaking in an emphatic and incredulous way, denounced the whole idea. . . . He gave a brave, old-fashioned American speech, honorable, sensible and strong; and he left everyone in the room, except me and perhaps the President, wholly unmoved.[48]

In the aftermath of the invasion's complete failure, Kennedy would say, "There is only one person in the clear—that's Bill Fulbright."[49]

Eighteen months later Cuba was again the focus of dramatic American policy decisions. This time the subject was missiles. Where earlier Fulbright had urged the view that Castro was "a thorn in the flesh; but

. . . not a dagger in the heart," he now reversed the metaphor and re-garded Castro as a mortal danger to America's well-being. In a meeting with Kennedy just two hours before the president was scheduled to in-form the nation by television of the frightening situation, Fulbright learned for the first time of the planned naval blockade. Urging a direct invasion instead, Fulbright succeeded only in arousing Kennedy's ire. Theodore Sorensen would later call this meeting "the only sour note of the day."[50]

Finding little satisfaction as a close-in advisor, Fulbright devoted the bulk of his energies to public discussions aimed at shoring up support for premises he largely shared with the Kennedy administration. In so do-ing, he frequently attacked those whose views he regarded as simplistic and dangerous.

His sharp attacks on right wingers and their call for total victory over communism made him a constant center of controversy.[51] If the steady torrent of invective from the political right bothered him, it was less as a personal matter than as what he regarded as a rising tide of intolerant extremism. Two weeks after the murder of John F. Kennedy, Fulbright delivered an important address examining "tendencies toward violence and crusading self-righteousness" in the nation's life. "It was in this pre-vailing atmosphere of suspicion and hate that the murder of the Presi-dent was spawned," he observed.[52]

His mournful fear of what he saw as mindless populism reinforced Fulbright's long-established belief in the necessity for elite rule, espe-cially in shaping the nation's foreign policy premises. Within a year, he would join with the elite heirs of Camelot to set the nation on a fateful, ultimately tragic course in Southeast Asia.

Prospects For The West

During April and May 1963, Fulbright commuted to Med-ford, Massachusetts, to deliver the annual Clayton Lectures at the Fletcher School of Law and Diplomacy. Later expanded and published under the title *Prospects For The West*, they offer perhaps the fullest account of his outlook as the brief Kennedy era neared its end. Scattered among the three lectures ("Russia and the West," "A Concert of Free Nations," and "The American Agenda") are revealing indications of Fulbright's thinking on five topics of recurring interest: the role of reason in human affairs, the making of American foreign policy, America's role and interests in the world, extant threats to those interests, and how best the nation can counter those threats.

Not since the heady, perhaps innocent, days of the Fulbright Resolution had the senator voiced much optimism about man's ability to control his secular fate through the use of reason. His Clayton Lectures are laced with sober admonitions on the limits of human reason and man's capacity to translate abstract design into concrete reality. His rummaging through history convinced him, he said, that "we must be cautious in our prescriptions and modest in our aspirations, not because grand designs and universal ideas are undesirable in the abstract, but because they are desirable only in the abstract, far exceeding the demonstrated limits of human capacity and human wisdom."[53]

The contemporary juxtapositioning of man's unlimited aspirations and his quite limited faculties is, in Fulbright's judgment, the wellspring of modern tragedy. In the name of their ideals, Marxist zealots enslave others and in turn fall prisoners to the barren intellectual trap of ideology. Americans are no less prone to the same forces: "having experienced virtual unanimity as to basic forms and values, (America) is inclined at times to regard unfamiliar opinions with intolerance and revulsion."[54] The very oneness of mind that has united us at home has hampered clarity in our dealings abroad: "we have not yet acknowledged the limitations of our perspective or accepted the proposition that our proper task is not to try to reshape the world in the American image."[55]

If ideology cloaks man's reason, substituting slogan for thought, it is through education that we can redeem ourselves.[56] Here it is Fulbright's aspiration that is truly universal. Not only can Americans learn to break out of their intellectual parochialism; Fulbright holds out the possibility of a Soviet Union defanged by the force of learning: "the cumulative impact of the real world of experience on the imaginary world of Marxian dogma will gradually bring about profound alterations in Marxian theory, in the character of Soviet society, and in the relations of Russia to the West."[57]

Reason, then, shrouded as it is by layers of ignorance and ideology, offers only limited hope for attaining a sane world order. Only through education can man hope to fulfill his potential for self-mastery.

At this point in his career, Fulbright's views on how foreign policy should be made were—even by his own prior standards—highly elitist. His Clayton Lectures contain several rhetorical swipes at the "intrusion" of popular currents in the determination of policy.[58] Approving references to de Tocqueville and Lippmann fortify Fulbright's own long-standing belief that decision makers must shape foreign policy according to rational criteria that transcend the "transitory preferences of public opinion."[59]

Within the governing elite, Fulbright argued, it is clearly the president who is "the source of an effective foreign policy under our system."[60] The Congress, he feels, lacks the resources and constitutional status to "initiate or shape policy."[61] In the lingering afterglow of the Cuban Missile Crisis, the president's dominant foreign policy role was widely hailed as necessary for the nation's survival. Certainly Fulbright shared in this view; interestingly, in view of his later role, in 1963 he was arguing that "we must contemplate the further enhancement of Presidential authority in foreign affairs."[62]

Future historians will arguably point to the early 1960s—after the missile crisis but before Vietnam—as the high water mark of America's fortunes. Certainly Fulbright shared in the contemporary celebration of the nation's power and accomplishments. In a departure from his usual detached skepticism, his Clayton Lectures include the exuberant boast that "by all standards of history that measure the success of nations, America is at the flood tide of growth and achievement. We have become preeminent in world power and responsibility."[63] Before the burdens of global primacy were apparent, Fulbright, like other political leaders of his generation, was loathe to look critically at what seemed in 1963 to be a position of unparalleled strength and opportunity.

Fulbright reveals a distinctly expansive concept of America's global role. In a rationale that could have come from Dean Rusk, Fulbright builds a case for American globalism. "Responsibility is inseparable from power," he notes. That power, in turn, may well have to be used at unpredictable points around the globe, since "the very credibility of our deterrent power depends upon our ability to deter lesser as well as greater provocations."[64] This line of reasoning would, of course, in time become a key rationale for maintaining the American commitment to Vietnam.

At another point, Fulbright defends an activist foreign policy on the grounds that America's security requires a congenial external environment. Thus defined as something other than—and greater than—defense in the physical sense, American security may well require global interventionism in order to advance, in the broadest sense of the term, the nation's way of life.[65]

In our dealings with the Third World, Fulbright argues that some repression needs to be accepted if it leads to desired development goals and, "in so doing, . . . contributes(s) to our own long-term purposes."[66] The equation between American security and a receptive international environment plus a concept of America's purpose that transcends physical security adds up to a vaguely imperial outlook characteristic of the times. Despite his reputation as an innovative thinker, in 1963 Fulbright was more archetype than architect of the American outlook.

To Fulbright it was clear that America's world interests faced one overriding threat: the Soviet Union and its communist allies. He shared freely in the then conventional view that the cold war was caused and sustained by Soviet imperialism. He explicitly denied that Russia's fears and hostility were based on western attitudes and behavior; instead, he insisted, it was the Soviet Union that had provoked the West to establish, among other things, a common defense through NATO.[67] The Soviets, in Fulbright's view, were propelled by unlimited aims and sought to establish a universal empire.[68] Russian imperialism "in some respects similar to Germany's two bids for world hegemony," originates in the messianic impulse of ideology,[69] he argued.

If America and the West were blameless in the origination of the Cold War, there are nonetheless steps we can take to cope with an unwanted situation. To Fulbright firmness and unflinching resolve are required if the West is to contain Russia's advances. Beyond containment in the physical sense, Fulbright holds out the long-term possibility of a Russia profoundly transformed by the weight of experience.[70] Like a stern pedagogue seeking to tame the schoolyard bully, the U.S. must teach the Soviets to "play the game of international relations by the traditional rules."[71] Fulbright believes Soviet moderation is a realistic possibility, but he has no doubt its emergence will be due primarily to the West's resolve and clarity of purpose.[72] The promise of vigilant containment lies in the gradual transformation of the Soviet adversary.

By the end of 1963, then, as the powerful and prosperous nation mourned the loss of its stylish young president, Fulbright was clearly supportive of the existing national consensus on the desirability of a globalist American world role. Within a matter of months, he would find himself at the center of a national debate on how best to secure that role.

4 *Myths Old and New*

FOR FULBRIGHT 1964 PROVED to be a year of contrasts. Spring brought unprecedented attention and praise in the wake of the single most famous speech of his career. By late summer, however, events pressed him to play a pivotal role in setting the nation on a course in Southeast Asia that would ultimately prove disastrous. Taken together, these two events—the celebrated "Old Myths and New Realities" speech and sponsorship of the notorious Gulf of Tonkin Resolution—reflect the incongruencies characteristic of a man in the midst of deep personal change. For Fulbright, the gnawing sense that America's diplomacy was much in need of fundamental rethinking existed alongside his own bedrock assumptions about America's role in the world that to some bore the marks of dogma. This tension between the eloquent call for new ideas and the stubborn adherence to old ones in time led Fulbright to undertake for himself the painful reexamination of assumptions that he had long been urging on his countrymen. But before that process of rethinking was fully underway, Fulbright would undergo the wrenching ordeal of guilt and self-doubt over his personal involvement in the escalation of violence in Southeast Asia.

Old Myths and New Realities

In late March of 1964 the U.S. Senate was in the grips of yet another Southern-led filibuster against a civil rights bill. As part of his contribution to the filibuster, Fulbright took the floor on the twenty-fifth for prepared remarks whose delivery would run a bit over one hour. For his topic he had chosen a theme that he had sounded throughout his adult life: the need for continual rethinking of the nation's foreign policy premises. Twenty years before, his maiden Senate speech had warned that "myths are one of the greatest obstacles in the formulation of national policy."[1] Today, before a nearly empty chamber, he returned to that theme once again.

In a matter of days it was clear that his words—first heard in such inauspicious circumstances—had touched a resonant chord throughout the nation. "Old Myths and New Realities" marked the initiation of a national debate over American foreign policy. Its fame—and the incessant invocation of its title—have somewhat obscured its actual arguments. In order to remind ourselves of what precisely it was that so aroused a wide national audience, we must reconstruct the logic of the original address.

Fulbright opened with the observation that "there is an inevitable divergence, attributable to the imperfections of the human mind, between the world as it is and the world as men perceive it."[2] The second paragraph then spells out more clearly the theme of the address:

> There has always—and inevitably—been some divergence between the realities of foreign policy and our ideas about them. This divergence has in certain respects been growing, rather than narrowing; and we are handicapped, accordingly, by policies based on old myths, rather than current realities. This divergence is, in my opinion, dangerous and unnecessary.[3]

This last point—that things need not be as they presently are—is worth noting; in Fulbright's ongoing internal debate over the efficacy of human reason and the potential for rational mastery, 1964 found him cautiously affirming the view that man can, to a considerable degree, avert catastrophe and attain self-direction through the conscious, clearheaded exercise of his mental faculties. He noted

> . . . two possible reasons for the growing divergence between the realities and our perceptions of current world politics. The first is the radical change in relations between and within the Communist and the free world; and the second is the tendency of too many of us to adhere to prevailing practices with a fervor befitting immutable principles.[4]

53

Particular emphasis is placed on the first factor. The Cuban Missile Crisis a year and a half earlier had apparently been a turning point; the Russians had presumably been sobered by the high cost of adventurism. Coupled with the test ban treaty and the continuation of America's strategic superiority, events seemed to indicate that

> . . . the character of the cold war has, for the present, at least, been profoundly altered: by the drawing back of the Soviet Union from extremely aggressive policies; by the implicit repudiation by both sides of a policy of 'total victory'; and by the establishment of an American strategic superiority which the Soviet Union appears to have tacitly accepted because it has been accompanied by assurances that it will be exercised by the United States with responsibility and restraint.[5]

Fulbright then argued that:

> these astonishing changes in the configuration of the postwar world have had an unsettling effect on both public and official opinion in the United States. One reason for this, I believe, lies in the fact that we are a people used to looking at the world . . . in moralistic rather than empirical terms.[6]

Having thus sounded the general theme that "we are clinging to old myths in the face of new realities," Fulbright proposes to "cut loose from established myths and . . . start thinking some 'unthinkable thoughts.' "[7] This is the burden of the main body of the speech, which diagnoses alleged myths and corresponding realities in our dealings with the Communist world, Latin America, and Southeast Asia. There are seven distinct "myths" which Fulbright in his speech specifically labels as such. Three have to do with Communist nations in general, another three pertain to our dealings with Cuba, and one concerns our relations with Panama. As an antidote to these explicitly named myths, Fulbright offers eight statements describing "new realities."

The first-named myth is "the master myth of the cold war . . . that the Communist bloc is a monolith composed of governments equally resolute and implacable in their determination to destroy the free world."[8] Note that this "myth" contains two distinct elements: one concerns the extent to which the United States faces a security threat from Communist nations, while the second involves the degree to which that threat is centrally directed. On both counts, Fulbright is relatively sanguine. Concerning the nation widely regarded as America's principal adversary, he argues that "the Soviet Union, though still a formidable adversary, has ceased to be totally and implacably hostile to the West."[9] With regard to unity of purpose among Russia's coideologists, Fulbright emphasizes that "the reality is that some Communist regimes pose a threat to the free world while others pose little or none."[10] Today the point would seem unexceptional, even banal, but it is worth remembering that as late as 1964 it was considered a bit daring to suggest outside elite circles that diversity rather than uniformity characterized the diplomatic calculus of the Communist nations. This, indeed, was Fulbright's deeper point: that we had steeled ourselves—mentally and materially—for so long against the starkness of international communism that our capacity for nuance had been weakened. The ringing clarity of purpose which anti-communism provides may have had as its price a debilitating loss of analytic clarity in comprehending local realities inside the Communist bloc. Here it is Fulbright's purpose to call attention to recent changes in the world and, incidentally, recent changes in his perception of the world.

The next two myths Fulbright takes on have to do with national attitudes toward protracted conflict. He argues that "there is little in history to justify the expectation that we can either win the cold war or end it immediately and completely. These are the favored myths, respectively, of the American right and of the American left."[11] With unintended irony, the man who gained fame as a critic of the cold war here critiques those who dissent from the mainstream view that little more can be expected of Soviet-American relations than an inconclusive duel of indefinite duration. Fulbright scoffs at those who would attempt a dramatic breakout from what John Kennedy called the "long twilight struggle." His proposed reality to supplant the myths of cold war critics comes close to constituting an apologia for the status quo: "we must . . . come to terms, at last, with the realities of a world in which neither good nor evil is absolute and in which those who move events and make history are those who have understood not how much but how little it is within our power to change."[12] Fulbright urges his countrymen to adopt a measure of philosophical resignation and to avoid what he regards as the dangerously architectonic designs of nonmainstream cold war critics.

Fulbright's fourth "myth and reality" concern our relations with Panama, especially the issue of the Panama Canal. In his detailed treatment of the historical, military, economic, and political dimensions of the controversy, Fulbright argues that Americans must break out of familiar mental molds and learn to understand the world as it looks to other people. His receptivity to the Panamian position is manifest. In words that are neatly prophetic of future national policy, he asserts that "we would . . . do well to disabuse ourselves of the myth that there is something morally sacred about the treaty of 1903," and thus of America's entire posture in Panama.[13] In place of the myth of the "rightness" and "lawfulness" of American ownership on remarkably favorable terms, we need to accept "the central reality . . . that the treaty of 1903 is in certain respects obsolete" and so, therefore, is our policy.[14]

The remaining three myths identified by Fulbright all relate to America's policy toward Cuba. He argues at some length that our policy of boycotting the Caribbean nation has conspicuously failed to attain its ostensible objectives of isolating Castro abroad and weakening him at home. In that failure, he argues, some valuable lessons can be gained, but only if we first succeed in casting off some crippling myths: "the boycott policy has not failed because of any 'weakness' or 'timidity' on the part of our government. This charge, so frequently heard, is one of the most pernicious myths to have been inflicted on the American people."[15] If our failure to enlist allied assistance in a Cuban boycott does not stem from want of trying on our leaders' part, the problem is perhaps more deeply rooted. Fulbright suggests we need to look at—and expunge from our thinking—"the myth that we can get anything we want if we only try hard enough."[16] These two myths need to be rejected in favor of "the basic reality . . . that it is simply not within our power to compel our allies to cut off their trade with Cuba."[17]

Beyond these tactical matters, Fulbright argues that fundamentally "we must abandon the myth that Cuban communism is a transitory menace."[18] In place of this myth, Fulbright would have us accept "two basic realities about Cuba: First that the Castro regime is not on the verge of collapse and is not likely to be overthrown by any policies which we are now pursuing or can reasonably undertake; and second, that the continued existence of the Castro regime, though inimical to our interests and policies, is not an insuperable obstacle to the attainment of our objectives."[19] A decade and a half later, Fulbright's matter-of-fact approach to Cuba seems prescient in its tone of wary acceptance of an unwanted neighbor. In 1964, though, his views were widely denounced.[20]

A final "reality" whose corresponding "myth" is implied but not explicitly stated concerns our China policy. Here Fulbright urges us to acknowledge existential "realites about China, of which the foremost is that there really are not 'two Chinas,' but only one—mainland China; and that it is ruled by Communists, and is likely to remain so for the indefinite future."[21]

Fulbright's concluding topic is Vietnam. Though he eschews listing specific "myths and realities," he argues, characteristically, that "the situation in Vietnam poses a . . . pressing need for a reevaluation of American policy."[22] But his own "reevalutation" reveals a conceptual range that seems suddenly cramped and curiously indifferent to the search for a transcendent vision which comprises the loudly announced purpose at hand. Fulbright takes up four possible courses of action for America. Withdrawal he curtly dismisses out of hand. Similarly, he argues that a negotiated solution offers little hope due to South Vietnam's military weakness: "it is extremely difficult for a party to a negotiation to achieve by diplomacy objectives which it has conspicuously failed to win by warfare."[23] That leaves two possibilities for the U.S.: "the expansion of the conflict in one way or another, or a renewed effort to bolster the capacity of the South Vietnamese to prosecute the war successfully on its present scale."[24] Fulbright avoids a clear-cut recommendation as to which of these two alternatives would best comport with the "realities" of the situation, but he leaves no doubt that the choice to be made concerns the question of how best to maintain a pro-American, non-Communist regime in South Vietnam, not whether that is both a valid and attainable goal for America: "whatever specific policy decisions are made, it should be clear to all concerned that the United States will continue to meet its obligations and fulfill its commitments with respect to Vietnam."[25]

The broad response evoked by "Old Myths and New Realities" began at once on the Senate floor. The most significant congressional reaction was that of Senator Wayne Morse of Oregon. As irascible as he was prophetic, Morse had long been a critic of America's Vietnam policy. Within minutes after Fulbright concluded his remarks, Morse delivered a lively rebuttal, focusing on the question of Vietnam. Taking a linguistic cue from Fulbright, Morse charged that "one of the myths is that the United States has a right to engage in unilateral action in the field of foreign policy."[26] Charging to the heart of his thesis, Morse asserted that "we cannot escape the realities. The difficulty in South Vietnam is a difficulty of the Vietnamese among themselves."[27] Morse did not content himself with differences over substantive policy questions; he proceeded to upbraid his chairman for allowing the Senate's foreign policy role to atrophy in the name of inter-branch harmony.[28]

Apparently stung by the sharpness of Morse's attack, Fulbright, in a rather halting colloquy, restated his overall support of America's Vietnam policy (". . . our motives are quite above reproach") and concluded flatly that "we are committed to the point where it would be quite disastrous for this country to withdraw."[29]

Other congressional criticisms were soon forthcoming, though most tended to rest on more superficial grounds than that of Senator Morse. Twice within the next month, for example, Senator Javits took the floor to chide Fulbright for the confusion and unsettling effects his remarks had allegedly had abroad.[30] Florida Senator Smathers labeled the speech "monumentally naive and unrealistic," though it was not a part of Smathers' purpose to show in any detail why this was so.[31] In a similar vein, New York Representative William Miller, then chairman of the Republican National Committee, blasted the speech as "a trial balloon which the Johnson Administration is sending up to prepare public opinion for the acceptance of a foreign policy that could lead only to disaster."[32]

For the most part, however, few members of Congress revealed publicly the "reactions of fear and foreboding" that Fulbright later attributed to them.[33] Most seemed content to accept at face value his stated purpose to "stimulate a general discussion, a rethinking and a reevaluation of our foreign policies in the light of changing circumstances."[34]

At his March 27 news conference, Secretary of State Rusk was questioned on four separate occasions about Fulbright's speech.[35] His overall tone was distinctly muted (". . . a thoughtful and thought-provoking statement"), though he did take exception to Fulbright's charge that our Cuban boycott policy had failed. Overall, Rusk's apparent objective was to disassociate Fulbright's comments from official administration thinking: "he was not speaking for the administration, he was speaking for himself; he was not floating a trial balloon for the administration."[36]

Recall that at the time of its delivery Fulbright regarded "Old Myths and New Realities" as a restatement of arguments he had often made before. He thus was startled and bemused by the national outpouring of attention and commentary that it triggered. Across the nation, reaction was almost instant. Within a week, fifteen thousand letters flooded the senator's office, most expressing approval of his call for rethinking foreign policy premises.[37]

Favorable notices were ubiquitous in the print media. The august *New York Times* lavished page-one coverage on the speech—thus certifying it for many as a genuine national event—and took the added step of reprinting the entire text on two inside pages.[38] Elsewhere, Walter Lippmann hailed his friend as a public leader "who says what he believes is true rather than what is supposed at the moment to be popular."[39] The *New Republic* took approving note of the speech;[40] the *Christian Century* labeled it a "daring, prophetic address."[41] "It was designed to start Mr. Johnson—and America—thinking," added *Newsweek*.[42]

Otherwise conservative voices attested to the significance of the speech, sharing, apparently, Kenneth Crawford's views that "the time obviously had come for Fulbright's idea that the Communist world is no longer a monolith."[43] *Business Week* agreed, noting that "Fulbright's speech reflects a growing feeling in Congress and the country that the political map of the world that has guided U.S. policymakers is out of date."[44]

Not all comment was favorable, but even writers who took issue with some of the arguments contained in the speech were quick to agree that it nonetheless constituted a major event for the nation. Hans Morgenthau praised Fulbright as one of "the ablest and most responsible members of the Senate" and expressed his admiration for "the high intellectual qualities of his speech."[45] He went on, however, to detail his reservations about Fulbright's analysis, especially the senator's core assumption that relations between the Soviet Union and the United States had undergone "radical change," in part due to changes in Soviet objectives and tactics. To Morgenthau, "the correctness of that assumption has not, to say the least, been proved."[46] In fact, he asserted, "the radical change in the relations between the United States and the Soviet Union which Senator Fulbright postulates turns out to be a myth rather than a reality."[47]

Another academic critic, Morton Kaplan, argued that Fulbright had "bought Khrushchev's myth of the great changes in Soviet foreign policy since Stalin."[48] The editors of *Commonweal* pursued a similar line of reasoning, arguing that "the Senator did . . . seem to overstate his case: one need not be a hopeless victim of cold-war mythology to believe that Communism must still be taken seriously as a world conspiracy and ideology."[49] Writing in the same publication, William V. Shannon sought to cast further doubt on Fulbright's central assumption. To Shannon, the speech constituted "a fashionable facile bit of analysis" which was "flawed by a shallow and opportunistic kind of 'realism.' "[50]

Surely the most incisive and subtle critique of the address was that of Richard Rovere. Acknowledging Fulbright's address to have been "an important discussion of American foreign policy," Rovere nonetheless took the senator to task in a fundamental way.[51] Far from believing in the "master myth" of the monolithic character of communism, Rovere argued, the nation's policymakers have for many years clearly grasped the fact that Communist nations vary in the degree of hostility and threat posed to the United States. If the dogma of a monolithic communist threat is rejected by foreign-policy elites, wrote Rovere, it nonetheless survives—and performs a needed function—among the mass public: "for the dogma is, in fact, the basis for popular and Congressional assent, and if Senator Fulbright or anyone else were to disabuse the public altogether of the 'old myths' that blind it to the 'new realities', the consequence might well be the withdrawal of assent from almost the whole of current American policy."[52]

Among the small chorus of critics, only the *Nation* criticized Fulbright's stand on Vietnam. Acknowledging that "Fulbright did the country a real if limited service," the editors went on to argue that "on the crucial question of the moment—American policy in Vietnam—he chose to go along with the Administration's policy, which grows more sterile with each passing month."[53]

Less than two weeks after his celebrated address, Fulbright journeyed to the University of North Carolina to deliver a speech entitled "The Cold War in American Life."[54] Appearing in the wake of its famed predecessor, the speech was bound to attract wide attention. Fulbright's thesis was straightforward enough: "of all the changes in American life wrought by the cold war, the most important by far, in my opinion, has been the massive diversion of energy and resources from the creative pursuits of civilized society to the conduct of a costly and interminable struggle for world power."[55] The cumulative effect of itemizing the cold war's costs was to further sharpen the senator's nascent reputation as a key national leader of foreign policy dissent.

Later that summer, these two widely cited speeches were published, along with two lesser-known addresses, in a volume entitled *Old Myths and New Realities*.[56] The added circulation given to Fulbright's views lent weight to the growing impression that here was a public official whose ideas could no longer safely be ignored.

Fulbright's message had thus struck a deep national urge to discuss and reconsider the nation's global role. While some of the nation's keenest minds doubted that he had got it quite right, there could be no mistaking the broad interest in the themes he had raised, an interest whose very eagerness seemed to betoken a vague, inarticulate sense that the nation stood on the verge of truly momentous decisions.

Far removed from the atmosphere and mood in which it first appeared, today's reader might wonder why "Old Myths and New Realities" drew such massive contemporary notice. Certainly any reader today would wonder at the claim to criticism and originality of an address whose comments on Vietnam utterly failed to transcend the most shopworn banalities then current in American life. Less obvious, but far more instructive, is the degree to which "Old Myths and New Realities" served to affirm the nation's consensual outlook on fundamental matters even while engaging in "dissent" on secondary concerns. More pointedly, it can be argued that in the course of leading the nation to look critically at its contemporary operational premises, "Old Myths and New Realities" deflected attention away from a reconsideration of the world role and interest presumably advanced by refashioned operational premises.

Nowhere does Fulbright define explicitly the fundamental ends he would have the nation pursue abroad. Were he to do so, there is little doubt that his vision of America's place in the sun would be virtually indistinguishable from that held by, say, Dean Rusk or, for that matter, John Foster Dulles. In regards to the Soviet Union, "a most formidable adversary," Fulbright believes "normal relations" will not be attainable until "Soviet leaders abandon the global ambitions of Marxist ideology."[57] Agreeing with the orthodoxy of the day that "the continued existence of the Castro regime in Cuba is inimical to the interests of the United States," Fulbright's "dissent" revolves around the practical inefficacy of the American-led boycott.[58]

On our role in Latin America, Fulbright poses this muliple-choice question:

But what if a violent social revolution were to break out in one of the larger Latin American countries? Would we feel certain that it was Cuban or Soviet inspired? Would we wish to intervene on the side of established authority? Or would we be willing to tolerate or even support a revolution if it was seen to be not Communist but similar in nature to the Mexican revolution or the Nasser revolution in Egypt?[59]

Absent from the list—because absent from Fulbright's and the nation's worldview—was the position that how Latin Americans choose to live is for Latin Americans themselves to work out. In Asia, Fulbright proceeds from the view that it is China's policies that must be changed, and that such change can be brought about by our own decisions on, say, whether to allow China into the United Nations or not.[60] Fulbright, incidentally, took the then-ritualistic stance that "unless it were accompanied by altered policies on the part of Communist China, recognition would have the distinct appearance of approval."[61] This amid a broader insistence that "we must dare to think 'unthinkable thoughts.' "[62]

Repeatedly, Fulbright urged the view that contemporary conditions provide "opportunities for American policy."[63] His purpose was to stimulate a retooling of the nation's operational premises so that it might seize those "opportunities" to secure its global sway. Far from constituting serious dissent against American foreign policy, "Old Myths and New Realities" underscored the massive weight of America's submerged consensus on underlying philosophical premises. It was the weight of that underlying consensus that would propel the nation headlong into Vietnam, where the "opportunities for American policy" would be heedlessly embraced.

The Gulf of Tonkin Resolution

Standing astride the crest of public attention and acclaim produced by his famed March 25 address, Fulbright had every reason to feel personally efficacious and optimistic about the future as the summer of 1964 approached. Lyndon Johnson, his long-time friend, was showing unsuspected gifts as a national leader. Moving firmly after Kennedy's death to win the nation's confidence, Johnson was now reaching beyond himself to enlarge and elevate the political vistas of the American public. A "Great Society"—first adumbrated in a speech at the University of Michigan on May 22—was now held to be within tantalizing reach.[64] The blight of poverty, pollution, ignorance, hunger, and discrimination could now be eliminated from our national life, insisted Johnson, and through an astonishing torrent of speeches to the public and messages to Congress he labored relentlessly to move the bold dream closer to reality.

To Fulbright, it was imperative that Johnson win a full term in the coming November elections.[65] For one thing, he viewed the Republican contender, Senator Goldwater of Arizona, as a dangerous extremist who must be defeated at all costs.[66] In the heat of the campaign, he would write of Goldwater:

> It is possible—just possible—that the nation could withstand the domestic effects of a Goldwater Presidency, but there seems little possibility that the nation could escape disaster under a Republican Administration committed to the kind of foreign policy proposed by Senator Goldwater.[67]

As importantly, Fulbright felt confident that his personal relationship with Johnson would insure that his own foreign policy views would be routinely welcomed in the inner councils of the executive branch. According to David Halberstam, Fulbright assumed that

> he would be consulted, his advice weighed; . . . . Being an adversary was not a role he had sought under any conditions; it was out of character, but it was particularly out of character with a fellow Democrat and friend in the White House.[68]

Fulbright's—and the nation's—buoyant summer mood was somewhat darkened by the war clouds then forming over Southeast Asia. Since the French defeat ten years earlier, successive administrations had gradually linked America's prestige to the survival of a pro-western regime south of the 17th parallel, but no Americans were as yet directly committed to combat roles. As the news out of Vietnam grew steadily worse—disunity in the south, mounting militance in the north—officials in the executive branch began formulating elaborate plans to salvage the deteriorating situation. As the so-called Pentagon Papers would later reveal, William Bundy, then assistant secretary of state for Far Eastern affairs, drafted and sent to the president in May a detailed scenario calling for steadily increasing American military pressure against North Vietnam as a means of shoring up the shaky regime in the south.[69] Bundy's secret plan would lead by stages to sustained American bombing of North Vietnam. Since this would decisively alter the nature of the American commitment, Bundy argued that a joint resolution should first be sought from Congress. On May 25, Bundy wrote a draft of the proposed resolution.[70]

Bundy's views soon took hold in the executive branch, so that "by June 10, there was firm support from most of the foreign-policy-making machinery of the Government for obtaining the resolution."[71] But Johnson's political instincts told him that a dramatic escalation of the war without a clear-cut "Pearl Harbor" provocation could prove costly in the fall elections. In June, therefore, he held back from implementing the hawkish recommendations of his advisors.[72]

Then, on the nights of August 2 and 4, there occurred off the Vietnamese coast a complex series of events whose exact nature has not to this day been fully established.[73] What matters to our study is how those events were perceived at the time, and on this point little ambiguity exists. As reported by the military, disseminated by the media, and accepted by the public, the American destroyer Maddox appeared to have been the victim of an unprovoked attack on August 2 by North Vietnamese torpedo boats while in international waters.[74] Avoiding a rash response, Johnson the next day took a two-prong step of issuing a stern warning to Hanoi and ordering an additional destroyer, the C. Turner Joy, to join the Maddox in the Tonkin Gulf.[75] Then on the night of the 4th, both destroyers reportedly were attacked by North Vietnamese torpedoes.[76]

Widespread acceptance of the view that American vessels had been attacked without provocation had a dramatic, catalytic effect here at home. What followed can only be understood as the coming together of the factors we have noted: Fulbright's own cold-war views on Vietnam, his strong, partisan support for Johnson in a presidential election year, and the unleashing within the executive branch of a secret plan to widen the war with explicit congressional approval.

Once Johnson decided to rally the Congress, he turned at once to Fulbright, who readily agreed to manage the proposed resolution in the

Senate.[77] On August 5, Fulbright formally presented to his Senate colleagues the measure that would prove so fatefully tragic. Amid the resolution's six paragraphs, two passages are of central significance.[78] The heart of the measure states that:

> . . . the Congress approves and supports the determination of the President, as Commander in Chief, to take all necessary measures to repel any armed attack against the forces of the United States and to prevent further aggression.[79]

A bit later, in Section 2, comes the assertion that:

> . . . the United States is, therefore, prepared as the President determines, to take all necessary steps, including the use of armed force, to assist any member or protocol state of the Southeast Asia Collective Defense Treaty requesting assistance in defense of its freedom.[80]

As soon as the resolution was read, even before it could be referred to a joint meeting of the Foreign Relations and Armed Services Committees, Senator Morse was on his feet to denounce it as a mindless ". . . predated declaration of war."[81] In this, his initial assault on the resolution, Morse focused on the underlying American policy: "our actions in Asia today are the actions of warmaking" and "we have threatened war where no direct threat to American security is at stake."[82]

At 9:00 A.M. the next day Fulbright presided over a secret joint meeting of the Foreign Relations and Armed Services committees. As the record of the hearing shows, Fulbright remained passive while Secretary of State Rusk, Secretary of Defense McNamara, and Chairman of the Joint Chiefs of Staff Wheeler proceeded to detail Hanoi's "aggression" for the assembled senators.[83] It is this passivity and credulity that would later cause him so much inner torment. "It never occurred to me it didn't happen that way," he would recall.[84] Later—too late—there would be reason to doubt the administration's version of what had transpired in the Gulf of Tonkin on those fateful August nights. It seems likely that Fulbright was indeed misled on the actual, immediate events of August 2 and 4. Fully as significant, however, was Fulbright's response to promptings whose soundness did not revolve around technical matters of who fired what at whom. In his recollection, "Rusk presented Vietnam as a conspiracy directed from Moscow. He thought it was our duty to intervene wherever the conspiracy surfaces."[85] But surely Rusk's was hardly an unconventional outlook in 1964. It was not Rusk, after all, who had received that very year massive notice by voicing, among other things, the view that

> . . . we have no choice but to support the South Vietnamese Government

and Army by the most effective means available. It should be clear to all concerned that the United States will continue to defend its vital interests in Vietnam.[86]

Clearly Rusk was preaching to an already converted Fulbright where Vietnam was concerned.

Later that day, Fulbright brought up the resolution for floor action in the Senate. Terming the August 4 incident involving the Maddox and the C. Turner Joy "without any doubt a calculated act of military aggression," he asserted that "the resolution now before the Senate is designed to shatter whatever illusions our adversaries may harbor about the determination of the United States to act promptly and vigorously against aggression."[87]

On the crucial question of the resolution's actual scope and intent, Fulbright, in response to a question by Senator McGovern, indicated his belief that "the policy of our Government not to expand the war still holds" and that nothing in the resolution would commit us to follow South Vietnamese leader Khan's stated desire that the war be carried to the North.[88] Moments later, in response to Senator Brewster's question as to "whether there is anything in the resolution which would authorize or recommend or approve the landing of large American armies in Vietnam," Fulbright initially responded that "there is nothing in the resolution, as I read it, that contemplates it." Then, in what might have been a devastating insight in a less crisis-ridden environment, Fulbright conceded that "the language of the resolution would not prevent it. It would authorize whatever the Commander-in-Chief feels is necessary."[89] This, indeed was the crux of the problem: what, precisely, was to be America's Vietnam policy and what, precisely, would the proposed resolution contribute to that policy? As Fulbright's remarks show, his own thinking on these momentous issues was not—at this crucial moment—entirely developed.

Senators Morse and Gruening were alone in denouncing the broad thrust of American policy in Southeast Asia.[90] To Morse, any president would already have sufficient authority to protect American ships and personnel; nothing in the resolution would enhance that authority, and thus the resolution would be superfluous.[91] The danger, as he saw it, was that the extremely broad language of the resolution (". . . all necessary measures . . . to prevent further aggression") contemplated no apparent limits, either on the substance of America's commitment or on the president's ability independently to define that commitment. Again and again, Morse pleaded with his colleagues to see that "what is proposed is to authorize the President of the United States, without a declaration of war, to commit acts of war."[92]

Fulbright's Hamlet-like, equivocal defense of the measure shows up again in separate colloquies with Senators John Sherman Cooper of Kentucky and Gaylord Nelson of Wisconsin. On August 6, Cooper and Fulbright had this exchange:

> *Mr. Cooper.* . . . In other words, are we now giving the President advance authority to take whatever he may deem necessary respecting South Vietnam and its defense, or with respect to the defense of any other country included in the treaty?
>
> *Mr. Fulbright.* I think that is correct.
>
> *Mr. Cooper.* Then, looking ahead, if the President decided that it was necessary to use such force as could lead into war, we will give that authority by this resolution?
>
> *Mr. Fulbright.* That is the way I would interpret it . . . .[93]

The next day, Senator Nelson, deeply troubled by the resolution's loose language, offered an amendment intended to make clear that "our continuing policy is to limit our role" and that "we should continue to attempt to avoid a direct military involvement in the Southeast Asian conflict."[94] Fulbright's response was one that would later come back to haunt him:

> I believe it is an accurate reflection of what I believe is the President's policy, judging from his own statements. That does not mean that as a practical matter I can accept the amendment. It would delay matters to do so.[95]

Throughout the records of the Senate debate there runs a skein of forlorn ambivalence that stands in stark contrast to the bold language of the resolution itself. Numerous senators rose to voice their anxiety about the apparent direction of American policy.[96] All but two, however, said that they would set those doubts aside and vote for the resolution in the belief that an hour of crisis was at hand which demanded the appearance, at least, of national unity and resolve.

Thus, on August 7, with only two dissenters—Morse and Gruening—the Senate followed Fulbright's lead and enacted the Gulf of Tonkin Resolution.[97] For his part, Lyndon Johnson now had the "blank check" that had secretly been contemplated since May. Later, in his memoirs, Johnson would dwell at length on the text of the Fulbright-Cooper exchange while avoiding altogether any reference to the instructive dialogue between Fulbright and Gaylord Nelson.[98] From this highly selective evidence, he wrenched the conclusion that "the record is clear. I wanted the Congress and the country to know what was being, or might have to be undertaken. The resolution served that purpose."[99] There was a brief, uneasy period when Johnson's "purpose" would win broad public support. Through the remainder of the year, Harris surveys found solid majorities in favor of the administration's steadily-hardening positions.[100]

For Fulbright, sponsorship of what was seen at the time as a patriotic measure was widely regarded as consistent with the new stature he had won in a single speech just months before. In time, however, as macabre "body counts" entered the language of everyday political discourse, he would look back on his role in passing the resolution with grief and bitterness. His biographers mark this as "his most humiliating moment in public life"; David Halberstam calls it "a move he would spend the rest of his life bitterly regretting."[101] How little does Fulbright reveal the pain when in 1966 he writes: "my role in the adoption of the resolution of August 7, 1964 is a source of neither pleasure nor pride to me today."[102] Years later, long after the last American helicopter had fled with its cargo of ignominy and pain, Fulbright would mourn his own failure to hold lengthy, public hearings before the resolution was adopted. With infinite sadness he says, "it could have been very different if we had just held hearings."[103]

5 *Fulbright's Dissent,*
1965–1966

THOUSANDS OF MILES separate Santo Domingo and Saigon. In 1965 fate would link them into familiar backdrops as America watched its military might flung into what were officially seen as tests of our resolve in halting the expansion of Communist rule through subversion and revolution. Fulbright's response to the galvanic events of 1965–66 would cast him in the unwanted role of public dissenter. By temperament and upbringing, he much preferred the comparative tranquility of routine Senate life to the turbulent stress of public controversy. His escalating outspokeness would earn him both lavish praise and bitter condemnation. In personal terms, his growing fame had as its price the contemplative serenity he so cherished. For Fulbright—as for the nation—1965–66 marked a season of fateful change.

The Dominican Incursion

The Dominican Republic shares the Caribbean Island of Hispaniola with Haiti. It has long known the familiar litany of sorrows common to most of the developing world: poverty, foreign domination, and domestic unrest. In April 1965, a severe crisis of public order arose following the overthrow of the pro-American civilian junta headed by Donald Reid Cabral. Leaders of the coup, both civilian and military, wanted a restoration of the constitutionally elected regime of Juan Bosch, a leftist reformer who had been forcibly deposed by the Reid junta. As Bosch's followers appeared on the brink of victory over the opposition Dominican military faction, the United States intervened militarily to suppress the disorder.[1]

Not until September 15, 1965, following lengthy Foreign Relations Committee hearings on the episode, did Fulbright rise in the Senate to present his critique of the administration's handling of the Dominican intervention. Though couched amid a carefully generous appraisal of President Johnson ("on the basis of the information and counsel he received, the President could hardly have acted other than he did"),[2] the thrust of the speech was bitingly critical: ". . . the United States turned its back on social revolution in Santo Domingo and associated itself with a corrupt and reactionary oligarchy," he charged.[3]

Central to Fulbright's analysis of the immediate question of the Dominican Republic was his deeper perception of hemispheric currents. "The movement of the future in Latin America is social revolution," he argued. "The question is whether it is to be Communist or democratic revolution and the choice which the Latin Americans make will depend in part on how the United States uses its great influence."[4] In light of this twin belief in the social volatility of Latin America and the apparently natural and proper role of this nation in shaping the internal fate of the region's members, Fulbright would have his countrymen sharpen their mental grasp of the operative dynamics: "we must try to understand social revolution and the injustices that give it rise because they are at the heart and core of the experience of the great majority of people now living in the world."[5] The needed task will require an uncommon intellectual effort since our own lives are separated from those of the Third World's poor by a vast existential chasm.

Our distaste for "uncouth revolutionaries" derives from the fact that "we are not, as we like to claim in Fourth of July speeches, the most truly revolutionary nation on earth; we are, on the contrary, much closer to being the most unrevolutionary nation on earth. We are sober and satisfied and comfortable and rich."[6] Our legacy of success and stability has left us somewhat unable to grasp fully the depth of revolutionary fervor in the poor nations. Add to this mix our reflexive anti-communism, and misguided interventionism becomes an ever-present possibility.

To Fulbright, this is precisely what transpired in the Dominican Republic. "The United States intervened forcibly in the Dominican Republic . . . not primarily to save American lives, as was then contended, but to prevent the victory of a revolutionary movement which was judged to be Communist-dominated. . . . This fear was based on fragmentary and inadequate evidence."[7]

Note that Fulbright is not offering up a generalized anti-interventionist rationale. Those who have emphasized Fulbright's dissent from contemporary foreign policy practice have too seldom noticed how narrowly based his dissent has typically been. Far from repudiating American interventionism, Fulbright wants rather to refine it into a pragmatic tool of sober purpose. In the case at hand, Fulbright's "dissent" includes the charge that "U.S. policy in the Dominican crisis was characterized initially by overtimidity."[8] Specifically, he believes that "the United States let pass its best opportunities to influence the course of events. The best opportunities were, on April 25, when Juan Bosch's party, the PRD, requested a 'United States presence,' and on April 27, when the rebels, believing themselves defeated, requested United States mediation for a negotiated settlement. Both requests were rejected."[9]

Clearly, it is not American interventionism *per se* that is being condemned, but rather what are judged to be clumsy, crude efforts based on intellectual slovenliness. Fulbright's preferred policy would have been no less imperialistic than that actually undertaken by the Johnson administration. It would have proceeded from the same expansive sense of the nation's rightful place in the world and would have led to an easy presumption in favor of a "United States presence" on the soil of a troubled near-neighbor. Its claim to distinction rests alone on its putatively more sophisticated grasp of the realities of the situation.

The exceedingly conservative character of Fulbright's dissent is clearly revealed in two passages near the end of the lengthy speech. In the first, he decries the fact that "the tragedy of Santo Domingo is that a policy that purported to defeat communism in the short run is more likely to have the effect of promoting it in the long run"[10] by alienating from us non-Communist progressives throughout Latin America. Clearly, it is the perceived counterproductiveness of the invervention that is being assailed, not the general concept of a forcibly-exported American order. The second statement comes amid the complaint that the administration's actions damaged the delicately-crafted inter-American system:

> The United States is a world power with world responsibilities and to it the inter-American system represents a sensible way of maintaining law and order in the region closest to the United States. To the extent that it functions as we want it to function, one of the inter-American system's important advantages is that it stabilizes relations within the Western hemisphere and thus frees the United States to act on its worldwide responsibilities.[11]

70

Here it is, neatly laid out in case we had somehow missed the point. Regional stability is the goal, it being a prerequisite to the nation's ability to fully enact its global visions. How can it be had? To Fulbright, by honing the acuity with which we apprehend the swirling currents of Latin America. Once we do so, we will surely see that "the movement of the future in Latin America is social revolution," a process which Fulbright emphatically proclaims is one that is amenable to American direction and control.[12]

The response to Fulbright's speech offers revealing clues about the way America discussed its place in the world in the middle of what would be remembered as a decade of self-conscious controversy and dissent. So utterly unaccustomed was the nation to public criticism of its foreign policy that a single critical speech representing the views of one Senator could and did trigger a nation-wide wave of discussion and commentary. The sheer volume of the response testifies to the sense of novelty with which Americans received Fulbright's critique.[13] Eric Sevareid's observation that "the Fulbright speech was a drama simply because it was unique in this period of consensus"[14] was undoubtly the most astute amid a veritable deluge of commentary, a good portion of which was semi-hysterical in tone and flagrantly obtuse in its inability to grasp the sharply conservative nature of Fulbright's dissent.

True to form the *Chicago Tribune* offered up the bombastic conclusion that "it is hardly necessary to say Fulbright is wrong. He is always wrong."[15] In the Senate, Russell Long of Louisiana rose immediately to denounce Fulbright's stand. "If the general philosophy of the Senator's speech had been followed," he argued, "Castro would have taken not only that island, but the Dominican Republic, also."[16] Florida's George Smathers weighed in with the remarkable argument that:

> I do not agree that too many were sent into the Dominican Republic. For that matter I do not believe we are sending too many troops to Vietnam. If one argued the same philosophy as that expressed by the Senator from Arkansas, perhaps he could say we are sending too many troops to Vietnam, because we are now beginning to win there.[17]

It fell to Connecticut's Thomas Dodd to deliver the formal, pro-administration rejoinder to Fulbright's criticisms. Addressing the Senate the day after Fulbright's speech, Dodd unleashed a vituperative barrage of personal invective. Fulbright, he charged, "suffers from an indiscriminating infatuation with revolutions of all kinds, national, democratic, or Communist."[18] Dodd added that Fulbright had "shut out from his mind all facts which failed to harmonize with the preconceived thesis that the rebels were right and the administration was wrong."[19] Having engaged Fulbright on this level, it was all but inevitable that Dodd would throw in

71

the ritualistic charge that by daring to dissent from contemporary orthodoxy Fulbright had given aid and comfort to the enemy: "I am certain that his speech will be picked up and played heavily by every
Communist and crypto-Communist and fellow traveler and anti-
American leftist who wields a pen in the Latin American press."[20]

In like vein, columnist William S. White, a close personal friend of
President Johnson, assailed Fulbright for speaking out against the administration. "To much of the world," wrote White, "his embittered testimony against this government's course in Latin America is turning
state's evidence and assisting the prosecution of his own side."[21] Evans
and Novak dismissed the Foreign Relations Committee hearings on
which Fulbright's remarks were based as a mere "quickie probe."[22] John
Chamberlain labeled Fulbright "a one-sided critic" who regularly uses
"double-standard thinking."[23] *Time* magazine's coverage of the brou-
haha triggered by one Senate speech included this remarkable cue to
help the reader see things *Time*'s way: "Fulbright's erratic attacks on the
Administration are no longer surprising."[24]

Not all comment was negative, Most, in fact, appeared to support
Fulbright's position, or, at least, his right to voice his views publicly.
Many newspapers echoed the editorial stance of the *New York Times*
that Fulbright "has now said a number of things about U.S. intervention
in the Dominican Republic that needed saying."[25] Columnist Joseph
Kraft assailed Fulbright's critics,[26] while Walter Lippmann praised the
Senator for opening up public debate.[27] The editors of the *Washington
Post* hailed Fulbright's "analytical powers" that "cut through the veneers
of cant and illusion."[28]

Much of the commentary dealt less with the specifics of Fulbright's
indictment than with the debate surrounding the propriety of his speaking out. As the editors of the *Nation* put it, in the course of praising
Fulbright's candor, "any American who says a critical word about U.S.
military or paramilitary operations anywhere on the globe is assured of a
generally bad press in his own land, and Senator Fulbright is no exception."[29] The *Washington Post*'s editors denounced Senator Dodd's
"tawdry if familiar tactic" of "trying to depict Mr. Fulbright as soft on
Communism."[30] Columnist Marquis Childs revealed a rare contemporary grasp of the essential issue in his observation that "on careful reread-
ing of the Fulbright speech it is hard to discover why the reaction was as
though it had been an offense against majesty."[31]

In the Senate, a number of Fulbright's colleagues rallied to his defense. Pennsylvania's Senator Clark argued that "the criticism of our
Dominican policy made by the Senator from Arkansas was healthy, salu-
tary, and in the long run will be helpful to the administration."[32] Senator

Young of Ohio reported that his own perusal of the documentary record led him to conclude that Fulbright's position was "corroborated and sound."[33] Minnesota's Eugene McCarthy lamented the fact that Fulbright's "thoughtful remarks" had only partially succeeded in prompting a thorough airing of the nation's Latin America policy. "In too great a measure," he argued, "they have been made the basis for raising questions about the relative authenticity of various sources of information or about the right or the propreity of the chairman to speak as he did on this matter."[34] Fulbright himself was moved to remark that "much of the discussion, I have noted to my surprise, has been about me rather than about the Dominican Republic and Latin America."[35]

Despite the distraction of extraneous issues, Fulbright had indeed prompted a national debate on the meaning of the Dominican invasion. In the nature of things, his *ex post facto* criticisms could not alter America's handling of the immediate crisis. This alone does not mean that his remarks were without effect; it does mean that their effect must be found, if it is to be found at all, in the formulation and conduct of future policy. One may perhaps concur with Andrew Kopkind's assessment that Fulbright "made his Senate speech not as a political leader but as an elder statesman-without-portfolio, an Arkansas de Tocqueville whose job it is not to make policy but to report it, and by reporting, influence in some small way its future course."[36] Indeed, this was the rationale that Fulbright himself would voice two weeks after delivering his now-famous address. "My main purpose in this case," he noted, "was to influence future actions."[37]

But what, in substance, would be the nature of Fulbright's desired influence? Certainly it would not, as Senator Dodd and others crudely suggest, be to render the nation's policy any more indifferent to the revolutionary designs of avowed Marxists. Still less would it be to yield a less interventionist American posture. Rather, the influence Fulbright sought was to inject a greater mental acuteness and selectivity into the external application of American power. In essence, the lesson he was trying to convey was that the nation could reduce the price of empire by substituting brainpower for firepower. Fulbright's mid-1960s world view did not in any important respect transcend this simple if subtle paradigm of the cost-effective tactician in the service of a consensual national outlook.

A full four years would pass before a new administration would enshrine as doctrine the Fulbright thesis that America could avoid the agony of interminable frontier wars and yet maintain its expansive global interests. But before that reformulation of foreign-policy premises would occur, the nation would wade into the moral and physical quagmire of Vietnam, where the ultimately convincing rebuttal to contemporary policy premises came wrapped in body bags. It is of the essence of Fulbright's torment that the lessons he so deeply yearned to impart to his countrymen would be learned, not through the civil pedagogy of his public instruction, but through the cruel, blood-soaked classroom of war.

Vietnam

Fulbright's star-crossed role in the Vietnam war came to bear all the traits of authentic tragedy. His sponsorship of the Gulf of Tonkin Resolution would be a recurring torment to him as President Johnson, citing the resolution's permissive language as his legal authority, dramatically escalated the level of violence in Indochina.

Throughout 1965 Fulbright maintained a cautious stance on the everwidening conflict; critcism of our now-militarized policy was left to others, especially Senators Morse and Mansfield. Fulbright's principal address on the subject that year was delivered to his Senate colleagues on June 15. The day before, Fulbright had spoken with Johnson, who, according to the *New York Times'* account, "told Mr. Fulbright that it would be helpful if he made a speech emphasizing that the Administration was committed to the goal of ending the war as soon as possible by negotiation without preconditions."[38]

There was still a warmth and closeness between the two men that had been nurtured by their long association in the Senate. Those personal bonds would later stretch and then snap under the avalanche of controversy aroused by Vietnam, but for now Fulbright's affection for Johnson helped check whatever doubts he entertained about the soundness of the president's course. In his well-publicized speech, Fulbright praised the "steadfastness and statesmanship" and the "restraint and patience" of President Johnson in resisting pressures for an even wider war.[39] He appeared to feel that the administration shared his own moderate views on the nation's proper course: "I am opposed to an unconditional American withdrawal from South Vietnam. . . . I am no less opposed to further escalation of the war."[40]

Within a few days of those remarks, Fulbright delivered a gloomy, foreboding address at a reunion of Rhodes scholars held at Swarthmore College. The tone of his remarks acutely reveals his own inner anxieties of the period. Fulbright offered the bleak assessment that "nations are sliding back into the self-righteous and crusading spirit of the cold war."[41] "Under these condition," he concluded, "the prognosis for peace with freedom is hardly favorable."[42] His dour mood is well captured by his use of Mark Twain's bitter, macabre "War Prayer": "for our sakes who adore thee, Lord," prays the protagonist before battle, "blast their hopes, blight their lives, . . . water their way with tears, stain the white snow with the blood of their wounded feet."

Clearly, this was a melancholy season for Fulbright. At the root of his distress was the mounting realization that events would soon force upon him a painful choice. On a personal level, he deeply wished to maintain close personal relations with Lyndon Johnson. More than friendship alone was at stake; by deep instinct Fulbright dreaded the thought of bringing on himself the firestorm of pressure and controversy that would certainly be triggered by publicly criticizing the war policies of a still-popular president. Yet, he could not much longer suppress his own gnawing doubts about the wisdom of committing America's power and prestige to the military determination of what he was coming to view as a localized political conflict.

As 1966 opened, Fulbright crossed a personal Rubicon, one that would secure his contemporary reputation as the nation's leading foreign policy dissenter. A supplemental foreign economic aid bill, S. 2793, was before the Foreign Relations Committee. Most of its $415 million would go to Vietnam. Fulbright's decision to hold public hearings on the measure created a compelling showcase for propagating his now-critical views on the war.

The Vietnam hearings, held on January 28, February 4, 8, 10, 17, and 18, 1966, created a national sensation. Lavish media coverage, including live television broadcasts of key sessions, served to focus much of the nation's attention on the committee's efforts.[43] What the nation saw was a steady stream of reasoned, articulate doubt about the soundness of the administration's war effort. That such doubt came from men of the stature of George F. Kennan and Lieutenant General James Gavin served to dispel the pernicious view that foreign policy dissent was the odious froth of a disreputable few.

For his part, Fulbright maintained a generally low-key stance throughout the hearings in order to minimize the inevitable public focus on personalities and the concomitant tendency to reduce momentous questions of public policy to mere personal antipathies. The popular press had recently noted Fulbright's conspicuous absence from recent White House functions and had stressed the view that, in *Time*'s words, "Fulbright is off Johnson's guest list because the President resents the Senator's criticism of Administration foreign policy."[44] Fulbright refused to respond in kind. "There's no war on with the White House," he stressed as the hearings got under way.[45] He had no wish to "embarrass" the administration, he said, but then added: "Is acquiesence the only thing that should be expected by any Administration? I do not view it that way."[46] The stage was thus set for an historic public dissection of the nation's foreign policy premises.

Carrying the banner for the administration in the hearings was Secretary of State Dean Rusk. Like Fulbright, Rusk was a product of the rural South and had attended Oxford University. But beneath such surface similarities lay massive differences between the two in temperament and outlook. Where Fulbright was cerebral, critical, and sometimes caustic, Rusk displayed the ponderous serenity of those who have stopped doubting the universality of their private conclusions.

To Rusk, Vietnam constituted a paradigm instance of the chronic problem of maintaining order in an anarchic global system.[47] "The underlying crisis of this postwar period turns about a major struggle over the very nature of the political structure of the world," he reasoned.[48] The next step in his world view comes from the argument that "what we face in Vietnam is what we have faced on many occasions before—the need to check the extension of Communist power in order to maintain a reasonable stability in a precarious world."[49] Our policy springs from eminently selfless motives: "the United States seeks no territorial aggrandizement. . . . We want no permanent military bases, no trade advantages," he insisted. Rather, "we wish only that the people of South Vietnam should have the right and opportunity to determine their future in freedom without coercion or threat from the outside."[50]

Fulbright's frequently-tense exchanges with the secretary marked the dramatic high point of the hearings. Yet it was by no means the case that Fulbright's critique arose from a fundamentally different concept of America's world role and interests than that so ably articulated by Secretary Rusk. In their bristling colloquy of February 18, Rusk's observation that "some of the things you said suggested that we should abandon the effort in South Vietnam" brought a pained denial from the chairman: "No, I am not suggesting we should abandon it." A paragraph later Fulbright announced "I am not questioning our motives. I think our motives are very good."[51]

The undertaking he labeled well-motivated and whose continuation in some form he has endorsed was nonetheless for Fulbright the source of great unease. "What bothers me," he said, "is that this is in one sense a relatively minor matter. In another sense it seems to be the trigger that may result in a world war, and I do not want that to happen. That is what we are really concerned with."[52]

Sharing in the main Rusk's broad views on the global sway of American power, Fulbright by 1966 had come to doubt the tactical operational premises of the war's architects. He doubted that Vietnam constituted an authentic challenge to the American-backed fabric of world order. If this doubt was valid, he reasoned, then surely Vietnam's intrinsic worth as a friendly nation was insufficient to justify the extraordinary price of a direct American combat role. He doubted, too, the "facile assumption" that the nation could continue to expend billions on a distant war and still devote adequate attention and resources to its domestic needs.[53]

In the midst of the hearings, CBS broadcast a special report entitled "Fulbright: Advice and Dissent," in which the Senator was interrogated by Eric Sevareid and Martin Agronsky.[54] The central issue of Vietnam was well-captioned in this brief exchange:

> *Mr. Sevareid:* The Secretary of State, Senator, seems to equate Communist China with Hitler's Germany of the thirties, that is, he feels that this is basically an aggressive force that unless one stops them in the early stage, as in Vietnam now, thinking again of Hitler's course of action, you will end up with a great big war. Do you subscribe to that analogy?

> *Senator Fulbright:* I am afraid I do not. This is a very complicated situation. In the first place, I think we have come to grossly exaggerate, at least the present power, of China to carry a war beyond her borders.[55]

Here, as in the case of the Dominican incursion, Fulbright was voicing his doubts about the intellectual soundness of the operational premises on which life and death decisions were based. "I do not question the motives," he would say in the Senate a month later; "all I question is the wisdom."[56] This, indeed, was the essence of Fulbright's much-misunderstood dissent. Ways must be found, he was insisting, to maintain our unrivaled place in the sun without the constant burden and danger of war. As he would put the point on another occasion, "the first consideration in developing a sound foreign policy should be the protection of your strength. When you dissipate it too widely and profligately, that is the thing that endangers you." The key need was for greater "wisdom." To Fulbright, the Rusk world view was the dangerous product of outmoded Cold War simplifications. The practical wisdom Fulbright would have his countrymen come to share was that Vietnam was simply unnecessary to the preservation of America's broader role and interests. "In the case of Vietnam," he wrote, "our honor and prestige are indeed involved, but they are involved principally because we laid them on the line and did so in a legally uncertain and politically casual way."[58]

The response to Fulbright's 1966 criticisms of American Vietnam policy was depressingly predictable. The editors of *Time* were outraged to the point of near-apoplexy. "The trait that has made him a Senate storm center for two decades is not hard to define," ran one story. "Put simply, it is an emotional and intellectual reluctance to believe that Communism is a monolithic doctrine of belligerance based on a fanatical dream of world domination. That blind spot has been manifested repeatedly through Fulbright's career."[59] Manifesting some striking blind spots of its own, *Time* offered up the singularly obtuse argument that "the testimony before Fulbright's committee pointed up a curious fact. Many liberal interventionists who were so ready to fight for Europe before World War II have become virtual isolationists today."[60] In *Time*'s telling, the Vietnam hearings had served merely "to bulwark the Administration's case that it is a necessary war."[61]

Right-wingers, having embraced the war as their own, were incensed by Fulbright's critique. Senator Goldwater repeatedly unleashed verbal broadsides against his colleague, even going so far as implying that Fulbright "lends support and aid and comfort to our enemies."[62] Columnist Kenneth Crawford publicly called upon Fulbright to resign as chairman of the Foreign Relations Committee. "This would free him to indulge the peevishness that characterizes his recent performance," Crawford wrote, adding that Fulbright then "could be as waspish as his apparently wounded vanity tells him to be."[63] Writer Henry Fairlie dismissed Fulbright as a mere "Cassandra."[64]

William Buckley's *National Review* outdid its well-nurtured penchant for mean-spirited invective in its campaign against Fulbright. "He should be curbed," ran one editorial; "others have to use the sidewalks too, you know."[65] The depth of Buckley's bitter passion is best captured in his response to Fulbright's Asian policy speech of July 22, 1966. It sought to smother the senator's policy criticisms beneath a vitriolic blanket of ridicule and contempt:

> Although the walls of the Senate have looked patiently down on its inmates for quite a long time now, and although they have witnessed and heard many rum characters and many fierce quarrels and many pointless, pitiful, and ridiculous words, they have seldom in our time seen any spectacle more grotesque than the 'Asian policy speech' that J. William Fulbright delivered July 22. . . . Did Senator Fulbright do the thing thoroughly? Did he accompany his words with wild gestures? Did his eyes wander erratically, did he skip and dance as he spoke? Did he enter the Senate that day dressed as a clown? Did he stick straws in his hair during the progress of his speech?[66]

This easy resort to the sobriquet was not untypical of the response to Fulbright's efforts.[67] His criticisms fell on a nation absorbed in fatuous superficialty. Rational debate tended to be crowded out by a mindless preoccupation with personalities. "If Fulbright pushes his attack on the

Administration to further extremes," one writer noted, "he will run the danger of becoming the center of a debilitating national controversy over American policy in the Far East."[68] Not until the weekly reports of American casualties reached grotesque proportions would it become clear that it was the war itself—and not the stylized exchanges that still passed for foreign policy debate—that was truly debilitating to the nation. Only then would Fulbright's tightly circumscribed dissent gain acceptance as the new conventional wisdom of the nation.

The Arrogance Of Power

In 1966 Fulbright published a book-length statement of his views. Entitled *The Arrogance Of Power*,[69] the volume grew out of a series of lectures delivered that spring at Johns Hopkins University's School of Advanced International Studies in Washington.[70] In it, Fulbright goes well beyond a simple commentary on the issues of the day. He reveals in more depth than on any previous occasion his deepest-held beliefs on fundamental political and diplomatic questions. In order to draw out those underlying beliefs and preceptions and to note points of constancy and change, *The Arrogance Of Power* is best observed through the same five organizing categories used to discuss his 1963 work, *Prospects For The West*. They are, first, Fulbright's fundamental concept of the nature and utility of political action, including especially his views on the role of reason in human affairs; second, his views on the making of American foreign policy; third, his informing vision of America's role and interests in the world; fourth, his perception of significant threats to those interests; and, finally, his prescriptive thoughts as to how the nation can best counter those threats.

Fulbright's long-standing skepticism appears to have deepened under the impact of what he regarded as the tragic and disastrous policies that the nation was pursuing in the mid-1960s. For years he had spoken out against the excesses and cruelties attending man's zealous pursuit of secular creeds. He returned to this theme in *The Arrogance Of Power*, bitterly assailing "men who believe in some cause without doubt and practice their beliefs without scruple, men who cease to be human beings with normal preferences for work and fun and family and become instead living, breathing embodiments of some faith or ideology."[71]

Fulbright renewed and extended his critique of ideology as a motive force in political life. In his estimation, ideology distorts our mental

79

workings by its inherent force in selecting, filtering, and ordering our perceptions of the outer world.[72] He debunks the normative content of ideology as well, arguing that "almost all of us acquire our ideological beliefs not principally as the result of an independent intellectual process but largely as the result of an accident of birth."[73] The political "truths" that so arouse and inflame domestic and world politics are thus for their adherents largely coincidental parts of one's life.

In place of romantic, transcendent visions, Fulbright advocates a sober politics of caution. "We must strike a balance between our aspirations and our limitations," he argues.[74] Sound policy must be grounded in "an approach that accepts the world as it is."[75] In his 1963 volume he had urged the view that "we must be cautious in our prescriptions and modest in our aspirations."[76] 1966 found him once again pleading for "skepticism in our judgments and restraint in our actions."[77]

Political action, it would follow, affords at best a slender outlet for the recurring human dream of consciously-planned change and progress. At one point Fulbright makes the point quasi-expicit: "insofar as the satisfactions of life have anything to do with politics at all, they have to do with domestic not foreign politics."[78] The conditional "insofar" suggests that for Fulbright the realm of the political ought not be seen as intimately related to man's deeper yearning for happiness.

The *Arrogance Of Power* contains Fulbright's fullest account of how he envisions that ultimate wellspring of political behavior: the concept of human nature. He does so in two ways. First, he restates and extends a view set forth two years earlier in the published version of *Old Myths And New Realities* that "the ultimate source of war and peace is human nature."[79] Emphasis is placed on "man's competitive instinct," which Fulbright insists is an "unalterable . . . element of human nature."[80] Under the condition of competitive state sovereignty, Fulbright believes the latent drive toward rivalry and conflict becomes manifest. Man's inherent hubris becomes collectivized, leading to what Fulbright calls "the arrogance of power," which he defines as "a psychological need that nations seem to have in order to prove that they are bigger, better, or stronger than other nations."[81]

This emphasis on the psychological origins of political behavior gives *The Arrogance Of Power* its distinctive case. Throughout the volume there runs a recurring theme of politics as tragedy, one whose roots lie in human nature. Competition and strife, rationalized and intensified by the distortions of ideology, are for Fulbright the natural order. That cheerless natural order is, in turn, squarely rooted in man's inherent nature, he argues.[82]

Fulbright's second set of comments on man's underlying nature occurs in this passage near the volume's end:

> . . . the essential strength of democracy and capitalism as they are practiced in the West is that they are relatively free of doctrine and dogma and largely free of illusions about man and his nature. Of all the intellectual achievements of Western civilization, the one, I think, that is most truly civilized is that by and large we have learned to deal with man as he is or, at most, as he seems capable of becoming, but not as we suppose in the abstract he ought to be. Our economy is geared to human acquisitiveness and our politics to human ambition. Accepting these qualities as part of human character, we have been able in substantial measure both to satisfy them and to criticize them.[83]

Fulbright seems unwilling to consider that acquisitiveness and ambition might themselves reflect the nation's thoroughly Lockean morality with its eminently doctrinal notions of individual competition for largely material rewards.[84]

In sum, then, *The Arrogance Of Power* presents Fulbright's basic views on politics, which emerges as an unrelieved expression of man's deeply flawed nature.

The book reflects graphically both the swiftness and the thoroughness of Fulbright's turnaround on the question of how American foreign policy ought to be made. A mere three years earlier Fulbright had written that "the source of an effective foreign policy under our system is Presidential power."[85] On that occasion it was Fulbright's conclusion that "we must contemplate a further enhancement of Presidential authority in foreign affairs."[86] A year later, in his foreward to the published version of *Old Myths and New Realities*, Fulbright had altered his emphasis a bit to argue that "Congress, and especially the Senate, does have a role in foreign policy. This role is to participate in shaping broad policies." "It is also a proper and important part of the Congressional role in foreign policy to take the lead in what ought to be a continuing national discussion and examination of the posture of the United States in the world, of our basic national interests, and of ways and means of advancing those interest," he added.[87] Still, this was by no means a clarion call for congressional activism. Set alongside this rather limited concept of what the Congress should do was Fulbright's critique of "a recurring tendency on the part of Congress to overstep its proper role."[88]

By 1966 Fulbright's attitude had undergone significant change, and he invoked constitutional provisions which—in his telling—*require* the Senate to "review the conduct of foreign policy by the President and his advisors, to render advice whether it is solicited or not, and to grant or

withhold its consent to major acts of foreign policy."[89] Alongside this
rather more expansive view of the congressional role in foreign policy-
making, Fulbright finds its recent performance to be wanting. "In recent
years the Congress has not been fully discharging these responsibilities
in foreign affairs," he notes, adding that "the Senate's constitutional powers of advice and consent have atrophied into what is widely regarded
as, though never asserted to be, a duty to give prompt consent with a
minimum of advice."[90] In order to reverse the trend toward the atrophy
of its role, Fulbright urges the Senate to strengthen its deliberative function, freely air whatever differences it may have with current policies,
protect its independence, and not hesitate to criticize the executive
branch.[91]

By 1966, then, Fulbright had come full circle. Here once again was the
insistence on a broad and independent congressional role that had
marked his single term in the House of Representatives more than
twenty years earlier.[92]

Although *The Arrogance Of Power* contains no systematic explication
of Fulbright's contemporary concepts of America's proper world role
and interest, there are occasional glimpses into his underlying beliefs
and perceptions. What is clear is that at this point in his career Fulbright's
criticisms of American foreign policy arose not because his concept of
the nation's deeper interest differed importantly from that held by the
objects of his criticisms, but rather grew out of different notions of what
actions the nation could and must undertake in the name of securing its
agreed position.

Nowhere does he advocate—or even seriously contemplate—the unilateral relinquishing of America's preeminent position in the global
community. At one point he matter-of-factly refers to "the United States
as the nation with principal, though not exclusive responsibility for
world peace and stability."[93] The uncritical acceptance of a view which
attributes to the nation a generalized superintending authority for the
functioning of the global system as a whole recurs—if only implicitly—
throughout *The Arrogance Of Power*. The identification of the national
interest with the attainment and maintenance of a preferred international order and the substantive specification of "stability" as a defining
feature of that order were central components of America's consensual
world view, circa 1966. As articulated by official administration spokesmen, sanctioned by respected academics, propogated by the media,
and accepted by virtually all segments of the mass public, America's
sense of self added up to the vaguely imperial outlook that perhaps in-
heres in the fact of being a superpower.

Once the goal of universal stability is admitted, it follows that vindication of the goal may well entail—in an environment of mounting global instability—the application of national power at unpredictable points around the globe. Too, deterrence of provocations to the global order with which one has equated the national interest renders imperative maintenance of unquestioned credibility of the nation's commitment, for the successful questioning of that commitment in any particular case could well call into question the entire fabric of international order whose very survival constitutes the agreed *sine qua non* of national security.

Fulbright was by no means the only "foreign policy dissenter" whose underlying premises turned out to be strikingly similar to those held by the objects of his criticisms. Former Kennedy aide Richard Goodwin had by 1966 acquired a reputation as a liberal critic of American diplomacy. Yet in the same year that Fulbright published *The Arrogance Of Power,* Goodwin wrote that "the bedrock vital interest of the United States . . . is to establish that American military power, once committed to defend another nation cannot be driven from the field."[94] And so too that year would Fulbright, in the book that secured his contemporary reputation as a "dissenter," write that "the United States cannot accept defeat or a disorderly withdrawal from South Vietnam."[95] So much for the charge that Fulbright proceeded from an isolationist concept of foreign policy!

Fulbright, in fact, explicitly takes up the question of isolationism and vigorously denies both the viability of the policy and its applicability as a pejorative appelation to his own views. He does so by first decrying "the over-involvement of the United States in certain parts of the world with the consequent neglect of important problems here at home. It is not true that this concern indicates a willingness to abandon vital American interests abroad and let the world go its way while we retreat into an illusory isolationism."[96]

Certainly Fulbright's own core notions about America's deeper role and interest in the world were anything but isolationist. He does not doubt the need to contain China's power in Asia.[97] In Latin America, he identifies America's interest with the evolution of democratic societies, an outcome whose realization "will depend in part on how the United States uses its great influence."[98] Elsewhere, the full breadth of the nation's global role is suggested in the observation that "the United States is a conservative power in the world in the sense that most of its vital interests are served by stability and order."[99] The cat, so to speak, is irretrievably out of the bag.

Although *The Arrogance Of Power* was widely perceived at the time as constituting a sharp assault on American foreign policy, it is clear that its criticisms do not, after all, rest on an unconventional concept of America's world role. Fulbright's own bedrock beliefs were nothing if not orthodox. If his observations are nonetheless found to sum up to a coherent critique, such claim must rest on the view that Fulbright's differences with contemporary policy are more a matter of the appropriate means required to attain goals he shares with those who are objects of his criticism. That Fulbright was in 1966 largely engaged in a debate over means is readily seen. It does not follow that his criticisms were therefore of little consequence; it does follow that they were not—contemporary opinion to the contrary—engaged in the task of fundamental inquiry and criticism.

On examination, Fulbright's 1966 commentaries and arguments turn out to rest upon and to be separated from official policy and public mood by fairly sharp differences over the nature and source of threat to the nation's paramount position and, hence, differences over the course of action that would best maintain the nation's global primacy.

It is not a part of Fulbright's 1966 world view to attribute to the Soviet Union any inordinate threat to America's interest and security. He explicitly announces his belief that Soviet leaders share the same commitment to maintaining existing global arrangements which he elsewhere defines as America's own core need: "Russia can now properly be regarded as a conservative power in international relations, as a nation whose stake in the status quo is a far more important determinant of her international behavior than her philosophical commitment to world revolution."[100] China, too, is characterized as posing little threat of physical aggression, the superheated rhetoric of its leaders notwithstanding.[101] If those nations widely viewed as America's principal adversaries individually pose little immediate threat to the nation's security and interests, their combined menace is held to be so slight as to be improbable. Fulbright repeatedly argues that the communist world is no longer monolithic. The fact of polycentrism in the former Soviet bloc means, in Fulbright's view, a significantly diminished Communist capacity to challenge American interest.[102]

Fulbright does warn of the dangers inherent in the turbulence wracking much of the developing world. Violence, authoritarianism, and revolution will be widespread for years to come, he notes. In this "extended time of troubles," it will be in America's interest to promote "peaceful and democratic social revolution in the underdeveloped world."[103] Yet it is not a part of Fulbright's purpose to endorse a bold new course of policy for the nation, for having conceded the nation's stake in the outcome of Third World instability, Fulbright quickly casts gloom on the prospects for the successful vindication of that stake: "we would do well

. . . to stop deluding ourselves about the likelihood of success," he writes.[104] Does this mean, then, that the nation stands in danger of defeat in maintaining what is held to be a legitimate interest? By no means, in Fulbright's telling, since the deeper force at work throughout the Third World is the force of nationalism, which—regardless of its several outstanding guises—does not immediately aid or damage the global weight of outside powers.

To be sure, America could, through its own incomprehension, alienate the leaders of Third World revolutions and thus open opportunities for local influence to our ideological opponents: "insofar as the United States makes itself the enemy of revolutionay movements, communism is enabled to make itself their friend."[105] Indeed, it is central to Fulbright's purpose at hand to argue that this very danger is by no means a hypothetical one but is, rather, at the core of much that is wrong with American diplomacy. The nation faces a dilemma throughout the Third World, he argues, one rooted in the incompatability of two of its operational premises: "We are simultaneously hostile to communism and sympathetic to nationalism, and when the two become closely associated, we become agitated, frustrated, angry, precipitate, and inconstant."[106] Fulbright believed the nation was responding more to its anti-Communist instincts than its pronationalist sentiments; central to his concern was the conclusion that

> . . . American interests are better served by supporting nationalism then by opposing communism, and . . . when the two are encountered in close association it is in our interest to accept a communist government rather than to undertake the cruel and all but impossible task of suppressing a genuinely national movement."[107]

If America's expansive global interests face a less than urgent threat from abroad, it remains the case that they are nonetheless menaced by a danger so great that their very survival cannot be assumed. That danger, in Fulbright's view, is that the nation will become so intoxicated by its own power that it will lose the capacity for nuance in its grasp of global currents. The coming together of unrivaled power, an overweening sense of purpose, and an impaired sense of proportion could make the United States a marauding force, recklessly intervening around the globe in order to promote its own preferred notions. This in essence is what Fulbright means by the provocative phrase, "the arrogance of power."[108] He believes that its symptoms are unmistakably evident in the nation, including an inflated sense of mission, "an excessive preoccupation with foreign relations," and a chronic inability to see the world as it is.[109] Taken together, they add up to the pervasively imperial mood that "has afflicted, weakened, and in some cases destroyed great nations in the past."[110]

Thus, it is Fulbright's belief that America's global interests are more likely to be undermined by our own mistakes than by the acts of external adversaries. It follows that the nation has it in its grasp—should it prove able to summon the clarity and the will—to avoid self-induced catastrophe and, by so doing, secure its expansive concept of its own global role and interest.

Fulbright's 1966 message was one of warning tempered by hope. At length he warns of the dangers of an overly ambitious foreign policy, one which proceeds from an exaggerated sense of the nation's purpose and all too easily resorts to force in pursuing its grandiose goals. The hope he holds out is that the nation can, by an act of will, throw off its mistaken notions and adopt in their stead a more pragmatic sense of its place in the sun. This is, indeed, the book's *raison d'etre*. Fulbright's world view reveals itself as one animated by a durable faith—albeit a faith characteristically cloaked in gloomy garb—that America can avert the dangers facing it and so prove master of its own fate.

Fulbright's broad prescription is for a reordering of the nation's priorities: "what is called for now is a redressing of the balance toward domestic affairs after twenty-five years of almost total preoccupation with wars and crises abroad."[111] He makes it clear that what is saved in wealth and energy now squandered abroad must be invested in social change here at home, not merely hoarded or frittered away in self-indulgent privatism.[112]

The immediate focus of a consciously-sought campaign of retrenchment would be, of course, Vietnam. Virtually all of chapter nine of *The Arrogance of Power* is given over to a detailed proposal whose core premise is that "the key to peace is mutual disengagement through political arrangements for the neutralization of Southeast Asia."[113] Fulbright's plan proceeds from a firm belief that "the tactical premise underlying the large-scale American military involvement has proven to be unsound."[114] To concede tactical error is not, however, to abandon a deeper interest. Under his plan, the United States "could and should retain its sea and air power around the periphery of Asia."[115] This follows from his acceptance of the central premise of the war's supporters, namely that "the central issue is the contest between Chinese and American power."[116] It is a matter of tactics, then, and not as a matter of fundamental disagreement with the nation's foreign policy orthodoxy that Fulbright urges the termination of military action in Vietnam.

Beyond Vietnam, Fulbright's 1966 prescription emphasizes avoiding in the future acts which might lead to similar entaglements. Among his specific targets is bilateral foreign aid, which, he argues, "has become a vehicle toward the involvement of the United States in matters lying far beyond its proper concern."[117] In its place, Fulbright advocates a multi-lateral program channeled through international agencies.[118] Fulbright believes that it is in our power to undertake "limited positive steps . . . toward improved relations with China," such as the exchange of scholars and abandonment of our opposition to Peking's admission to the United Nations.[119] Such steps would by no means entail the giving up of our overall position in Asia, however; his call for what Professor A. Doak Barnett termed a policy of "containment without isolation" would entail significant changes in diplomatic style while entailing no apparent change in strategic interest.

Fulbright's comments on the Soviet Union similarly stress the need to undertake practical steps, such as cultural exchanges and trade, to help build a "habit of cooperation."[120] He argues that "the reconciliation of East and West is primarily a psychological problem, having to do with the cultivation of cooperative attitudes and of a sense of having practical common objectives."[121] These sought changes in East-West atmospherics do not proceed from any call for unilateral American withdrawal from its global role, nor do they entail any lessening of the rigors of containment. Rather they are designed to moderate the intensity of the Soviet-American duel, thus creating the very climate of relaxed tensions which is held to be the necessary precondition to the nation's return to a more domestic-oriented stance.

It is in these ways, Fulbright argues, that the nation can free up the energies to address its long standing needs at home. That they entail stylistic more than substantive changes in the nation's approach to the outer world is abundantly clear. That this was almost universally missed in 1966 is a signal comment on the quality of the nation's foreign policy dialogue. *The Arrogance Of Power* established, once and for all, Fulbright's reputation as a foreign policy dissenter. His was still at this point a dissent built more on appearances than on matters of fundamental import.

6 *The Limitationist Critique and the End of the Johnson Consensus*

FULBRIGHT'S 1965–66 EMERGENCE as an outspoken critic of American diplomacy was, as we have seen, a halting, reluctant process of personal growth and change. Sharing in the main the broad sense of American purpose held by the objects of his criticism, he grew increasingly disenchanted with the methods used to advance that purpose, and it was largely to those methods that his highly vocal dissent was addressed. Viewed solely as a singular instance of intellectual evolution, Fulbright's mounting dissent constitutes an episode of more than passing interest, if only because of the public prominence of its subject. Its larger significance, however, lies in the fact that the changes taking place in Fulbright's outlook were by no means isolated events in an idiosyncratic life. Rather, they were part of, and partly a cause of, a pronounced national mood-swing of the late 1960s and early 1970s wherein the nation came to reject the foreign policy style and outlook imperfectly summed up by the term "globalism." Installed in its place was a new set of operational premises loosely grouped under the banner of "limitationism." First appearing in the guise of a protest ideology linking key elements of the nation's political and intellectual elite, the limitationist critique became by 1970 both the conventional wisdom of a majority of Americans and the informing presence behind efforts of succeeding administrations to reformulate America's world role.

The Limitationist Critique

The first and most basic argument made by publicists of the limitationist critique is that the nation has attempted too much in its foreign policy and that it thus became, at some point, badly over-extended. "The nation is burdened,"[1] they argue, by a vast array of commitments that exceeds the bounds of prudence. Arguing for an appreciation of the limits of American power, Henry Steele Commager wrote that "it is not our duty to keep peace throughout the globe, to put down aggression wherever it starts up, to stop the advance of communism or other isms which we may not approve of."[2] As the range of its commitments grew, so too did the nature of the nation's purpose change, so that in time the national interest became transformed into an imperial interest. We acquired, in the words of Stillman and Pfaff, "that sense of total involvement and responsibility which . . . results in a global American interventionism."[3]

Secondly, it is not a part of the limitationist critique to impugn the motives behind what is otherwise found to be an objectionable diplomacy. Indeed, the nation and its leaders are judged to have been remarkably, perhaps uniquely, free of the rapacious impulses that animate the diplomacy of other nations.[4] If its instincts have been decent, even benevolent, the nation's foreign policy is nonetheless found wanting, not least on the grounds that its putatively humane ends have been invoked in the defense of actions that can only undermine the credibility of the nation's professed values.[5]

What is it that motivated the vigorous, sometimes violent outward projection of American power? To limitationist writers, it is the nation's reflexive anti-communism.[6] Born of cold war realities but later applied indiscriminately, without regard to the nation's own interests or capabilities, anti-communism is held to be at the root of much that is wrong with our foreign policy. As one distinguished critic put it, "The anti-Communist crusade had its origins in the Truman Doctrine . . . (which) transformed a concrete interest of the United States in a geographically defined part of the world into a moral principle of world-wide validity, to be applied regardless of the limits of American interests and of American power."[7] The desire to curb the spread of a totalitarian ideology is readily acknowledged to be a worthy, even noble aspiration. It is the alleged elevation of that desire to central, dogmatic status in the nation's diplomatic calculus that critics depict as outmoded and mindless.

A third point advanced by limitationist critics reflects their view of the root intellectual error behind the nation's foreign policy. They believe that the very universalism of our anti-Communist animus weakens our ability to comprehend local realities, the chief of which is the force of particularistic nationalism. The limitationist school insists that the very fact of nationalism renders outdated policies based on the core premise that monolithic communism comprises the overriding international threat to the nation's interests.[8]

It is this insistence on the sheer wrongheadedness of American foreign policy that gives the limitationist critique its distinctive bite. In a much-quoted passage, Hans Morgenthau argued that:

> If one should characterize American foreign policy in a sentence, one could say that it has lived during the last decade or so on the intellectual capital which was accumulated in the famous fifteen weeks of the spring of 1947 when the policy of containment, the Truman Doctrine, and the Marshall Plan fashioned a new American foreign policy, and that this capital has now been nearly exhausted.[9]

In like vein, Stillman and Pfaff argued that "if there is a single indictment of the multiple and self-contradictory forms that American globalism takes, it is simply that its arguments and rationales are out of date."[10] To Ronald Steel, "our diplomacy remains frozen in the posture of two decades ago and mesmerized by a ritual anti-communism that has become peripheral to the real conflict of power in today's world."[11] "We are the last of the ideologues," he adds, "clinging to political assumptions that have been buried by changing time and circumstances."[12]

By the late 1960s foreign policy critics were placing heavy emphasis on the fact of disunity in the Communist world. Titoism and the Sino-Soviet split seemed to show, they argued, the irrelevance of old policies based on opposition to a presumed Communist monolith directed from Moscow.[13] To critics, the dramatic resurgence of nationalism compelled the adoption of a new American outlook which assessed other nations according to their particular stance toward concrete American interests rather than their domestic ideological preferences. According to Arthur Schlesinger, Jr., "the fallacy—and tragedy—of current United States policy . . . is that we are trying to deal with polycentrist Communism today in terms of stereotypes and strategies left over from the fight a generation ago against Stalinism. We have thus permitted rational anti-Communism to yield to obsessive anti-Communism."[14]

A fourth point raised by limitationist critics in the late 1960s addresses the results of what they regard as the erroneous operational premises behind official policy. In their view, the effort to actualize the universal aspirations of our instinctive crusade against communism has given rise to a militarized, interventionist policy, often where U.S. interests aren't truly at stake. "America, whether most of us realize it or not, has become the interventionist power par excellence," wrote Ronald Steel.[15] To Theodore Draper, the mounting use of military force as a tool of interventionism reflects a deep crisis in our approach to the outer world.[16]

The upshot, to critics, has been the growth of the very anti-American, pro-socialist sentiment that our policy ostensibly seeks to thwart.[17] This "momentous change"[18] in policy is contrasted with the allegedly more sober, pragmatic style of the earlier cold war.

A fifth and final element of the limitationist critique entails its prescription for remedying the foreign policy errors it claims to have discerned. In essence, limitationist writers wish to deideologize our diplomatic outlook. Beyond this, and in consequence of it, they would have the nation scale down the range of its global undertakings and, in particular, would curb the reliance on military force, particularly in Third World nations undergoing internal struggles for power.[19] A more fluid policy, responsive more to local realities than to universal ideological measures, is what the limitationist school prescribes. In place of ideological standards, critics would have the nation think in terms of concrete American interests. Once such a change in our foreign policy outlook is accomplished, they insist, a less interventionist policy will follow, for a pluralistic world is held to be ultimately a safer world than one animated by the deadly standoff of opposed ideological blocs.

From the available evidence it is abundantly clear that the public's foreign policy outlook underwent striking change during the late 1960s and early 1970s. It is equally clear that the direction of that change was along the lines staked out by publicists of the limitationist critique. On Vietnam, the issue that can safely be said to have occasioned the broader rethinking of the nation's foreign policy premises, antiwar feeling rose as inexorably as the grim weekly tabulations of death. As early as October 1967, Gallup surveys revealed a plurality agreeing that "the U.S. made a mistake sending troops to fight in Vietnam."[20] By March 1968 more Americans called themselves "doves" than "hawks" on the war.[21] By August of that year, solid majorities had come to regard our military intervention as a mistake,[22] an assessment that would, by January 1973, reach an overwhelming two-to-one proportion among the populace.[23] The despised and rejected undertaking that was defended at official levels as necessary to the maintenance of American credibility and power was judged by a crushing five-to-one majority to have actually weakened our position in world affairs.[24]

Vietnam, then, became a bitterly unpopular war with the American people. But if Vietnam entailed, as has often been suggested, more basic questions about our foreign policy premises that went beyond the war itself,[25] we would expect to find evidence of changing foreign policy attitudes on questions other than Vietnam. Polling data from the period offers ample evidence to confirm that expectation. In the spring of 1969 a Harris survey uncovered "widespread skepticism about the uses of military power."[26] In Harris's words, "the mood of the American people is to take a hard look at the limits of U.S. military power in the world."[27] By the early 1970s five times as many Americans felt the country was spending too much on the military as felt it was spending too little.[28] On specific applications of the nation's armed might, the mood was similarly skeptical. Asked in 1968 what the U.S. should do in the event of a full-scale Mideast war, six times as many Americans wished us to "stay out" as favored "supporting Israel."[29] By 1973, solid support was found for reducing the nation's forces stationed in Europe as part of our NATO commitment.[30] This represented a sharp turnabout from three-to-one approval found in 1968 for maintaining troops in West Germany.[31] Indicative of a broadly growing sentiment to limit the use of American military might abroad was the mounting approval given to proposals to restrict the president's ability independently to commit troops to action. In 1973 Gallup found that "by a vote of 5 to 1, the public favors curbing the President's war-making powers."[32]

There is no gainsaying the fact that the cold war consensus had come unravelled and had taken with it the public's ready willingness to support global interventionism. If, as one writer put it, the American people previously had "accepted without question the official rationalizations of U.S. policy," that mood now appeared to have dissolved in the monsoon of failure in Southeast Asia.[33]

But what did the new mood add up to? To some, it was the unwanted recrudescence of isolationism, an older strain in American international thought that had suffered a direct hit at Pearl Harbor. James Johnson, addressing readers of the prestigious quarterly *Foreign Affairs*, announced that "the decade of the sixties has produced a new school of isolationism."[34] Found disproportionately among the young, it reflects the fact that "young Americans are disillusioned about what good America can do abroad."[35] In like vein, Harvard's Graham Allison, writing in the first number of *Foreign Policy*, argued that "Vietnam has produced a major shift in American public opinion. The silent majority's willingness to 'fight Communism' in every part of the globe has been sapped."[36] Amid this flux in foreign policy thinking, particular attention must be given to the young, argued Allison, for "the attitudes of young Americans today are a harbinger of the future."[37] If Allison is correct, then notice must be taken of a Gallup survey—conducted, incidentally, the very month that Lyndon Johnson handed to Richard Nixon the weighty foreign policy powers of the presidency—which purports to have unearthed evidence that "isolationist sentiment in the U.S. has grown steadily during the Vietnam conflict" and that "young persons . . . are chiefly responsible for the growth in the isolationist viewpoint."[38] Here, it would appear, is confirmation of the oft-voiced charge that the discredited premises of an earlier day were staging a comeback. It can be argued, however, that the threat of a "new isolationism" growing out of our misbegotten Vietnam venture was somewhat exaggerated all along. In the first place, the much-cited Gallup survey could find scarcely more than a fifth of the nation who fit its understanding of isolationism, and they were disproportionately young, poor, and uneducated, hardly the type ordinarily courted by the State Department.[39] More to the point is the question of what it means to believe in isolationism. That the term was seldom used after World War II except as a sobriquet makes it all the more important that it be defined with care so as to minimize its polemical potential.[40] As its sole measure of "isolationism," the Gallup survey posed this single question: "Would it be better for the United States to keep independent in world affairs—or would it be better for the United States to work closely with other nations?"[41] Clearly, the question is of such generality that one must doubt its ability to measure much of anything.

We must doubt, then, that the evident changes occurring in the nation's foreign policy outlook in the late 1960s and early 1970s sum up to a new isolationism in any meaningful sense of the term. Do they, nonetheless, amount to a meaningful change from the hitherto secure cold war consensus? On one level, they plainly do. The increased skepticism towards far-flung global involvements, especially where military force is contemplated, alters in significant ways the characteristic premises of pre-Vietnam days. The near-unanimity behind the view that at all costs the nation must avoid "another Vietnam" is bound to shape official thinking and decision making on the permissible applications of American power.

What is less evident, however, is the lasting meaning of the nation's mood swing attending Vietnam. In essence, it appears to rest less on any major rethinking of basic, philosophical premises concerning the nation's place in the sun than on a revised estimate of the operational realities—both extant dangers and credible tools to counter those dangers—affecting the nation's global role. In the case of our Asian policy, for example, the public's mounting opposition to the unilateral application of American armed might in the region arose not so much from any clear redefinition of American interests in the Pacific basin, but rather followed logically from a sharply reduced perception of the threat actually posed by China to those interests.[42] Similarly, the much-noticed 1969 Harris survey ought not be held aloft as proof of the existence of a new national concept of our interests in the world; what it does suggest is a new sense of the dangers of relying on unilateral military force to vindicate those interests.

Untold hours of cocktail chatter were prompted by Harris's findings that the American people were simply unwilling to use nuclear weapons in the defense of other nations. Less noticed but arguably of greater import were the findings that suggest a new mood of mature pragmatism. Nearly two to one agreed that "we cannot go it alone in the world any more."[43] While 82 percent agreed that small nations face security threats if left to their own devices, more (64 percent) favored addressing that problem within the framework of allied action than favored a unilateral American guarantee.[44] In nonnuclear situations, ample support was found for the defense of traditionally-defined American interests. For example, 64 percent would extend U.S. help to defend Berlin, that venerable symbol of "commitment" in earlier days. Nor would the public insist on defining the national interest solely in terms of the nation's physical security. Bonds of sentiment, ideology, and culture are clearly still admissible, as evidenced by the finding that a plurality favored "going to the aid of the Israelis should Soviet-aided Arabs threaten to overrun them."[45]

Like the limitationist intellectuals whose critiques hinge more on matters of means than of ends, the mass public came gradually to feel that ways surely must exist to maintain America's global sway without the constant burden and danger of war.[46] This was, of course, precisely the position Fulbright was striving to erect in the political arena. From 1965 onward Fulbright functioned as the main political spokesman for the limitationist view. Throughout the last half of the Johnson Administration, the nation's outlook at both elite and mass levels swung sharply Fulbright's way. Much preferring his accustomed role of solitary critic, he was both bemused and discomfited to find himself at the head of an historic shift in the national climate of opinion.

Acting in informal concert with like-minded political figures, including Senate colleagues Church, McGovern, Hatfield, Mansfield, Bayh, Gore, Harris, and Kennedy, Fulbright used his Senate role to inject the limitationist outlook into the play of power. Where men like Hans Morgenthau and Ronald Steel were confined in their efforts to influence policy by the uncertain armory of the publicist, Fulbright could seize the inherent advantages of Senate membership to function as both publicist and powerbroker. Through speeches, articles, books, television appearances, and highly publicized hearings staged by his Foreign Relations Committee, he became one of the most visible and effective advocates of change in our foreign policy along the lines developed by the limitationist outlook. In addition to public advocacy, Fulbright sought through the legislative process to apply directly the limitationist prescription.

Fulbright In The Twilight
Of The Johnson Years

By 1967 Fulbright's late-blooming dissent on the Vietnam war had become a near-obsession with him. Haunted by his role in the Gulf of Tonkin Resolution, he now seized every opportunity afforded by his growing fame to rally opponents of the war and, in so doing, attempt to pressure the administration into a reversal of what he now regarded as an unrelieved disaster. The transcript of his January 22, 1967, appearance on "Meet the Press" clearly captures his overriding preoccupation with the war and, more to the point, offers strikingly clear insights into the structure of his own foreign policy premises. At the fundamental level of how the nation's world role and interest ought to be defined—what we have called philosophical premises—Fulbright reveals to all who would listen his continued adherence to the outsized national self-concept that lay at the core of postwar American thought and action. In the course of arguing that Vietnam entails little or no vital interest for this nation, Fulbright offers this instructive distinction:

> I think our interests there are marginal, that we have never before considered that a land warfare in the land mass of Asia was justified or that a permanent position on the land mass was in our—was essential to our interests, as distinguished from our military, our naval power on the oceans and in the island fringes along the periphery of Asia and particularly in our bases. I still think that is sound.[47]

The maintenance of American armed might an ocean away, albeit not necessarily on the Asian mainland, is held by Fulbright as self-evidently required to fulfill the national purpose. Unstated but unmistakable is the presumption that that purpose is one which goes well beyond merely maintaining the physical security of the nation.

To Fulbright, the American enterprise in Vietnam became dubious only when its costs became clear. His opposition arises, then, not from the view that America ought to avoid intervening in distant disputes, but stems rather from the impersonal calculus of cost effectiveness. In response to Lawrence Spivak's pointed question, "What has led you to change your mind on the soundness of the policy? Is it the size of the war?" Fulbright allowed that "well, yes that is partly it."[48] Like the limitationist critics and like most of his countrymen, Fulbright did not oppose the war because he had come to acquire a down-sized set of philosophical premises about the nation's place in the global scheme of things. Rather, his opposition arose from his operational premises which differed fundamentally from those held by the Johnson administration in their estimate of the relevance of Vietnam to the maintenance of America's global sway. Where Secretary Rusk insisted tirelessly that the fundamental issue involved in Vietnam was armed aggression which, if left unchecked, would invite further challenges to the fabric of world order whose preservation constitutes the nation's overriding need, Fulbright and his fellow limitationists insisted with equal fervor that Vietnam was primarily a civil conflict with little significance to the broader structure of world order. It is as an eminently practical matter that Fulbright's fabled antiwar dissent must be understood. Desiring above all else to maintain America's awesome world role, he came to see Vietnam more as victimizer than vindicator of that role.

As he would put the point in a Senate speech late in 1967, "far from demonstrating America's readiness to discharge all of its prodigal commitments around the world, the extravagance and cost of Vietnam are more likely to suggest to the world that the American people will be hesitant indeed before permitting their government to plunge into another such costly adventure."[49] Coming at the same point another way, he added that "if America ever does withdraw into the neoisolationism of which our policymakers are so fearful, it will not be because of the influence of those of us who advocate selectivity in foreign commitments, it will be in reaction to the heedless interventionism of Vietnam."[50]

Here, then, are the essential elements of Fulbright's outlook as he neared the apogee of his fame and influence as a leader of foreign policy dissent: given that "heedless interventionism" leads to both "neoisolationism" at home and doubts abroad about our long-term credibility, and given that both of these factors call into question the nation's continued ability to discharge its global role as conservator of world order, it follows that one must oppose, as effectively as one is able, the temptation to commit the nation's might to "heedless interventionism." It became Fulbright's passion and commitment to hold this message aloft, forcefully and relentlessly, during the last half of the Johnson era.[51]

In his opening statement before yet another televised hearing on the war, this one in March 1968, he denied that Vietnam is "an exemplary war . . . which will prove to the Communists once and for all that so-called wars of national liberation cannot succeed."[52] At the heart of his critique was the forlorn assertion that "by committing half a million of our young men to bloody and endless combat in these distant jungles our leaders have converted a struggle between Vietnamese for possession of the Vietnamese land into a struggle between Americans for possession of the American spirit."[53] By now the acknowledged leader of the Senate's antiwar rebels,[54] Fulbright was still unwilling to contemplate unilateral abandonment of the enterprise whose cruel futility he has so vigorously denounced. What he proposed was, in his words, "an honorable compromise, not a total victory and certainly not a surrender."[55]

The discomfort he felt in his role of public dissenter was intensified by the personal anguish of seeing his long and hitherto warm personal relationship with Lyndon Johnson degenerate into ill-concealed rancor and disdain.[56] Stung by Fulbright's public criticisms, Johnson alternately ignored his old friend altogether or, when the senator's comments could no longer be ignored, engaged in small, mean-spirited attempts to deflate Fulbright's reputation.[57] It became a journalistic cliché to speak of the nation's growing polarization during the late 1960s. More than most, Fulbright knew the melancholy human reality behind the facade of impassioned public discourse. Longing as always for high-minded discourse governed by the gentleman's code of civility, he was both hurt and depressed by the mounting coarseness of public discussion.[58]

Long a favorite target of right-wing bile, he was stung nonetheless by the morose viciousness that now routinely turned up in the pages of the *National Review*. "In a competition of slow-learners," went a typical sneer, "Senator Fulbright would awe the most experienced veterans of Operation Head Start."[59] It hurt him to be reviled on the other side of the spectrum, too, whether by former friends now irrevocably committed to the president's war policies or by firebrands of the New Left who viewed as suspect his past stands on civil rights and who generally disdained his determinedly nonradical style. Equally, though, he was embarrassed by his celebrity status in trendy liberal circles. Relishing neither the bonfire nor the limelight, Fulbright privately grieved for the nation in its wrenching ordeal and publicly set himself to the task of limiting the likelihood that it would again be drawn into a needless, self-defeating war.

It was with an eye to preventing future Vietnams that Fulbright turned his attention to the question of the role and procedures of the Congress in the foreign policy-making process. In February 1968, his

Foreign Relations Committee held hearings to review that symbol of promiscuous congressional consent, the Gulf of Tonkin Resolution of 1964. With Secretary of Defense McNamara in the witness chair, Fulbright delivered a remarkable, impromptu revelation of the private guilt and anguish he had carried for over three years:

> If I had had enough sense to require complete evaluation I never would have made the mistake I did. . . . [N]ormally this committee does have hearings and questions. I don't know why, what possessed me, the background was such that I went along, of course I wasn't the only one. . . . I mean, this is not a small matter that we are in Vietnam, and I think for the future the least I can do and the committee can do is to alert future committees and future Senates that these matters are not to be dealt with in this casual manner. I feel very badly about it, about the matter.[60]

Fulbright concluded his poignant emotional release with a verbal sigh: "well, I delivered myself." And he would continue to "deliver himself" in the new-found cause of recapturing for Congress a vigorous, independent role in shaping the nation's foreign policy.

His efforts, in fact, had begun in earnest the previous summer. In July 1967, Fulbright submitted to the Senate a proposed resolution which, in its entirety, read as follows:

> Whereas accurate definition of the term, national commitment, in recent years has become obscured: Therefore be it

> Resolved, that it is the sense of the Senate that a national commitment by the United States to a foreign power necessarily and exclusively results from affirmative action taken by the executive and legislative branches of the U.S. Government through means of a treaty, convention, or other legislative instrumentality specifically intended to give effect to such a commitment.[61]

Rightly characterizing the proposal as arising from a "conservative position," Fulbright went on to stress that it "seeks to recover in some degree the constitutional role of the Senate in the making of foreign policy—a role which the Senate itself has permitted to be obscured and diminished over the years."[62]

Few observers seemed able to grasp Fulbright's "conservative position" at face value. To the editors of the *Washington Post*, the measure was a mere "gesture," one which fit a pattern of "continued harassment of the Administration because of its Vietnam policy." Lest its position be missed, the *Post* added that "there is little hope for a smoother working relationship between the White House and Congress so long as Mr. Fulbright retains his present position."[63] *Newsweek* taunted Fulbright by depicting his proposal as a guilt-assuaging substitute for repealing the

Gulf of Tonkin Resolution. As they put it, "no one believes that Senator Fulbright, for all the vehemence of his dissent, could possibly muster the votes to undo what he did so eagerly three years ago."[64] Similarly, the *Reporter* sought to cast doubt on Fulbright's motives, arguing that "he has yet to account fully for this drastic revision of his views."[65]

In the event, Senate Resolution 187 proved to be but a preliminary skirmish in a much broader struggle between the executive and legislative branches. Although favorably reported by the Foreign Relations Committee in November 1967, it never came before the full Senate for debate and decision. Not until the Nixon years would the Congress rally to Fulbright's "conservative position" and enact limits on the power of the Executive independently to draw the nation into a ruinous war. For the balance of the Johnson years, Fulbright continued to hammer home his new focus on congressional prerogatives along with his now-familiar dissent against the war itself. In March 1968, in the midst of pervasive rumors that the war would be escalated still further, Fulbright touched off a rhetorical free-for-all in the Senate with remarks that included the argument that

> . . . these pending decisions raise a basic and most important constitutional issue which must concern every Member of this body, regardless of whether he supports or disagrees with the administration's war policy. This issue is the authority of the administration to expand the war without the consent of Congress and without any debate or consideration by Congress.[66]

Within a few days, Fulbright's Foreign Relations Committee opened two days of long-anticipated hearings on the war with Secretary Rusk as the prime witness. Millions watched the live television coverage. What they saw was a replay of positions long since staked out by the principal actors, Rusk and Fulbright, but with a new twist. On the second day of the hearings, Fulbright angrily rejected Rusk's claim that the Congress had been adequately consulted on Vietnam. "We are in very serious difficulty," he exclaimed. "I am proposing that we not follow the old system of just accepting anything the Administration sends down here without questions which we have done and did in August, 1964. We had entirely too much confidence, in my opinion, in the wisdom of this or any Administration."[67]

If his advocacy of a revivified congressional role in the making of foreign policy marked a new concern for Fulbright, his general ruminations on America and the world continued themes that were by now familiar. In remarks delivered in far-flung locales, he extended lines of reasoning that had been staked out in *The Arrogance of Power*. Repeatedly he stressed the counter-utility of armed interventionism as an operational means of securing the nation's global position. As he put the point in a colloquy following Henry Steel Commager's presentation to the Foreign Relations Committee in 1967,

> this great country . . . has had such promise. And I personally have felt that it had great promise of becoming a unique world power, that I am very puzzled about why we have . . . turned aside from the policies which I thought we were pursuing until recently, and that was to make ourselves . . . an example for the rest of the world, and thereby exercise influence far beyond what I think we can do by the exertion of military force.[68]

Fulbright never doubted that America should "exercise influence" throughout the world; his doubts centered around the efficacy of force in securing that influence. In his view, the nation's mounting reliance on external coercion was symptomatic of the abiding need for a heightened national acuity regarding international affairs. Through sheer intellectual slovenliness, he argued, the nation and its leaders were unable to grasp the subtleties of world currents. Our self-willed lack of nuance, in turn, raised the likelihood of relying on violent interventionism in a blind, misguided effort to shore up a presumably pro-American status quo.

In a revealing exchange with Harvard's Louis Hartz during the 1968 hearings, Fulbright inquired whether Hartz would concur "that because of this lack of experience in a revolution in the French sense, that this makes it difficult for us to understand either the need for, or perhaps the outbreak in some cases of, revolutions in Latin America or anywhere else in the world?" Hartz, of course, agreed that "this is a great interfering element in our understanding of revolutions elsewhere," adding that "to the extent that a nation is conditioned by its history, we are not conditioned to understand this peculiar kind of experience."[69]

Beyond his preoccupation with self-defeating interventionism and what he regarded as the nation's chronic misperception of international patterns, Fulbright's gloomy, foreboding reflections on the rise and fall of nations figured prominently in a number of his much-reported public comments. In August 1967, he traveled to Hawaii to address members of the American Bar Association. His remarks, entitled "The Price of Empire,"[70] contained this dour warning:

> We are well on our way to becoming a traditional great power—an imperial nation if you will—engaged in the exercise of power for its own sake, exercising it to the limit of our capacity and beyond, filling every vacuum and extending the American 'presence' to the farthest reaches of the earth. And, as with the great empires of the past, as the power grows, it is becoming an end in itself, separated except by ritual incantation from its initial motives, gov-

erned, it would seem, by its own mystique, power without philosophy or purpose.[71]

It became a recurring theme with him that America seemed headed toward the decline that has been the fate of other nations whose quest has been for ever-greater power. The theme of the tragic fall from power caused by the mindless lust for power became a near-fixation. "Powerful nations have always devoted their main part of their resources to building empires," he wrote in a piece for the *New York Times*.[72]

Yet his deeper argument was that the nation might yet hold onto its great power, for while other nations appear to have had "fates," America has "choices." "If ever a nation was free to break the cycle of empires, America is that nation," he insisted.[73] Breaking will require some genuine changes in our approach to the outer world, but they apparently entail matters of style and method more than bedrock substance. "By using our power like a giant," he told his listeners in Hawaii, "we are fostering a world environment which is, to put it mildly, uncongenial to our society."[74] If the greatest danger to our power is our own reckless use of it, then it follows that we can conserve that power, and thus avoid the "fate" of great powers past, by casting off the coarse, club-wielding style of the brawny, brainless "giant."

Once we follow the guide of reason rather than indulge the primitive instinct for ever-expanding powers, we will see the need for a new global framework to ensure the preservation of peace and, presumably, the broad global sway that America carved out of the postwar chaos. To members of the *Pacem in Terris* convocation in Geneva, Switzerland, Fulbright delivered an eloquent plea for "international community, for arrangements in the world that will restrain the arrogance of power."[75] Proceeding from the view that "the power drive of men and nations traditionally has been checked by the power drive of other men and other nations," Fulbright insisted that the reality of nuclear weapons means that "the principle of unregulated countervailing force is no longer an acceptable basis for organizing the world."[76]

In its place, he proposed "a principle of *Community*, one which will end the no longer tolerable anarchy of unlimited national sovereignty."[77] As a Washington newcomer more than two decades earlier, he had voiced similar assaults on the principle of national sovereignty, but the heady, architectonic outlook of his early efforts had arisen from an outlook of qualified idealism. Now, in the personal and political prime of his life, his call for a radical remaking of the world system arose from an acute sense that it offered a way for his own nation to conserve the unrivaled place it had won but, like earlier giants, could not forever main-

101

tain. As he put the point in Geneva, "whether such arrangements can be devised will depend in no small part on the wisdom of the most powerful, on whether they can be brought to understand the terrible danger of their power—and that not least to themselves."[78]

Believing deeply that the nation was suffering cruelly from its own unwisdom, Fulbright took on an air of melancholy dismay as he watched the slow collapse of Lyndon Johnson's once-mighty political reputation. The tug of old bonds heightened the sadness with which he viewed the strewn wreckage of a dream he had so recently shared. That dream—social change at home, prudent primacy abroad—was being consumed by the very uncaution of men whose excessive pride and zeal led them to overstep the bounds of what could practically be attained. Their recklessness, in turn, threatened the stability of the postwar order whose dominance Fulbright and the nation had long since taken for granted. Its preservation, Fulbright could see, would require new men with new operational premises incorporating the view that only by limiting its global role could the nation hope to maintain its massive but vulnerable place in the sun.

7 Fulbright in the Nixon Years

Nixon's Revision Of The Nation's Foreign Policy Premises

RICHARD NIXON'S IMPROBABLE political comeback of 1968 owed much of its success to the electorate's collective unease over the management of America's vast informal empire.[1] Though hardly awarded a clear mandate in the sense of overwhelming voter approval, Nixon's assumption of power in the midst of a sharp drop in public support for the use of American power abroad meant that some fresh thinking would have to be done about the premises underlying American foreign policy.[2]

Yet, given the entire thrust of Nixon's long career, there was virtually no possibility that the mandated rethinking would entail a wholesale rejection of the expansive philosophical premises undergirding American foreign policy throughout the postwar era. "I could see," Nixon later wrote,

> that the central factor in 1968 on the eve of my presidency was the same as it had been in 1947 when I first went to Europe with the Herter Committee: America now, as then, was the main defender of the free world against the encroachment and aggression of the Communist world.[3]

103

Nor was the evidence conclusive that the apparent flux in public sentiment necessarily summed up to a coherent critique of those long-familiar philosophical premises.[4] What was "perfectly clear" was that the costs of maintaining the nation's world role must be sharply reduced.

Thus it became Nixon's self-defined mandate somehow to fashion a new set of operational premises that was compatible with the new mood and yet would preserve substantially intact the large global role envisioned by the nation's still-habitual philosophical premises. That this would be a delicate undertaking was abundantly clear. There is no gainsaying the fact that the wish to pursue constant ends by merely altering the means is far easier said than done.

Should, for example, the conclusion be accepted that the war in Vietnam must be terminated "as quickly as was honorably possible"[5] due to its unacceptably high costs and that it further must be the nation's abiding policy to avoid "future Vietnams" throughout the Third World so as to conserve that nation's strength; this would be, presumably, an instance of the revision of means in order to enhance the unquestioned end of American paramountcy, or, in Nixon's formulation, the maintenance of America's role as "the main defender of the free world."[6] Yet it is inescapably true that a decision to forego "future Vietnams" as a means strongly suggests a willingness to accept a somewhat reduced definition of the ends—that is, the global role and interest—that presumably would have been vindicated by those means. Once the argument is accepted that certain means must be avoided due to the limits of their practical efficacy, it is but a short step to the view that the nation might well need to impose new limits on the sought ends of its global undertakings.

It was of the essence of Nixon's much-dissected diplomacy to obscure the logic of the nation's new-found respect for the limits of its coercive capabilities. His abiding conviction was that America's global role and interest must retain the outsized proportions of the giant, one that is neither pitiful nor helpless, and he set out to fashion a doctrine of means to accomplish that end.

To aid in his projected reformulation of the nation's foreign policy, Nixon recruited Harvard professor Henry Kissinger, a man of Teutonic pedantry whose inflated sense of self nicely matched that of his adopted nation. It has become a commonplace to attribute to Kissinger authorship of the intellectual framework of Nixonian diplomacy.[7] In fact, key elements of what would assume later the guise of official doctrine were unveiled in an article Nixon had written for the October 1967 issue of *Foreign Affairs*.[8]

Here, more than a year before he first met Kissinger, is Nixon's preliminary adumbration of his, and increasingly the nation's, revised operational premises. Affirming America's permanent role in Asian affairs and defending the nation's Vietnam venture on the grounds that it had emboldened non-Communist forces throughout the region, Nixon sought nonetheless to show that past operational premises would no longer suffice. The direct containment and virtual isolation of China were proving to be too costly. Within the nation, Nixon noted the incipient fatigue of a people grown weary of ceaselessly projecting their might to the outer frontiers of the American imperium:

> One of the legacies of Viet Nam almost certainly will be a deep reluctance on the part of the United States to become involved once again in a similar intervention on a similar basis.[9]

Domestic resistance means, in turn, that foreign leaders must be forewarned of our new mood of temperance: "other nations must recognize that the role of the United States as world policeman is likely to be limited in the future."[10]

Does this mean, then, that America must abandon the broad concept of its global—or, in the case at hand, Asian—interests in whose name the Vietnam war was waged? To Nixon, this conclusion would hold only if no other means were in sight to shore up the region's stability, stability being the prerequisite to the maintenance of American interests.

In actual fact, he argued, we must be aware of the existence of two new means by which Asian stability may yet be attained. The first involved changes already occurring along China's periphery which promise to attain America's goals even while permitting a scaling down of the direct commitment of American means. Those changes—essentially, in Nixon's view, a heightened awareness of the dangers posed by militant communism—coupled with a "rising complex of national, subregional and regional identifications and pride," were producing "an increasing disposition to seek Asian solutions to Asian problems through cooperative action."[11] Operationally, then, America's Asian purposes could yet be attained while the nation shifted away from the role of front-line guardian and assumed the still active but less risky role of supporter of non-Communist regional undertakings.

The second new means to traditional ends involved a preview of Nixon's most dramatic act: the encouragement of Chinese participation in a diverse array of international relationships, thus ending its isolation and, hopefully, diminishing its hostility. In Nixon's words,

> . . . we simply cannot afford to leave China forever outside the family of nations, there to nurture its fantasies, cherish its hates and threaten its neighbors. There is no place on this small planet for a billion of its potentially most able people to live in angry isolation.[12]

If Nixon's new outlook was the product of an acceptance, however grudgingly, of the evident limits of American power, it is no less the case that the form of its presentation betrayed a hardy fidelity to the nation's long-standing sense of its place in the sun. Change in China's international style was to be sought because *we* decide that "there is no place" for an unreconstructed China. Its introverted stance must be altered because "we simply cannot afford" it otherwise.

From this 1967 mix of constant philosophical premises and revised operational premises emerged a solid preview of the now-familiar themes of Nixon's foreign policy: America would remain a great power but would avoid another Vietnam; existing regional trends plus the imaginative use of diplomacy provide a way to perpetuate a pro-American stability even while lessening our direct costs.

This germinal "Nixon Doctrine" gradually took on a fuller, more global character during Nixon's first thirteen months in office. It did so in three stages. The first took the form of a background briefing Nixon conducted for the press during his July 1969 stopover on the island of Guam.[13] Though his remarks focused on Asia, they incorporate a set of premises that would later be projected onto a global framework. Emphasizing that "we will keep our treaty commitments" and will "continue to play a significant role," Nixon went on to stress that in the future "we must avoid that kind of policy that will make countries in Asia so dependent upon us that we are dragged into conflicts such as the one that we have in Vietnam."[14] Noting "a very great growth of nationalism" and of "regional pride," Nixon emphasized that non-Communist Asia could and must look more to its own devices for its future defense, the sole exception being "the threat of a major power involving nuclear weapons."[15] In Nixon's overall characterization of his new Asian doctrine, we would have henceforth "a policy not of intervention but one which certainly rules out withdrawal."[16]

Any substantive change arising from Nixon's Guam pronouncement would be confined clearly to a reluctance to take on hypothetical new interests at some future point. The American nuclear umbrella emphatically would be preserved, as would the vast array of commitments previously made.

The second step in the formulation of the Nixon Doctrine came on November 3, 1969. In a televised address focusing on Vietnam, Nixon gave a formal rendition of the nation's new operational premises. For the first time, Nixon broadened the themes he had first applied to Asia into a new global doctrine:

First, the United States will keep all of its treaty commitments.

Secondly, we shall provide a shield if a nuclear power threatens the freedom of a nation allied with us or of a nation whose survival we consider vital to our security.

Third, in cases involving other types of aggression, we shall furnish military and economic assistance when requested in accordance with our treaty commitments. But we shall look to the nation directly threatened to assume the primary responsibility of providing the manpower for its defense.[17]

Finally, in February, 1970, Nixon issued the first of what would be annual foreign policy reports to Congress. In it, he spelled out as fully as any president ever had his perception of contemporary international currents. Stressing the theme of changing external circumstances, Nixon concluded that "the postwar period in international relations has ended."[18] Five changes were identified as particularly important: the economic and political recovery of Japan and Western Europe, the new determination to resist Communist penetration among the new nations, the fracturing of Communist-bloc unity on the shoals of nationalism, the loss of American supremacy in strategic weapons, and the declining vitality of the rival cold-war ideologies.[19]

Amidst this historic change, Nixon argued, his new doctrine offered a coherent way for America to secure its interests in the midst of swirling external currents. "Its central thesis," he wrote,

> is that the United States will participate in the defense and development of allies and friends, but that America cannot—and will not—conceive *all* the plans, design *all* the programs, execute *all* the decisions and undertake *all* the defense of the free nations of the world. We will help where it makes a real difference and is considered in our interest.[20]

To his doctrine of sobriety, Nixon added the concept of détente with major adversaries to be pursued through creative diplomacy. As elaborated in subsequent annual foreign policy reports, détente emerged as the necessary corollary of the Nixon Doctrine.[21]

In a widely read book, Henry Brandon wrote that "the Nixon Doctrine was a signal to everybody, heralding an end to the containment policy against the Soviet Union and China."[22] In fact, as Nixon himself later insisted in his memoirs, "the Nixon Doctrine was not a formula for getting America out of Asia, but one that provided the only sound basis for America's staying in."[23] Brandon clearly had missed the significance of a comment Nixon made to him in a February 1970 interview. The reformulation of operational premises, Nixon had said then,

> must be seen as an effort to withstand the present wave of new isolationism as embodied in such moves as the Mansfield Resolution for the withdrawal of

American troops from Europe. . . . What we had to do first was to make it plain to the American people that in fact we cannot opt out of the world, and second, to seek their support in continuing a policy even though it is a revised policy of involvement.[24]

Henry Kissinger's rather petulant account of the Nixon Doctrine—reflecting, one surmises, his peripheral role in its formulation—nonetheless underscores the doctrine's clearly intended thrust: "Domestically," writes Kissinger, "it supplied a coherent answer to the charges of overextension."[25]

Indeed it did. Nixon's "revised policy of involvement" had deftly co-opted the essential arguments of the limitationist critique. To be sure, the weight of personal and partisan considerations meant that in co-opting their critique Nixon had by no means co-opted all the critics. Their dissent, however, henceforth would display a curious ambivalence: alternately bemoaning the inadequacies of the doctrine Nixon had purloined from them and yet decrying the administration's failure to act consistently on it, limitationists were uncertain whether to acknowledge their paternity or call the new thing a bastard.[26]

None displayed this ambivalence more than J. William Fulbright. Watching while premises he had long advocated were voiced not only officially but regularly invoked in the defense of dramatic and hopeful new diplomatic initiatives, he welcomed the Nixon-Kissinger approach as an improvement over the crusading style that presumably had now been supplanted. But what he readily conceded to be an improved diplomacy could not, in the end, satisfy him. He thus devoted himself during what would prove to be his final Senate term to a belated attempt to formulate his own fundamental, philosophical premises about America's rightful place in the sun. By so doing, he returned in spirit to the international ideals of his political youth.

The Crippled Giant

In 1972 Fulbright published what likely will prove to be his final book-length commentary on American foreign policy.[27] It drew a notably more tepid response than its famed predecessors, especially *Old Myths and New Realities* and *The Arrogance of Power*. That response can be taken as a succinct measure of Fulbright's Nixon-era role. His dissent had been stripped of its distinctive mien by Nixon's wholesale takeover of the limitationist stance. No longer the *de facto* head of a

broad intellectual and political rebellion, and indisposed by temperament to serve as Nixon's and Kissinger's cheerleader, he was groping for
a coherent set of premises that would satisfy his lingering, visceral discontent with contemporary currents.

The Crippled Giant contains his summary of that endeavor. Our discussion focuses on two aspects of Fulbright's outlook as revealed in the
volume: his beliefs concerning reason and the nature of politics, and his
premises concerning America's world role.

Fulbright's familiar skepticism about what man might attain through
consciously planned political action resurfaces in *The Crippled Giant*.
"The human mind is limited and imperfect," he again argues.[28] He de-
velops, more starkly than ever, his belief that man by nature is propelled
toward competition and conflict. "As a species, we do not really like
each other all that well," he insists, and refers repeatedly to "our instinct
for competition," "our competitive impulse," "this appetite for contest,"
and man's "competitive and destructive impulses."[29] Politics, to Fulbright, is thus the grim arena where our unattractive, often self-
destructive nature finds its natural expression.

That Fulbright's very good mind is not always a consistent one is
shown by the fact that the opening pages of the volume contain an elaborate lament that

> the conception of politics as warfare seems to have shaped the outlook not
> only of Mr. Nixon's Administration but, as far as international relations is con-
> cerned, of every Administration since World War II. It is assumed, a priori,
> that the natural and inevitable condition of the world is one of basic
> antagonism.[30]

Unwilling, at least at this stage of the argument, to endorse that assumption, Fulbright insisted that "if indeed politics is warfare, it is not because
the Lord decreed it but because nations, including our own, have made
it so."[31]

When it does not otherwise serve his polemical purpose of the moment, Fulbright remains reasonably faithful to his long-expressed view
of politics as a cheerless, conflict-laden product of human nature. Far
from enhancing our lives, politics—both in its domestic and international forms—interferes with the more desirable concerns of life. He
detects "a new myth: that politics is life and everything political is highly
consequential."[32] If domestic politics is often irrelevant, international
politics is usually destructive: it "draws upon but for the most part does
not replenish the resources of the nation." Flatly, he insists that "the real
life of a nation is the life of its people as a society."[33]

As in years past, Fulbright in 1972 ridicules the notion that it is through politics that man seeks to actualize his transcendent beliefs and ideals. Bluntly he argues that the reverse more typically occurs: "in politics we feel a compulsion to dress up our contentious impulses in the vocabulary of ideals and ideology."[34] Our ideals, he insists, "are far less controlling than we like to believe; . . . more often than not what we take for principle is not principle at all but rationalization."[35]

As in his earlier writings, *The Crippled Giant* contains no systematic exegesis of Fulbright's concept of America's proper international role and interest. Its recurring theme is "the necessity of fundamental change in the way nations conduct their relations with each other."[36] Fulbright specifically links the national purpose with a global one; repeatedly he urges "the dedication of our foreign policy to the single overriding objective of forging the bonds of international community."[37] He had, of course, been saying this for three decades, but now there was a new intensity and centrality to his plea for "an international community which is capable of making and enforcing civilized rules of international conduct"[38] that he had not displayed since 1946.

That Fulbright is a man of good will and laudable ideals has seldom been doubted. That his revived crusade for international community involves a good bit more than the disinterested quest for global benevolence has seldom been noticed. Nowhere does he explicitly connect the pieces to reveal the structure of his intellectual mosaic; but neither has he attempted to hide the crucial pieces.

Begin with his notion that "what is vital to us in our foreign relations is the by-product of what is valuable to us in our own society."[39] Despite relentless attacks by him on the crusading style of American globalism, Fulbright has never insisted on defining the national interest solely in terms of utilitarian calculations of security. No less than a Dulles or a Rusk, he has insisted on the transcendent character of the American purpose.

Consider next the prospects of a unilateral vindication of that purpose. To Fulbright, the lesson of recent years has been the sheer improbability of any nation—no matter how great its might—proving able to master the direction of global currents. Our own extreme activism of the postwar era had posed a "material and spiritual drain"[40] on the nation while yielding results that were cruelly counterproductive: "by using our power like a giant we are fostering a world environment which is, to put it mildly, uncongenial to our society."[41]

Turn now to the Nixon-Kissinger enterprise, understood essentially as the triumph of the limitationist view that America could preserve its primacy while reducing its costs by avoiding the intellectual error of indiscriminate commitment. Acknowledging that "the Nixon-Kissinger policy has represented a significant departure from the ideological anti-communism which so strongly influenced the foreign policy of American Presidents from Truman to Johnson,"[42] and conceding it to be "an enormous improvement on the ideological crusade which it appears, step by step, to be supplanting,"[43] Fulbright insists nonetheless on the highly qualified character of the improvement. "With its careful, dispassionate analyses of threat and interest and advantage,"[44] it may keep the present system going with fewer violent upsets, thus enhancing the purposes of the system's dominant members. But even with nonmessianic manipulators at the controls, the old international system "has always broken down in the end."[45]

This gets us precisely to where Fulbright would have us go: to the view that international institutions—in whose direction our own voice would be a mighty one—offer an eminently practical way to "free ourselves from the costs, both material and spiritual, which three decades of war and cold war have extracted from us."[46] It is not merely the rhetoric of salesmanship that Fulbright is using when he speaks of "the practical idealism of the United Nations Charter."[47] It is nothing less than the clear-headed calculus of national interest as envisioned by Fulbright's subtle scheme.

Recall that it is on purely practical grounds that he doubts the long-term viability of the Nixon formulation as a guarantor of American primacy; its dependence on an unending display of diplomatic pyrotechnics defines its implausibility. More plausible, in Fulbright's view, is the eminently "practical idealism" of "a system of laws rather than of men, a system that does not depend upon the cleverness or benevolence of the men who run it."[48]

Whether his conclusions are judged to be sound or unsound, there is no mistaking the hidden agenda that led Fulbright to them. If the hidden agenda behind Nixon's vision of a "full generation of peace" was the wish to maintain America's superpower status by more affordable means, no less does Fulbright's vision of a "system of laws" camouflage a sublimated pro-American order. Such, indeed, is the essence of Fulbright's "practical idealism."

To show that Fulbright's idealism was thoroughly practical in character is not to confirm its practicability. What *The Crippled Giant* accomplishes, no doubt unintentionally, is to demonstrate why it is that we shall likely not be able to erect the kind of global community capable of stabilizing the world and thus securing American paramountcy. War, militarism, armed crusades, power politics—these are the demonic forces that threaten the order on which American primacy depends, and which to Fulbright are drives rooted in the very nature of man. They are, in the jargon of modern social science, dependent variables, rising and falling by rhythms set up on another, more basic plane.

It is of course true that these forces take on the character of independent variables where their effects are concerned, and it is precisely those destructive effects that Fulbright seeks to curb. But one must assume that in order to effect change downstream in the causal chain, all the links in that chain must be susceptible of reform. Alas, it is the hope of this assumption that Fulbright has closed off, for having argued so laboriously that our "competitive and destructive impulses"[49] are powerful engines of human action while our capacity for rational self-mastery is slender indeed, he effectively precludes the kind of self-conscious global reform he otherwise so longingly seeks.

Even if he had not insisted on grounding his causal model on his gloomy notions of human nature, the end result Fulbright seeks—global reform—would still face formidable barriers. Such reform could occur by one of two ways: it could be the agreed result of existing consensus, or it could be the imposed result of irresistible coercion. On Fulbright's own evidence, neither way is in sight at the international level.

At one point he appears to elevate the American constitution to the status of global example: "the genius of the American Constitution," he asserts,

> is that . . . it has kept the game going and the competitors in competition. . . . with unsentimental realism, the Framers of our Constitution faced up to the universality of the human drive to self-aggrandizement, recognized it for the creative but dangerous force that it is, and harnessed it into a system of regulated rivalries, free enough to generate political energy, restrained enough to protect the people from despotism.[50]

But surely the Framers had a good bit more on their side than merely the "unsentimental realism" Fulbright admires. Not least were their labors buoyed up by the undercurrents of a shared national outlook. In the absence of what Louis Hartz has called the nation's "submerged Lockean consensus," the Constitution would remain to America precisely what Fulbright's vision of "a system of laws" will remain to the world: an aspiration merely.[51]

As to global reform by way of unilateral coercion, it is no exaggeration to say that Fulbright's fame arose from his eloquent demonstrations of the practical limits of American power in securing and maintaining its preferred notions of world order. Countless times since the mid-1960s he had sounded the refrain that "the nation has been weakened by the material and spiritual drain of an overly ambitious foreign policy,"[52] and that further unilateral exertions are to be avoided rather than advocated.

With more consistency of philosophy than of logic, Fulbright gives evidence of a back-up position pending the nation's unlikely commitment to seeking a global rule of law. Though not formally presented, the outlines of the provisional position Fulbright would have the nation take emerge clearly from comments scattered throughout his book.

In the first instance, Fulbright would strip the nation's diplomacy of any residual ideological cast it might still possess. Much of *The Crippled Giant* is given over to a revisionist account of postwar diplomacy in which the Truman Doctrine is seen as the archetypal expression of the nation's crusading style, "the charter for twenty-five years of global ideological warfare and unilateral military intervention against Communist insurgencies."[53] His critique of our cold-war hostility toward Communist powers fails to note that the attitudes so thoroughly condemned from the vantage point of 1972 are attitudes which Fulbright fully shared at the time.[54]

A diplomacy shorn of its millennial style would not be a diplomacy of passivity. Isolationism, he insists, "will not happen because it cannot happen."[55] What Fulbright is getting at, of course, is what he has been saying for many years: that the nation will benefit greatly from a heightened intellectual acuity where the conduct of its vast global role is concerned. Bluntly, he asserts that "as long as we are going to continue to play the old game of power politics we might as well play it intelligently."[56] That he would prefer a less risky global mode to "the old game of power politics" does not detract from his gloomy hunch that the "game" will go on and that our side must therefore learn to "play it intelligently."

As to the premises that would guide an intelligent player, Fulbright urges "selectivity in our international commitments—selectivity according to our own needs, our own capacities."[57] Clearly, it is precisely the definition of those "needs" that occasions the debate in which Fulbright is participating. On occasion Fulbright sounds as if it is the nation's most fundamental, philosophical premises with which he is quarreling. On the still-smoldering issue of Vietnam, for example, he asserts flatly that "the United States has no vital security interest in the preservation of South Vietnam as an independent, non-communist state."[58] By 1972, of course, few would hold otherwise.

Does this mean that Fulbright—and the nation—had foresworn committing the nation's power to the attainment of goals not directly related to the spartan standard of "vital security interest?" It does not. In a number of instances Fulbright refuses to confine his own philosophical premises concerning America's world role to the narrow criteria of physical security. On Vietnam, he notes that

> the interest of the United States in Southeast Asia is something less than a 'vital interest': nothing much that happens—or is likely to happen—in that part of the world is a matter of life and death for the American people. We do have an 'interest' in the region, but in the less cataclysmic sense of advantage or preference. In this sense we have an interest in the continued freedom of the countries of Southeast Asia from domination by China or any other great power.[59]

Again, in another context comes the argument that

> from the standpoint of America's security and interests, the central fact about Indochina is that it does not matter very much who rules in those small and undeveloped lands. We have preferences, to be sure, but they are a product of sentiment and habit.[60]

What is held to be a less-than-vital interest is not, for that reason, rejected as valid to the national purpose. The key to this essential point comes amid a discussion of the Middle East. Noting that "we are tied to Israel by bonds of culture and sentiment," Fulbright specifically allows that "these bonds represent a perfectly valid basis for the definition of a 'national interest'."[61]

Clearly, these and other "perfectly valid" bonds arise from a broad national sense of purpose that refuses to limit the national interest to purely security considerations. It is in this context that Fulbright's now-perennial admonition for "selectivity in our national commitments"[62] must be seen. His is a selectivity born solely from a sober sense that the nation's coercive power is finite. He has never—all appearances and public perceptions to the contrary—conceived of the nation's *purpose* in terms of the principle of selectivity. The universality of the American example is to him entirely self-evident.[63] His is not, after all, a dissent against the nation's expansive philosophical premises, but rather a caution against the unlikelihood that we can attain the global order envisioned by those premises by continuing to rely on our "chronic unilateralism."[64]

The Crippled Giant was Fulbright's final attempt to help the nation find a way out of its dilemma of unlimited wants and limited means. The collapsing logic of his plea for a universal "system of laws rather than men"[65] added one more layer to the intellectual rubble of foreign policy concepts in the postwar era.

Fulbright And The Nixon Approach

Like so many of his fellow limitationists, most of whom were Democrats, Fulbright displayed a chronic ambivalence toward the broad thrust of the Nixon-Kissinger foreign policy. On the one hand, he had to concede that the new mood and style of nonevangelical restraint in the Third World coupled with creative diplomatic overtures to major adversaries constituted a more promising, less costly means of conducting the nation's global role. Indeed, Nixon and Kissinger were following paths that Fulbright had previously staked out in numerous speeches and writings.

On the other hand, his now-institutionalized role as the nation's most visible foreign policy dissenter inclined him to voice regular criticisms, both of the administration's failure consistently to follow its own neolimitationist vision and what he perceived as inadequacies of the vision itself.

Typical of the latter was his comment in October 1973 on "the nub of both my concurrence with, and dissent from, the Nixon-Kissinger foreign policy."[66] "I concur, strongly," he said, "in the efforts toward a 'structure of peace,' but I am concerned with the flimsiness of the structure. It is makeshift and fragile, too dependent on agility and cleverness, too delicate to work for dull leaders or withstand incompetent ones."[67]

With no apparent embarrassment, the man who had made it his life's work to warn of the deficiencies of "dull leaders" was now constructing a brief on their behalf. And what is it that Fulbright would have us—and, presumably, future dull leaders—adopt in place of the Nixon approach? "I remain," he went on, "a Wilsonian, a seeker still of a world system of laws rather than of men, a believer still in the one great new idea of this century in the field of international relations, the idea of an international organization with permanent processes for the peaceful settlement of international disputes."[68]

Truth to tell, Fulbright's activities as a "seeker" of a Wilsonian order were confined to occasional rhetorical flourishes tacked onto other, more practical concerns. Those concerns, often as not, dealt with the immediate, operational aspects of contemporary diplomatic currents. Here it was Fulbright's objective to shore up support for the administration when he agreed with its efforts and generate pressure on them when he did not. His task was complicated by the emotionalism that now routinely attended the nation's ongoing dialogue concerning its proper international role. No public figure was entirely immune from its sting, but there was something about Fulbright that seemed to magnify the wrath

115

of those who disagreed with him. It became a commonplace among those who found his views uncongenial or merely incomprehensible simply to dismiss him as a hopeless isolationist. The evident absurdity of the charge did little to deter its frequent use, whether by hostile columnists or hostile presidents. *Newsweek*'s Kenneth Crawford wrote that Fulbright was "facing toward an isolationist mecca," echoing Nixon's famous address at the Air Force Academy a few weeks earlier.[69] It thus became something of a set piece in Washington's stylized foreign-policy "debates" for Fulbright to preface his critical commentaries with a firm reassurance that, indeed, he was no isolationist.[70]

Never was the instrumental, means-oriented nature of Fulbright's dissent more apparent to all who would but listen than during the Nixon years. On Vietnam, for example, he continued to emphasize the now-consensual view that "there is no vital security interest of the United States at stake and, accordingly, that the nature of the government of South Vietnam is not a matter of vital interest to the United States but only one of strong preference."[71] As a purely practical matter, he argued in a nationally-televised address, "the war in Indo China is a bad investment of our resources and our talents."[72] Given that the nation had come to reject Vietnam as a means to its broader foreign-policy ends, the debate now revolved around how best to liquidate its "bad investment."

To Fulbright, the gradual withdrawal of American forces would unnecessarily compound the wasted investment. "I accept the administration's statement as to its purpose and intention," he told his Senate colleagues in 1970. "All we are saying is that . . . the means now being used are not going to work."[73]

Later that year, appearing on "Face the Nation," Fulbright repeated that "it's only [Nixon's] judgment as to the means that he seeks to achieve the end that I raise questions about," adding that "I'm bound to say in his statements there creeps into it the idea of—that we are still on a crusade against Communism as an ideology."[74] Here is the devout limitationist chiding Nixon for the incompleteness of his conversion. While awaiting a Wilsonian transformation of the world order, Fulbright would consistently espouse the limitationist view that the nation must seek less costly, less risky, more astute ways of maintaining its essential postwar role.

When not criticizing Nixon's and Kissinger's inconstancy as limitationists, Fulbright vigorously praised their efforts which arose from essentially limitationist premises concerning how best to preserve our world role. A real warmth developed between Fulbright and Kissinger, leading Stanley Karnow to characterize them as "locked in an affectionate embrace" by late 1973.[75] Karnow argues, correctly, that "Fulbright's approbration of Kissinger stems, first of all, from agreement with his policies. The Senator has long favored detente with the Soviet Union and a rapprochment with China."[76] There is no mistaking the essential identity between Fulbright's rhetoric and Kissinger's deeds.

Fulbright displayed no partisan reluctance to credit Nixon and Kissinger with major advances. He was quick to applaud the opening to China ("a potentially important breakthrough")[77] and repeatedly stressed that "I have approved of the policy that was initiated by President Nixon . . . the policy of detente with Russia."[78] With an appreciative Secretary Kissinger in the witness chair, Fulbright commented in Foreign Relations Committee hearings that "I do not see how we can expect to make real progress . . . if we do not have what you have already described so well, detente."[79]

Urging the view that we must "build upon the cooperative measures initiated by President Nixon and Dr. Kissinger,"[80] Fulbright watched with dismay as Nixon became ever more grimly impaled on the stake of Watergate. He developed a saddened sympathy for the one-time red-baiter with whom he had never been close. Criticizing media excesses, Fulbright insisted that in destroying the Nixon presidency the real victim would be the nation's newly astute diplomacy. In late June, 1974, Fulbright rose in the Senate to assail the "enemies of detente"[81] and underscore his own support of Nixon's "justified pride of the many agreements reached with the Soviet Union during his period in office."[82]

In the final months of his own career and with Nixon's resignation but weeks away, Fulbright bitterly assaulted "the cold warriors in the Pentagon and in Congress" who, "emboldened by the President's domestic difficulties," "have mounted a concerted offensive, both against arms control and trade with the Soviet Union."[83] In a rare display of public emotion, Fulbright revealed the depths of the frustration he felt watching the limitationist victory slip away on a tide of national distraction: "If Watergate is hampering the Administration's foreign policy," he argued, "it is not the doing of the Russians but of the cold warriors at home."[84]

Much of Fulbright's activity during the Nixon years was devoted to a virtual crusade to strengthen the Senate's voice in the making of foreign policy. It is true that he had at one time felt otherwise. In a 1961 article he had written:

> I wonder whether the time has not arrived, or indeed already has passed, when we must give the executive a measure of power in the conduct of world affairs that we have hitherto jealously withheld. . . . It is my contention that for the existing requirements of American foreign policy we have hobbled the President by too niggardly a grant of power.[85]

It is also true that he would later give evidence of having second thoughts over the extremes displayed by a newly assertive Congress. Four years after leaving the Senate he wrote:

> I confess to increasingly serious misgivings about the ability of the Congress to play a constructive role in our foreign relations. . . . Those of us who prodded what seemed to be a hopelessly immobile herd of cattle (Congress) a decade ago, now stand back in awe in the face of a stampede.[86]

Still, there is no convincing evidence to support Daniel Yergins' argument that "for Fulbright, the 'Senate's role' was not an important issue in itself, no matter what his orations suggested, but merely a tool with which to attack a policy—Vietnam—with which he did not agree."[87] That he held an inconstant view on the subject does not detract from the evident sincerity with which his views were held.

Central to his Nixon-era campaign for an enlarged congressional role was his insistence that the Congress itself was failing to exercise its rightful, lawful role. "[T]he Senate refuses to use the power it has," he told his colleagues in 1972.[88] He did not exempt himself or his committee from the charge of negligence. As he admitted on the Senate floor in 1970, "for many years the role exercised by the Committee on Foreign Relations was that of the unquestioning advocate of policies and programs submitted to the Senate by the executive branch of the Government."[89]

The result, he argued, was a derangement of constitutional roles. As he expressed the point to students at the University of South Florida in 1971:

> Out of a well-intentioned but misconceived notion of what patriotism and responsibility require in a time of world crisis, Congress has permitted the President to take over the two vital foreign policy powers which the Constitution vested in Congress: the power to initiate war and the Senate's power to consent or withhold consent from significant foreign commitments.[90]

On both counts, he worked for change. Shortly after Nixon was inaugurated Fulbright reintroduced his "sense of the Senate" resolution on national commitments. Arguing that it was the resolution's purpose "to reassert . . . the legitimate function of the Senate in participating in the making of commitments by the United States," Fulbright viewed the measure as one of his principal legislative efforts.[91]

He had proposed an identical resolution in 1967. On that occasion, he had gathered solid support within the Foreign Relations Committee only to find his Senate colleagues unwilling to deal with the issue at all for fear of appearing to undercut President Johnson's Vietnam policy. By 1969, however, the national climate had undergone distinct change. Now, Fulbright felt, the Senate would be ready to address the long-muted question of its rightful role in the foreign policy process. Accordingly, on February 4, he formally submitted Senate Resolution 85, soon widely known as the national commitments resolution. Inherently, the measure would have little legal significance since its provisions would not be binding upon the executive branch. As both statement and warning, however, its actual effect could well be substantial. Henceforth, Fulbright reasoned, presidents would be less likely to commit the nation to foreign regimes in the absence of prior and explicit Senate approval since passage of the measure would convey the sense of the Senate:

> That a national commitment by the United States to a foreign power necessarily and exclusively results from affirmative action taken by the executive and legislative branches of the United States Government through means of a treaty, convention, or other legislative instrumentality specifically intended to give effect to such a commitment.[92]

Despite stiff Staff Department opposition to the resolution, the Foreign Relations Committee voted its near-unanimous approval on March 12.[93] Noting that the executive branch had acquired "virtual supremacy over the making as well as the conduct" of foreign policy, the committee report stressed the need to restore a more equal balance of power between the two branches.[94] Between release of the committee's report on April 16 and the final Senate vote on June 25, there appeared a steady barrage of public commentary and debate on the measure. Typical of conservative critics was *Newsweek*'s Kenneth Crawford who insisted upon seeing the isolationist ghost of Senator William Borah in Fulbright's every effort. The Senate, he wrote, has a new "band of willful men determined to reassert their authority in foreign policymaking. This time the band is led by Sen. J. William Fulbright."[95] Taking a less inflammatory tack, President Nixon at a June press conference expressed sympathy for the resolution's "sentiment," but argued that the president should not "have his hands tied in a crisis."[96]

Despite these and other opposing voices, however, it became clear that Fulbright had rightly gauged the Senate's temper. Undoubtedly it was the war's mounting unpopularity that lay behind much of the enthusiastic support awaiting the resolution in the full Senate. No doubt, too, simple partisanship was at work. A Democratic Senate would find it far easier to jab a legislative thumb in the eye of a Republican president than a Democratic one. In any case, following five days of debate, the Senate on June 25 voted its overwhelming approval of a somewhat revised version of Senate Resolution 85.[97] In the immediate afterglow of the vote, Senate majority leader Mansfield claimed that "simply stated, the Senate has acted to reassert its historical and constitutional role."[98] But surely the Senate had merely begun to act. A more realistic assessment of the resolution's actual significance had been offered by Idaho's Frank Church on the first day of Senate debate. He quite candidly admitted that "the purpose of the resolution is political; that is to say, we would hope its passage would help to create a new congressional attitude toward foreign policy."[99] And so it did.

The passage of the so-called National Commitments Resolution stands as a notable watershed in the history of legislative-executive relations in the foreign policy process. For nearly three decades the initiative in foreign affairs had gravitated increasingly into executive hands, while lawmakers had seen their impact diminish to the point of near-impotence. It is true, of course, that the legislators—Fulbright among them—had allowed the constitutional imbalance to occur, had even urged its acceleration. Much has been made of Fulbrights' notable change of heart on the subject.[100] As a scholarly account put it, "upon first reading the public pronouncements and writings of Senator J. William Fulbright concerning the question of the proper role of the President in foreign-policy formulation the impression of some sort of conspicuous inconsistency is gained. Probably no other authority has articulated both sides of the issue in such full form as has Fulbright."[101] But Fulbright was hardly alone in deferring to presidents during periods of consensus and then rediscovering Madisonian logic in the face of policy conflict. His turnaround on congressional prerogatives accurately mirrors a larger national rethinking that led to the intense congressional activism of the 1970s.[102] His National Commitments Resolution of 1969 was a pivotal event marking his and the nation's unwillingness to give the executive a nearly unrestricted hand in foreign affairs.

Four years later, as he presented to the Senate the conference committee report on the historic War Powers Act, he stressed the continuity of congressional purpose in recent years: "I feel that this legislation is a follow-on from the commitments resolution passed by the Senate some 4 years ago."[103] Congressional adoption of the landmark measure showed conclusively that the lawmakers would, in Fulbright's words, "reclaim the mastery of . . . the domain of deciding when our country is to be committed to war." [104]

By late 1973 Fulbright had every reason to feel that his long years of dissent had begun to pay off. Limitationist premises he had long espoused were now routinely invoked in defense of official policy, and now the Congress was asserting itself after a long season of passivity. The satisfaction he was starting to feel, however, would soon be overcome by the hurt of rejection inflicted by his fellow Arkansans.

8 *Autumnal Perspectives*

AS 1974 DAWNED Fulbright weighed a decision that soon must be made: whether to retire from politics or seek reelection to a sixth Senate term. The choice was proving to be surprisingly difficult. Certainly the thought of retirement was by no means an unattractive one. Never much absorbed by the routine details of legislative life, his three decades in the Congress had left him in "kind of a rut," he would later concede.[1]

Too, he would be nearly seventy when the next Congress was sworn in. Though still in good health, he knew he could not indefinitely postpone the hoped-for leisure of private life. Watergate had about finished what Vietnam had begun as far as the public's affection for its political leaders was concerned. Perhaps he should join the swelling ranks of incumbents who would voluntarily step down that year, men who, like Sam Ervin, simply concluded that they had done their duty and now would make way for a younger generation.

On the other hand, Fulbright clearly relished his role as chairman of the Senate's most prestigious committee. Long accustomed to the limelight, he rather enjoyed the courtly rituals of public hearings, Sunday interview shows, campus appearances, and international travel. When he thought of private life, he thought of the opportunities it would afford him to read, write, travel, and make the kind of elegant addresses he so loved to labor over. Truth to tell, he could do those things as well—

121

better, perhaps—by staying in the Senate. In the end, the lure of power, or, at least, its ornate trappings, proved irresistible; Fulbright decided to run.

Like the authors of a much-hailed political reference work who breezily wrote that "he seems likely to win another term,"[2] Fulbright, it turned out, had not done his homework on Arkansas politics. He was, quite simply, out of touch, belonging more to the urbane elegance of Georgetown than the bucolic homeliness of Arkansas.

It was not just that he seldom visited the state. His problem was that he had lost touch with his constituents' sensibilities. His group ratings traced a sudden veer to the left in the early 1970s. In a state whose congressional delegation averaged an approval rating by the liberal Americans for Democratic Action of around twenty, Fulbright had jumped from an A.D.A. score of fourteen in 1968—the last time had been up for re-election—to an eye-popping eighty-five in 1971.[3]

Dale Bumpers, the state's popular young governor, sensed Fulbright's vulnerability and joined the primary race. When the votes were counted on May 28, Fulbright had been defeated by a humiliating margin of nearly two-to-one.

In the aftermath, millions who admired Fulbright would curse the caprice of political tides that had swept him away. "Bumpers is to Fulbright as somebody in Bristol was to Edmund Burke," wrote columnist Tom Braden.[4] To the editors of the Arkansas Gazette, "it is not Fulbright who is the loser; alas, the loser is the Republic."[5]

But what, precisely, had been lost? On one level the answer seems clear enough: Fulbright had been among the major public figures of the postwar era, and now he was gone.

By wide agreement, he was one of the most complex and interesting politicians of his age. As one writer had puckishly noted, "he is really an uncomplicated Rhodes Scholar from Arkansas interested in the price of chickens and international relations."[6] He was indeed a man of many parts.

By his own dignified example he had legitimized foreign policy dissent for a generation seared by the tragedy of Vietnam. Without him the nation might have forgotten that love of one's country and forceful dissent against its policies are not exclusive tendencies. It misses the point to say that a healthy democracy requires both patriots and dissenters. What is required are citizens who combine both tendencies in their own lives. Few had ever made the point so well as Fulbright, and he had done it best by his own memorable example.

But his dissent had come to be seen by Arkansas voters as a dissent against them, and they had turned him out. In an age when blow-dried glibness was routinely mistaken for leadership, his high intellect, stubborn courage, and uncompromised forthrightness would be sorely missed.

More problematic is the matter of his long-term legacy. That he will be remembered is a certainty. Frank Church was not merely indulging the lawmaker's penchant for hyperbole when he remarked: "when all of us are dead, the only one they'll remember is Bill Fulbright."[7] The international exchange program alone assures him of a niche in the memory of his times. The titles of his two most famous works—*Old Myths and New Realities* and *The Arrogance of Power*—have entered the idiomatic repertoire with which the nation discusses its relation to the outer world. If only for these reasons, he will be remembered.

But how will he be remembered? We have shown why it would be unwise to remember him as an architectonic foreign-policy thinker. The weight of received perception to the contrary, he was not a particularly creative thinker, nor was it his purpose to design and promote a radically new concept of America's place in the sun. At bottom he fully shared the pervasive postwar belief in the natural primacy of American might and the natural supremacy of the American example. He deeply wanted the nation to maintain its paramount world position and so devoted himself to an ongoing search for the best means of accomplishing that end.

That his contemporaries chronically misunderstood his purpose does not detract from the seriousness with which he undertook it. Removed from the hue and cry occasioned by his dissent, we have little excuse today for perpetuating that misunderstanding.

If upon learning of his purpose we feel a certain sense of disappointment, toward whom ought that disappointment be directed? Toward Fulbright for betraying our exalted image of him? But surely it is Fulbright who is the object and not the source of our chronic incomprehension. He has been nothing if not prolific in his advocacy. It would be hard to find another twentieth century figure who had left behind a larger record of interviews, speeches, articles, and books for all who would examine them. To do so is to see Fulbright whole. But to strip away the caked layers of incomprehension is not thereby to unmask a pretense. Fulbright never pretended to be other than a critic of means who shared the nation's consensual ends. His difficulty in making himself understood tells us something about ourselves, especially about how we approach discussions of our world role. A nation unaccustomed to rational public self-scrutiny is bound to mistake its own friendly critics either for utopian visionaries or enemy apologists. We have insisted on revering Fulbright as the former or reviling him as the latter. In fact he was neither.

Few men had better used the Senate as a public forum than Fulbright. Now that forum had been denied him. In subsequent years he has surfaced occasionally on the op-ed page of the nation's newspapers[8] while privately lamenting the absence of a forum for his views.[9]

Three days before his seventy-fifth birthday the *New York Times* ran his none-too-subtle plea for just such a forum: "There are many individuals," he wrote,

> who have had substantial experience in governmental and foreign-policy affairs and whose integrity and character is beyond question. A panel of senior foreign-policy statesmen could be selected and funded by a nonpolitical organization such as a public foundation and could develop procedures and policies designed to restore consistency and direction to our nation's foreign policy.[10]

Even as we wince at the poignancy of his autumnal plea, we recall with no little affection the long effort to bring "consistency and direction to our nation's foreign policy" by a good and decent man whose "integrity and character" are indeed "beyond question." There could be no better epitaph for the public career of J. William Fulbright.

Notes

Introduction

1. Haynes Johnson and Bernard M. Gwertzman, *Fulbright the Dissenter* (Garden City, N.Y.: Doubleday, 1968).
2. Kurt Tweraser, *Changing Patterns of Political Beliefs: The Foreign Policy Operational Codes of J. William Fulbright, 1943–1967* (Beverly Hills: Sage, 1974), p. 67
3. Daniel F. Trask, "The Congress as Classroom: J. William Fulbright and the Crisis of American Power," in Frank J. Merli and Theodore A. Wilson, eds., *Makers of American Diplomacy* (New York: Charles Scribner's Sons, 1974), p. 650.
4. Daniel Yergin, "Fulbright's Last Frustration," *New York Times Magazine*, November 24, 1974, p. 14.
5. Johnson and Gwertzman, p. 7.
6. Tristram Coffin, *Senator Fulbright: Portrait of a Public Philosopher* (New York: Dutton, 1966), p. 13.
7. "Debate and Disquiet," *Newsweek*, February 6, 1967, 35.
8. "The Ultimate Self-Interest," *Time*, January 22, 1965, 18.
9. Henry Fairlie, "Old Myths and New Realities," *Reporter*, June 16, 1966, 21.
10. "The Crackdown," *Nation*, October 11, 1965, 205.
11. Eric Sevareid, "Why Our Foreign Policy is Failing: An Exclusive Interview with Senator Fulbright," *Look*, May 3, 1966, 24.

12. Roy Reed, "Fulbright, the Scholar in Foreign Affairs, *New York Times,* June 2, 1974, sec. 4, p. 3.
13. Kenneth W. Grundy, "The Apprenticeship of J. William Fulbright," *Virginia Quarterly Review* (Summer 1967), 382.
14. Stanley Karnow, "The Kissinger-Fulbright Courtship," *New Republic,* December 29, 1973, 16.
15. Charles McCarry, "Mourning Becomes Senator Fulbright," *Esquire,* June, 1970, 116.
16. Russell Baker, "An Ozark 'Professor' Studies Wall Street," *New York Times,* March 6, 1955, p. 17.
17. Brock Brower, "The Roots of the Arkansas Questioner," *Life,* May 13, 1966, 117.
18. "Advice and Dissent," *Newsweek,* February 21, 1966, 30.
19. See George Liska, *Quest for Equilibrium: America and the Balance of Power on Land and Sea* (Baltimore: Johns Hopkins Press, 1977); Morton A. Kaplan, *System and Process in International Politics* (New York: Wiley, 1957).
20. See James A. Robinson and Richard C. Snyder, "Decision-Making in International Politics," in Herbert C. Kelman, ed., *International Behavior: A Social-Psychological Analysis* (New York: Holt, Rinehart, and Winston, 1965); Richard C. Snyder, H. W. Bruck, and Burton Sapin, eds., *Foreign Policy Decision-Making* (New York: Free Press, 1963); Richard W. Cottam, *Foreign Policy Motivation* (Pittsburgh: University of Pittsburgh Press, 1977).
21. See Ole R. Holsti, "The Belief System and National Images: A Case Study," *Journal of Conflict Resolution,* 6 (1962), 244–52; Robert Jervis, *Perception and Misperception in International Politics* (Princeton, N. J.: Princeton University Press, 1976).
22. See Henry A. Kissinger, "Domestic Structure and Foreign Policy," *Daedalus,* 95 (Spring 1966), 503–29; Felix Gilbert, "Bicentennial Reflections," *Foreign Affairs,* 54 (July 1976), 635–44.
23. "The Ultimate Self-Interest," 18.
24. Quoted in Karnow, "The Kissinger-Fulbright Courtship."

Chapter 1

1. Author's interview with J. William Fulbright, Washington, D. C., March 9, 1981.
2. Tristram Coffin, *Senator Fulbright: Portrait of a Public Philosopher* (New York: E.P. Dutton, 1966), p. 41. Coffin's book must be used with some care. While basically accurate in his facts, Coffin paints an embarrassingly eulogistic portrait, e.g., p. 23, "Senator Fulbright is a modern Prometheus. He

defies the gods and myths of modern society to save man from the horror of atomic doom."

3. Quoted in Haynes Johnson and Bernard M. Gwertzman, *Fulbright The Dissenter* (Garden City, N.Y.: Doubleday, 1968), p. 18.
4. Ibid., p. 15.
5. Author's interview with J. William Fulbright, Washington, D.C., March 9, 1981.
6. Quoted in Johnson and Gwertzman, p. 27.
7. Ibid.
8. See E. H. Carr's classic discussion in *The Twenty Years' Crisis, 1919–1939*, 2d ed. (New York: Harper and Row, 1964), pp. 22–62.
9. On Fulbright's ambivalence toward the role of reason in human affairs see, illustratively, *Prospects for the West* (Cambridge: Harvard University Press, 1963), p. 2, 14; *Old Myths and New Realities* (New York: Vintage Press, 1964), p. 3; *The Arrogance of Power* (New York: Vintage Press, 1966), p. 206.
10. J. William Fulbright, "Economic Problems of Arkansas," speech delivered before Chamber of Commerce, Little Rock, October 18, 1940; cited in Johnson and Gwertzman, p. 28.
11. Fulbright's outlook thus combines into a synthetic whole two distinct leadership styles which James MacGregor Burns has recently labeled "transactional" and "transforming". See his *Leadership* (New York: Harper and Row, 1978), p. 4.
12. See, for example, Charles B. Seib and Alan L. Otten, "Fulbright: Arkansas Paradox," *Harper's*, June, 1956, 61.
13. U.S. Senate, *Congressional Record*, February 19, 1946, p. A 1284.
14. Ibid.
15. Author's interview with J. William Fulbright, Washington, D.C., March 9, 1981.
16. For representative statements of Fulbright's abiding belief in the primacy of a nation's domestic life, see *Prospects For The West*, p. 79; *Old Myths And New Realities*, p. 110; *The Arrogance Of Power*, p. 222; *The Crippled Giant*, p. 152.
17. Author's interview with J. William Fulbright, Washington, D.C., March 9, 1981.
18. Johnson and Gwertzman, pp. 48–49.
19. For the period covered in this and the preceding paragraph, see Johnson and Gwertzman, pp. 37–39; Coffin, p. 49.
20. Johnson and Gwertzman, p. 41.
21. Fulbright, "Economic Problems of Arkansas."
22. Author's interview with J. William Fulbright, Washington, D.C., March 9, 1981.
23. Quoted in Johnson and Gwertzman, p. 44.
24. Ibid., p. 47.
25. This event is recounted by Johnson and Gwertzman, pp. 48–50.

Chapter 2

1. Haynes Johnson and Bernard M. Gwertzman, *Fulbright the Dissenter* (Garden City, N.Y.: Doubleday, 1968), p. 53; see also Brock Brower, "The Roots of the Arkansas Questioner," *Life*, May 13, 1966, 98.
2. Brower, "The Roots of the Arkansas Questioner."
3. Johnson and Gwertzman, p. 54.
4. Walter Davenport, "Just a Boy From the Ozarks," *Colliers*, February 10, 1945, 14ff.
5. J. William Fulbright, "The Legislator," *Vital Speeches*, May 15, 1946, 468–72.
6. Charles B. Seib and Alan L. Otten, "Fulbright: Arkansas Paradox," *Harper's*, June, 1956, 63.
7. Johnson and Gwertzman recount the event, pp. 63–66.
8. For the text and subsequent colloquy, see U.S. House of Representatives, *Congressional Record*, February 16, 1943, pp. 1011–12.
9. Ibid., p. 1011.
10. Ibid.
11. Ibid.
12. Ibid., p. 1012.
13. Ibid.
14. Typical was the *New York Times'* stress on an exchange of "caustic words" during which "the House was tense." See "Exchange Over Airways," *New York Times*, February 17, 1943, p. 13.
15. *Congressional Record*, p. 1012.
16. Inis L. Claude, Jr., *Power and International Relations* (New York: Random House, 1962), p. 204.
17. See Johnson and Gwertzman, p. 66.
18. Text in Karl E. Meyer, ed., *Fulbright of Arkansas: The Public Positions of a Private Thinker* (Washington, D.C.: Robert B. Luce, 1963), p. 10: This is the language adopted by the House of Representatives on September 21, 1943. For Fulbright's original version, see p. 12.
19. Fulbright's premises during his single term in the House are treated with insight by Kurt Tweraser, *Changing Patterns of Political Beliefs: The Foreign Policy Operational Codes of J. William Fulbright, 1943–1967* (Beverly Hills: Sage, 1974), pp. 25–28, 38, 43, and 72–73.
20. "Planning for Peace Seen Gaining in U.S.," *New York Times*, February 28, 1943, p. 33.
21. Tweraser, p. 26.
22. For his somewhat disingenuous handling of the question of national sovereignty, see Fulbright's article: "Congress and the Peace," *Journal of the National Education Association*, (November 1943), 218.
23. J. William Fulbright, "The United Nations Today and Tomorrow," deliv-

ered May 10, 1943, at Constitution Hall Washington D.C.; text in Meyer, ed., p. 11, 13; see also Fulbright's discussion of "Sovereignty and the Charter," *New Republic*, August, 1945, 158–59.

24. For the full text of Fulbright's House speech, see U.S. House of Representatives, *Congressional Record*, September 20, 1943, pp. 7659–60, quote at p. 7659. The text of this speech is virtually identical to one delivered in Chicago before the American Bar Association a month earlier (see "War Not Crusade, Taft Tells Bar," *New York Times*, August 27, 1943, p. 2) and, again, before a New York audience several days after the House speech (see *New York Times*, September 25, 1943, p. 1). Portions of the text surfaced yet again as two different magazine articles. See J. William Fulbright, "Power Adequate to Enforce Peace," *New York Times Magazine*, October 17, 1943, pp. 9, 38–39, and "Congress and the Peace," *Journal of the National Education Association* (November 1943), 217. Academics facing the familiar "publish or perish" syndrome can only marvel at the politician's knack for getting maximum mileage out of a single work.

25. Text in Meyer, ed., p. 11.

26. Fulbright, House speech of September 20, 1943.

27. "War Not Crusade, Taft Tells Bar," *New York Times*, August 27, 1943, p. 2.

28. "Fulbright Fears Isolationist Fight," *New York Times*, October 19, 1943, p. 8.

29. See Nelson Polsby, Miriam Gallaher, and Barry Rundquist, "The Growth of the Seniority System in the U.S. House of Representatives, *American Political Science Review* (September 1969), 787–807.

30. "House Group Backs World Peace Plan," *New York Times*, June 16, 1943, p. 1, 4.

31. "House Votes 360–29 For Collaboration in Peace After War," *New York Times*, September 22, 1943, p. 1, 14. For the House debate and vote on the measure, see U.S. House of Representatives, *Congressional Record*, September 21, 1943, pp. 7705–29.

32. See George's comments, *Congressional Record*, September 21, 1943.

33. This was the critique of among others, Arthur Krock, "In the Nation," *New York Times*, June 18, 1943, p. 20.

34. "Vandenberg Gives New Post-War Idea," *New York Times*, July 3, 1943, p. 6.

35. See "Senators Draw Up A Post-War Pledge of Collaboration," *New York Times*, October 14, 1943, p. 1, 11; "Post-War Pledge Put Up to Senate," *New York Times*, October 15, 1943, p. 1, 9.

36. See "President Favors A General Pledge," *New York Times*, October 30, 1943, p. 5.

37. "Senate Votes 85 to 5 to Cooperate in Peace," *New York Times*, November 6, 1943, p. 1.

38. Johnson and Gwertzman, p. 71.

39. Harry S. Truman, *Memoirs: Year of Decisions* (New York: Doubleday, 1955), pp. 70–71.

40. Ibid., p. 552; the quote is from Truman's January 5, 1946, letter to Secretary of State Byrnes.
41. On this point see John Lewis Gaddis, *The United States and the Origins of the Cold War* (New York: Columbia University Press, 1972), p. 317.
42. The text of Kennan's cable is in U.S. Department of State, *Foreign Relations of the United States: 1946*, vol. 6 (Washington, D.C.: Government Printing Office, 1970), pp. 696–709. Kennan discusses the matter in his *Memoirs, 1925–1950* (Boston: Little, Brown, 1967), pp. 68–69; 292–93.
43. Gaddis, p. 304.
44. Harry S. Truman, *Memoirs: Years of Trial and Hope, 1946–1952* (Garden City, N.Y.: Doubleday, 1956), p. 100.
45. Acheson's account of this session is in his *Present at The Creation: My Years in the State Department* (New York: W. W. Norton, 1969), ch. 12, p. 219; see also Joseph M. Jones, *The Fifteen Weeks* (New York: Viking, 1955), pp. 138–42.
46. Acheson, p. 219.
47. See Truman's account in his *Years of Trial and Hope*, pp. 105–06. ("This was, I believe, the turning point in America's foreign policy . . . .")
48. Gaddis, p. 317, 350.
49. [George Kennan], "The Sources of Soviet Conduct," *Foreign Affairs* (July 1947), pp. 566–82.
50. Ibid., p. 575.
51. Ibid., p. 576.
52. Ibid., p. 582; Kennan's somewhat mournful reflections on the article are in his *Memoirs: 1924–1950*, pp. 354–67.
53. Gabriel Almond, *The American People and Foreign Policy* (New York: Harcourt, Brace, 1950), pp. 94–95.
54. See, generally, Louis Hartz, *The Liberal Tradition In America* (New York: Harcourt, Brace, & World, 1955), ch. 11; consult also Edward Weisband, *The Ideology of American Foreign Policy: A Paradigm of Lockian Liberalism* (Beverly Hills, Sage, 1973).
55. J. William Fulbright, Address before the Foreign Policy Association, New York City, October 20, 1945; text in Meyer, ed., pp. 34–44; quote at p. 35.
56. More than thirty-five years later, Fulbright vividly recalls how deeply affected he was by the awesome force of the atomic bomb. "It looked as if the human race would surely do something about it," he reflects. Author's interview with J. William Fulbright, Washington, D.C., March 9, 1981.
57. Fulbright, Address of October 20, 1945, p. 40.
58. Ibid., p. 43; see also "Sovereignty Gone, Fulbright Holds," *New York Times*, December 12, 1945, p. 6.
59. Ibid., p. 40.
60. Ibid., pp. 36–37.
61. J. William Fulbright, "Law: The Basis of World Peace," address over NBC, November 23, 1945; text reprinted in *NEA Journal* (February 1946), 61–62. See also "Fulbright, Hatch Now Hit UNO Veto," *New York Times*, November 24, 1945, p. 5.

62. Ibid., "Law: The Basis of World Peace," p. 62.
63. Ibid. At his next press conference, Truman dismissed the "playing by ear" charge with a curt "I think it's playing by music." *Public Papers of the Presidents, Harry S. Truman, 1945* (Washington: U.S. Government Printing Office), p. 513, cited by Johnson and Gwertzman, p. 100.
64. Fulbright, "Law: The Basis of World Peace," p. 62.
65. Tristram Coffin, *Senator Fulbright: Portrait of a Public Philosopher* (New York: E.P. Dutton, 1966), p. 91.
66. Author's interview with J. William Fulbright, Washington, D.C., March 9, 1981.
67. J. William Fulbright, Address Before a Joint Meeting of the American Academy of Arts and Letters and the National Institute of Arts in New York City, May 17, 1946; text in Meyer, ed., pp. 48–52.
68. Ibid., p. 49.
69. Ibid., p. 51.
70. See Tweraser, pp. 28–30.
71. Walter Lippmann, *The Cold War: A Study in U.S. Foreign Policy* (New York: Harper, 1947).
72. Quoted in Gaddis, p. 339.
73. Ibid., pp. 339–40.
74. Nearly thirty years later Fulbright would rue his own uncritical adherence to the Cold War consensus and belatedly acknowledge Wallace's prescience. "After World War II," he recalled, "we were sold on the idea that Stalin was out to dominate the world. I didn't have the knowledge or the foresight to make a judgment at that time. . . . Henry Wallace sensed it, he had a feeling about it, but he was ridiculed for being a visionary, an appeaser, unrealistic." Quoted in Daniel Yergin, "Fulbright's Last Frustration," *New York Times Magazine*, November 24, 1974, p. 87.
75. Anthony Leviero, "Vandenburg Move Clarifies Aid Plan," *New York Times*, April 8, 1947, p. 5.
76. Ibid.
77. McArthur's response: "I disagree with you completely." See *Military Situation in the Far East, Hearings Before the Committee on Armed Services and Committee on Foreign Relations*, U.S. Senate, 82nd Cong., 1st Sess. (1951), vol. I, p. 142. Fulbright repeated his point a bit later at pp. 298–99 and again, this time in a colloquy with Secretary of State Marshall, at pp. 642–43.
78. An interesting group of articles on the phenomenon, including the Fulbright program, is found in the March 1976 issue of *The Annals of the American Academy of Political and Social Science;* the issue is entitled "International Exchange Programs: A Reassessment."
79. Don Oberdorfer, "Common Noun Spelled f-u-l-b-r-i-g-h-t," *New York Times Magazine*, April 4, 1965, p. 80.
80. Walter Johnson and Francis J. Colligan, *The Fulbright Program: A History* (Chicago: University of Chicago Press, 1965), p. 13.
81. Fulbright's bill enabled foreign countries to buy American surplus war

material, using their own currencies rather than then-scarce dollars. The resulting revenue could then be used to pay for the varied activities of the exchange program. See Johnson and Colligan, ch.2; see also Thomas J. Hamilton, "Plan To Sell War Stocks For Foreign Scholarships, "*New York Times*, December 20, 1945, p. 1.

82. See Johnson and Gwertzman, pp. 108–11.

83. "Common Noun Spelled F-u-l-b-r-i-g-h-t," p. 82.

84. J. William Fulbright, "The Most Significant and Important Activity I Have Been Privileged to Engage in During My Years in the Senate," *Annals of the American Academy of Political and Social Science* (March 1976), 2.

85. Author's interview with J. William Fulbright, Washington, D.C., March 9, 1981.

86. For attempted explanations, see Nelson W. Polsby, "Towards an Explanation of McCarthyism," *Political Studies* (October 1960), 250–71, and Michael Paul Rogin, *The Intellectuals and McCarthy* (Cambridge, Mass.: M.I.T. Press, 1967).

87. Author's interview with J. William Fulbright, Washington, D.C., March 9, 1981.

88. Ibid.

89. See Edgar Kemler, "The Fulbright Fellow," *Nation*, (February 20, 1954), 146.

90. Fulbright's testimony, and his frequent colloquies with McCarthy make highly entertaining reading. See U.S. Senate, Committee on Appropriations, *Hearings on the Supplemental Appropriation Bill of 1954*, 83rd Cong., 1st Sess., 1953, pp. 613–42.

91. Johnson and Colligan, pp. 102–03.

92. Johnson and Gwertzman, p. 136; this judgment is shared by Richard Rovere, *Senator Joe McCarthy* (New York: Harcourt, Brace, 1959), pp. 34–35.

93. "McCarthy v. Welch," (Wilmette, Ill: Films Incorporated, n.d.).

94. Anthony Leviero, "Fulbright Offers Specific Charges Against McCarthy," *New York Times*, August 1, 1954, p. 1.

95. For a good overview, see James A. Nathan and James K. Oliver, *United States Foreign Policy and World Order.* 2nd ed. (Boston: Little, Brown, 1981), ch. 5. See also the interesting treatment in Robert Divine, *Eisenhower and the Cold War* (New York: Oxford University Press, 1981), ch. 1.

96. Dulles' views were set out in his "A Policy of Boldness," *Life*, May 10, 1952, 146–60.

97. For the text of Dulles' speech, see John Foster Dulles, "The Evolution of Foreign Policy," *Department of State Bulletin*, January 25, 1954, p. 108.

98. Nathan and Oliver, p. 178.

99. Divine, *Eisenhower and the Cold War*, pp. 38–39.

100. *Arkansas Gazette*, April 18, 1954. Cited in Tweraser, p. 43.

101. For a good discussion of Fulbright's criticisms of Eisenhower-Dulles policies, see Kenneth W. Grundy, "The Apprenticeship of J. William Fulbright," *Virginia Quarterly Review* (Summer 1967), 382–99.

102. J. William Fulbright, Senate speech, U.S. Senate, *Congressional Record*, February 27, 1956, p. 3369; see also "Criticism and Praise for Dulles' Views," *U.S. News and World Report*, March 9, 1956, 111–13; William S. White, "Dulles Assailed in Senate on View Soviet is Losing," *New York Times*, February 28, 1956, p. 1.

103. *Congressional Record*, February 27, 1956, p. 3370.

104. Ibid.

105. U.S. Senate, *Congressional Record*, April 15, 1956, p. 6501.

106. Quoted in Nathan and Oliver, pp. 215–16.

107. Allen Drury, "Fulbright Terms Foreign Policy 'Unwise' and Harmful to West," *New York Times*, December 15, 1956, p. 13.

108. William Harlan Hale, "The Man from Arkansas Goes After Mr. Dulles," *Reporter*, April 18, 1957, 31.

109. Ibid.

110. William S. White, "Dulles Faces Fire on Mideast Plan; House Unit for It," *New York Times*, January 25, 1957, p. 1.

111. "Texts of Fulbright and Truman Statements on Mideast Policy," *New York Times*, January 25, 1957, p. 6.

112. J. William Fulbright, Senate address, U.S. Senate, *Congressional Record*, August 14, 1957, pp. 14701–10.

113. Ibid., p. 14708.

114. Ibid.

115. Hale, 30.

116. Grundy, 398.

117. James Reston, "Dulles and Fulbright—Feud or Truce," *New York Times*, February 1, 1959, p. 10E.

118. J. William Fulbright, "The Dangerous Apathy," U.S. Senate, *Congressional Record*, June 20, 1958, p. 11844.

119. Ibid., p. 11846.

120. Ibid., p. 11845.

121. Ibid., p. 11847.

122. J. William Fulbright, "On the Brink of Disaster," U.S. Senate, *Congressional Record*, August 6, 1958, p. 16319; see also "Fulbright: 'Mistaken Policies' Behind U.S. Troubles in World," *U.S. News and World Report*, August 15, 1958, 86.

123. Fulbright, "On the Brink of Disaster," p. 16317.

124. Ibid., p. 16318.

125. J. William Fulbright, Senate speech of August 21, 1958, U.S. Senate, *Congressional Record*, August 21, 1958, p. 18903. The speech was recast as an article entitled "Challenge To Our Complacency," *New York Times Magazine*, September 14, 1958, pp. 24ff.

126. *Congressional Record*, August 21, 1958, p. 18903.

Chapter 3

1. Russell Baker, "Green, 91, Quits as Senate Chief of Foreign Policy," *New York Times*, January 31, 1959, p. 1.
2. Beverly Smith, Jr., "Egghead from the Ozarks," *Saturday Evening Post*, May 2, 1959, 116.
3. E. W. Kenworthy, "The Fulbright Idea of Foreign Policy," *New York Times Magazine*, May 10, 1959, pp. 10–11.
4. "New Age in the Senate," *New York Times*, January 31, 1959, p. 4.
5. See J. William Fulbright, "What Makes U.S. Foreign Policy?" *Reporter*, May 14, 1959, 18–21.
6. Sidney Hyman, "The Advice and Consent of J. William Fulbright," *Reporter*, September 17, 1959, 24.
7. U.S. Senate, Committee on Foreign Relations, *Hearing*, "What is Wrong with our Foreign Policy," 86th Cong., 1st Sess., April 15, 1959, pp. 18–19.
8. Ibid.
9. See, for example, "Fulbright's Leadership," *New Republic*, May 4, 1959, 5–6.
10. *Executive Sessions of the Senate Foreign Relations Committee*, Historical Series, vol. 11, 86th Congress, 1st Session (1959), p. 222.
11. Ibid., pp. 222–23.
12. J. W. Fulbright, "Where Do We Stand?" address delivered at the 77th Annual Dinner of the Harvard Club of Washington, D.C., March 12, 1960; text in U.S. Senate, *Congressional Record*, March 28, 1960, pp. 6715–17; quote at p. 6715.
13. Ibid.
14. Ibid., p. 6717; Fulbright had used nearly identical rhetoric in Senate floor remarks on March 5. For his comments and an interesting round of colloquies, see U.S. Senate, *Congressional Record*, March 5, 1960, p. 4555–72.
15. J. William Fulbright, "Some Aspects of American Foreign Policy," address before American Bar Association, Washington, D.C., September 1, 1960; text in U.S. Senate, *Congressional Record*, September 1, 1960, pp. 19207–9.
16. Ibid., pp. 19208–9.
17. Ibid., p. 19208.
18. Ibid.
19. See "As Fulbright Sees U.S. Policy Abroad," *U.S. News and World Report*, February 15, 1959, p. 87.
20. *Executive Sessions of the Senate Foreign Relations Committee*, vol. 11, p. 414.
21. David Halberstam, *The Best and the Brightest* (New York: Random House, 1972).
22. Arthur M. Schlesinger, Jr., *A Thousand Days* (Boston: Houghton Mifflin, 1965), p. 210.
23. Ibid., p. 214.

24. For the complete text, see Theodore C. Sorensen, *Kennedy* (New York: Harper and Row, 1965), pp. 245–48; quote at p. 246.
25. Robert A. Divine, "The Education of John F. Kennedy," in Frank Merli and Theodore Wilson, eds., *Makers of American Diplomacy* (New York: Scribners, 1974), p. 621.
26. Quoted in Sorensen, p. 245.
27. Ibid., p. 248.
28. See Seyom Brown, *The Faces of Power* (New York: Columbia University Press, 1968), p. 162–63.
29. For germinal statements of the new premises, see Walt Rostow, *The Stages of Economic Growth: A Non-Communist Manifesto* (London: Cambridge University Press, 1960), and John Kenneth Galbraith, "A Positive Approach to Foreign Aid," *Foreign Affairs* (April 1961), 444–57.
30. For a critical survey of Kennedy's foreign policy, see Richard J. Walton, *Cold War and Counterrevolution: The Foreign Policy of John F. Kennedy* (New York: Viking, 1972).
31. See W. H. Lawrence, "Kennedy Planning to Give Bowles Foreign Policy Job," *New York Times*, November 30, 1960, p. 1.
32. Schlesinger, p. 139.
33. Ibid., p. 140.
34. Quoted in "The Dilettante," *Nation*, September 7, 1970, 166.
35. Russell Baker, "Fulbright Calls for Calmness in Race to Match Gains by Reds," *New York Times*, June 30, 1961, p. 1. These remarks triggered a vigorous rebuttal from Arizona's Senator Goldwater, who called Fulbright's reasoning "patently ridiculous." See Russell Baker, "Goldwater Says Kennedy Drifts," *New York Times*, July 15, 1961, p. 12.
36. J. William Fulbright, "American Foreign Policy in the 20th Century Under an 18th-Century Constitution," *Cornell Law Quarterly*, 47 (Fall 1961), 1.
37. J. William Fulbright, "The Elite and the Electorate: Is Government by the People Possible?" in Edward Reed, ed., *Challenges to Democracy: The Next Ten Years* (New York: Frederick A. Praeger, 1963), pp. 84–85.
38. J. William Fulbright, address before the American Philosophical Society, Philadelphia, April 20, 1961; text in Karl E. Meyer, ed., *Fulbright of Arkansas: The Public Positions of a Private Philosopher* (Washington: Robert B. Luce, 1963), pp. 188–94, quote at p. 190.
39. Ibid., p. 189.
40. J. William Fulbright, Doherty Lecture, University of Virginia, April 21, 1961; text in Meyer, pp. 263–73, quote at p. 273.
41. J. William Fulbright, "For a Concert of Free Nations," *Foreign Affairs* (October 1961), 3.
42. Arthur Krock, "In the Nation," *New York Times*, May 2, 1961, p. 36.
43. Ibid.
44. "Fulbright Hints U.S. Weighs Use of Troops in Asia," *New York Times*, May 5, 1961, p. 1.
45. The earliest and still one of the best accounts of his role is Sidney Hyman,

"Fulbright: The Wedding of Arkansas and the World," *New Republic*, May 14, 1962, 19–26.

46. The memorandum is reprinted in Meyer, pp. 195–205.
47. Ibid., p. 201.
48. Schlesinger, p. 252.
49. Ibid., p. 289.
50. Sorensen, p. 702.
51. See E. W. Kenworthy, "Fulbright Becomes a National Issue," *New York Times Magazine*, October 1, 1961, pp. 21ff. See also Kenneth Crawford, "Fulbright's Rightness," *Newsweek*, October 16, 1961, 32.
52. J. William Fulbright, "The American Character," address delivered at Rockefeller public service awards presentation luncheon, Washington, D.C., December 5, 1963; text in U.S. Senate, *Congressional Record*, December 6, 1963, pp. 23726–28, quote at p. 23728.
53. J. William Fulbright, *Prospects For The West* (Cambridge, Mass.: Harvard University Press, 1963), p. 2; see also p. 33, 35.
54. Ibid., p. 97; see also p. 11. Fulbright seems to have been deeply influenced by Louis Hartz's well-known interpretation of America's "Lockean consensus;" he shares Hartz's concerns about the limiting effect domestic unanimity can have when we deal with other nations, few of whom share our outlook. (See Louis Hartz, *The Liberal Tradition in America* [New York: Harcourt, Brace & World, 1955].) Fulbright cites Hartz in *Prospects*, p. 96–97.
55. Ibid., p. 97.
56. Ibid., p. 94.
57. Ibid., p. 14.
58. Ibid., pp. 107ff.
59. Ibid., pp. 109–10; see also Kurt Tweraser, *Changing Patterns of Political Beliefs: The Foreign Operational Codes of J. William Fulbright, 1943–1967* (Beverly Hills: Sage, 1974), pp. 20–24.
60. *Prospects*, p. 112.
61. Ibid., p. 113; see also Tweraser, pp. 50–57.
62. *Prospects*, p. 114.
63. Ibid., p. 76.
64. Ibid., p. 51.
65. Ibid., p. 67. ("Foreign aid is one of a number of instruments of policy by which the West seeks to bolster its own security, by fostering a world environment in which our kind of society, and the values in which it is rooted, can survive and flourish.")
66. Ibid., pp. 70–71.
67. Ibid., p. 10, 26.
68. Ibid., p. 6, 10, 14, 19, 36.
69. Ibid., p. 1, 5, 6.
70. Ibid., p. 7, 9, 10, 14, 21, 26.
71. Ibid., p. 9.
72. Ibid., p. 10.

Chapter 4

1. Haynes Johnson and Bernard M. Gwertzman, *Fulbright the Dissenter* (Garden City, N.Y.: Doubleday, 1968), p. 186.
2. J. William Fulbright, "Old Myths and New Realities," U.S. Senate, *Congressional Record*, March 25, 1964, p. 6227.
3. Ibid.
4. Ibid.
5. Ibid.
6. Ibid.
7. Ibid.
8. Ibid., p. 6228.
9. Ibid.
10. Ibid.
11. Ibid., p. 6229.
12. Ibid.
13. Ibid.
14. Ibid.
15. Ibid., p. 6230.
16. Ibid.
17. Ibid.
18. Ibid., p. 6231.
19. Ibid.
20. See his rebuttal to that criticism in "Let's Talk Sense About Cuba," *Saturday Evening Post*, May 16, 1964, 8ff.; reprinted in U.S. Senate, *Congressional Record*, May 22, 1964, pp. 11734–35.
21. Fulbright, "Old Myths and New Realities," p. 6231.
22. Ibid., p. 6232.
23. Ibid.
24. Ibid.
25. Ibid.
26. U.S. Senate, *Congressional Record*, March 25, 1964, p. 6238.
27. Ibid.
28. Ibid., p. 6241.
29. Ibid.
30. Jacob Javits, "U.S. Foreign Policy and Chile," U.S. Senate, *Congressional Record*, April 22, 1964, p. 8748; "Uneasiness in Germany," U.S. Senate, *Congressional Record*, April 25, 1964, pp. 9070–71.
31. "Growing Foreign Policy Row: Two Top Democrats Urge Changes," *U.S. News and World Report*, April 6, 1964, 19.
32. Ibid.
33. Fulbright, "Let's Talk Sense About Cuba," p. 11734.
34. Ibid.
35. "Secretary Rusk's News Conference of March 27," *Department of State Bulletin*, April 13, 1964, pp. 570–76.

36. Ibid., p. 570.
37. Johnson and Gwertzman, p. 187.
38. *New York Times*, March 26, 1964, pp. 1, 12–13.
39. Walter Lippmann, "A Senator Speaks Out," *Newsweek*, April 13, 1964, p. 19.
40. "We and They," *New Republic*, April 18, 1964, 3–4.
41. "Chinks in Fulbright's Armor," *Christian Century*, April 22, 1964, 509.
42. "U.S. Policy: Old Myths, Mixed Voices," *Newsweek*, April 6, 1964, p. 17.
43. Kenneth Crawford, "Democratic Dialogue," *Newsweek*, April 13, 1964, 32.
44. "Are Our Policies Turning Obsolete?" *Business Week*, April 4, 1964, 28.
45. Hans Morgenthau, "Senator Fulbright's New Foreign Policy," *Commentary*, May, 1964, 68.
46. Ibid.
47. Ibid., 69.
48. Morton A. Kaplan, "Old Realities and New Myths," *World Politics* (January 1965), 339; Kaplan's biting attack was directed at the published volume entitled *Old Myths and New Realities*, not just the famous speech of that name.
49. "Fulbright and Myths," *Commonweal*, April 17, 1964, 101.
50. William V. Shannon, "New Myths For Old," *Commonweal*, April 17, 1964, 103.
51. Richard Rovere, "Letter From Washington," *New Yorker*, April 11, 1964, 149.
52. Ibid., 150.
53. "Fulbright's Progress," *Nation*, April 13, 1964, 357.
54. Reprinted in U.S. Senate, *Congressional Record*, April 7, 1964, pp. 7093–97.
55. Ibid., p. 7093.
56. J. William Fulbright, *Old Myths and New Realities* (New York: Random House, 1964).
57. Ibid., p. 9, 10.
58. Ibid., pp. 25, 29–32.
59. Ibid., p. 37.
60. Ibid., pp. 38–39.
61. Ibid.
62. Ibid., p. 45.
63. Ibid., p. 11, 40.
64. See Doris Kearns's good account in *Lyndon Johnson and the American Dream* (New York: New American Library, 1976), ch. 8.
65. Johnson and Gwertzman, pp. 185–92.
66. See J. William Fulbright, *The Arrogance of Power* (New York: Vintage Books, 1966), p. 52: "An election campaign was in progress and I had no wish to make any difficulties for the President in a race against a Republican candidate whose election I thought would be a disaster for the country."

67. J. William Fulbright, "Dangerous Delusions: A Note on Senator Goldwater," *Saturday Review*, October 24, 1964, 24.

68. David Halberstam, *The Best and the Brightest* (New York: Random House, 1972), p. 415.

69. Neil Sheehan, "The Covert War and Tonkin Gulf: February-August, 1964," in *The Pentagon Papers as Published by the New York Times* (New York: Quadrangle Books, 1971), pp. 244–78.

70. Ibid., p. 257.

71. Ibid., p. 265.

72. Ibid.

73. For the best available account, blending evidence and logic, see Joseph C. Goulden, *Truth Is The First Casualty: The Gulf of Tonkin Affair—Illusion and Reality* (Chicago: Rand, 1969).

74. Arnold H. Lubasch, "Red PT Boats Fire at U.S. Destroyer on Vietnam Duty," *New York Times*, August 3, 1964, p. 1.

75. See Neil Sheehan's account drawn from the Pentagon Papers, pp. 267–68.

76. It is this episode that later aroused so much doubt; see ibid., pp. 268–69; Goulden, ch. 5. For a contemporary account, see Tom Wicker, "U.S. Planes Attack North Vietnam Bases; President orders 'Limited' Retaliation After Communists' PT Boats Renew Raids," *New York Times*, August 5, 1964, p. 1.

77. See E. W. Kenworthy, "President Requests Support of Congress," *New York Times*, August 6, 1964, p. 1.

78. The full text is in U.S. Senate, *Congressional Record*, August 5, 1964, p. 18133.

79. Ibid.

80. Ibid.

81. Ibid.

82. Ibid., p. 18134, 18136.

83. Consult "Southeast Asia Resolution," *Joint Hearing Before the Committee on Foreign Relations and the Committee on Armed Services*, U.S. Senate, 88th Cong., 2d Sess., August 6, 1964.

84. Author's interview with J. William Fulbright, Washington, D.C., March 9, 1981.

85. Ibid.

86. Fulbright, *Old Myths and New Realities*, pp. 43–44.

87. U.S. Senate, *Congressional Record*, August 6, 1964, p. 18399, 18400.

88. Ibid., p. 18402.

89. Ibid.

90. For Gruening's comments, see ibid., pp. 18413–4.

91. Ibid., p. 18425.

92. Ibid., p. 18427, p. 18430, and at greater length the next day: U.S. Senate *Congressional Record*, August 7, 1964, pp. 18442–49.

93. U.S. Senate, *Congressional Record*, August 6, 1964, p. 18409.

94. U.S. Senate, *Congressional Record*, August 7, 1964, p. 18459.

95. Ibid.
96. Representative comments are those of Senator Church on August 6, U.S. Senate, *Congressional Record*, p. 18415; Senator Gore, ibid., p. 18416; Senator Bartlett, ibid., p. 18422; Senator Aiken, U.S. Senate, *Congressional Record*, August 7, 1964, pp. 18456–57; Senator McGovern, U.S. Senate, *Congressional Record*, August 8, 1964, pp. 18668–69.
97. Technically, in the end, the Senate tabled its own resolution, S.J. Res. 189, and passed the identically-worded measure (H.J. Res. 1145) that the House had already passed on a 416-to-0 vote. U.S. Senate, *Congressional Record*, August 7, 1964, p. 18470.
98. Lyndon B. Johnson, *The Vantage Point* (New York: Holt, Rinehart and Winston, 1971), pp. 118–19.
99. Ibid., p. 119.
100. Louis Harris, "Americans are 85 Pct. With Johnson On Ordering Vietnam Air Strikes," *Washington Post*, August 10, 1964; Louis Harris, "58 Pct. of Public Backs U.S. Course in Viet-Nam," *Washington Post*, December 21, 1964.
101. Johnson and Gwertzman, p. 196; Halberstam, p. 416.
102. J. W. Fulbright, *The Arrogance of Power* (New York: Vintage Books, 1966), p. 52.
103. Author's interview with J. William Fulbright, Washington, D.C., March 9, 1981.

Chapter 5

1. Among the best older studies of the revolt and subsequent U.S. intervention is Theodore Draper, *The Dominican Revolt: A Case Study in American Policy* (New York: Viking, 1968). A good recent account, written from a distinctly critical, pro-Bosch perspective, is Piero Gleijeses, *The Dominican Crises: The 1965 Constitutionalist Revolt and American Intervention* (Baltimore: Johns Hopkins, 1979).
2. J. William Fulbright, "The Situation in the Dominican Republic," U.S. Senate, *Congressional Record*, September 15, 1965, p. 23855.
3. Ibid., p. 23859.
4. Ibid., p. 23856.
5. Ibid.
6. Ibid.
7. Ibid., p. 23859.
8. Ibid., p. 23855.
9. Ibid., p. 23859.
10. Ibid., p. 23860.
11. Ibid., p. 23861.
12. Ibid., p. 23856.

13. Representative press comments inserted into the *Congressional Record* by Fulbright run to twenty-seven pages of triple-column, fine-print type. See U.S. Senate, *Congressional Record*, October 22, 1965, pp. 28379–406.

14. Eric Sevareid, "Congress: Soul Searching in Order," *Washington Evening Star*, October 4, 1965.

15. "Senator Fulbright's Wave of the Future," *Chicago Tribune*, September 17, 1965.

16. U.S. Senate, *Congressional Record*, September 15, 1965, p. 23862.

17. Ibid.

18. U.S. Senate, *Congressional Record*, September 16, 1965, p. 24172.

19. Ibid., p. 24170; see also John M. Goshko, "Supporters of U.S. Dominican Stance Lower Boom on Fulbright's Criticism," *Washington Post*, September 17, 1965.

20. Ibid., p. 24173.

21. William S. White, "Fulbright's Folly—An Irresponsible Speech," *Washington Post*, September 17, 1965.

22. Rowland Evans and Robert Novak, "Inside Report; The Fulbright Furor," *Washington Post*, September 20, 1965.

23. John Chamberlain, "These Days—Fulbright's Chancy Bet On History," *Washington Post*, September 25, 1965.

24. "Dominican Republic—Erratic Attack," *Time*, September 24, 1965, 44.

25. "Fulbright on the Dominican Crisis," *New York Times*, September 18 1965.

26. Joseph Kraft, "Insight and Outlook—Fulbright and His Critics," *Washington Post*, September 25, 1965.

27. Walter Lippmann, "Soviet-American Relations," *Washington Post*, September 28, 1965.

28. "Stemwinder," *Washington Post*, September 16, 1965.

29. "Senator Fulbright Dissents," *Nation*, October 4, 1965.

30. "Panic Button," *Washington Post*, September 17, 1965.

31. Marquis Childs, "Tyranny of the Majority in the United States," *Washington Post*, September 27, 1965.

32. U.S. Senate, *Congressional Record*, September 17, 1965, p. 24245.

33. U.S. Senate, *Congressional Record*, September 22, 1965, p. 24733.

34. U.S. Senate, *Congressional Record*, September 30, 1965, p. 25620.

35. U.S. Senate, *Congressional Record*, October 22, 1965, p. 28372.

36. Andrew Kopkind, "The Speechmaker," *New Republic*, October 2, 1965, 15. E. W. Kenworthy similarly noted that "his advice . . . has more effect after the event than on it." See his "Fulbright: Dissenter," *New York Times*, October 31, 1965, sec. 4, p. 4.

37. U.S. Senate, *Congressional Record*, September 30, 1965, p. 25623.

38. E. W. Kenworthy, "Fulbright Urges a Holding Action in Vietnam War," *New York Times*, June 16, 1965, p. 1.

39. J. William Fulbright, "The War in Vietnam," U.S. Senate, *Congressional Record*, June 15, 1965, p. 13656, 13657.

40. Ibid., p. 13656.

141

41. J. William Fulbright, "Prospects for Peace With Freedom," address delivered June 19, 1965, at Swarthmore College; text in U.S. Senate, *Congressional Record,* July 1, 1965, pp. 15460–61; quote at p. 15460.
42. Ibid., p. 15461.
43. For the full record of the hearings see U.S. Congress, Senate, Committee on Foreign Relations, *Supplemental Foreign Assistance, Fiscal Year 1966-Vietnam, Hearings on S. 2793;* 89th Cong., 2d Sess., 1966; major portions of the hearings were published in paperback form for the reading public: *The Vietnam Hearings* (New York: Vintage Books, 1966).
44. "The Disinvited Guest," *Time,* December 31, 1965, p. 14; see also "The Absentee," *Newsweek,* January 3, 1966, pp. 15–16.
45. E. W. Kenworthy, "McNamara Balks at Public Inquiry," *New York Times,* February 5, 1966, p. 1.
46. E. W. Kenworthy, "Fulbright Fears Conflict With China Over Vietnam," *New York Times,* February 8, 1966, p. 1.
47. See E. W. Kenworthy, "Rusk Says Peace of World is Issue in Vietnam War," *New York Times,* February 19, 1966, p. 1.
48. *The Vietnam Hearings,* p. 230.
49. Ibid., pp. 230–31.
50. Ibid., pp. 240–41.
51. This exchange is in the full transcript of the hearings, at p. 666.
52. Ibid.
53. Homer Bigart, "Fulbright Warns of 'Fatal' Course by U.S. in Vietnam," *New York Times,* April 29, 1966, p. 1.
54. The transcript is reprinted in U.S. Senate, *Congressional Record,* February 2, 1966, pp. 1941–43.
55. Ibid., p. 1942.
56. U.S. Senate, *Congressional Record,* March 1, 1966, p. 4383.
57. U.S. Senate, *Congressional Record,* May 3, 1966, p. 9615. This comment occurs amid a freewheeling Senate discussion on China. In a fascinating exchange with Senator McGovern, Fulbright poses this revealing query: "Will not the Senator agree that if there is any basis for the fear of China being able to take us over, it will result because such countries as ourselves and others will have exhausted their resources . . . in just such wars as we have now going on in the jungles of Vietnam?" McGovern, of course, agrees with Fulbright's stand.
58. J. William Fulbright, "We Must Negotiate Peace in Vietnam," *Saturday Evening Post,* April 9, 1966, p. 10.
59. "Portrait of the Chairman," *Time,* February 18, 1966, p. 22.
60. "The New Realism," *Time,* February 18, 1966, p. 20.
61. "Exhaustive, Explicit and Enough," *Time,* February 25, 1966, 21.
62. "On the Subject of Arrogance," *Time,* May 13, 1966, 31.
63. Kenneth Crawford, "Replacement Needed," *Newsweek,* October 10, 1966, 44.
64. Henry Fairlie, "Old Myths and New Realities," *Reporter,* June 16, 1966, 21.

65. "Should Fulbright Be Muzzled?" *National Review*, August 24, 1965, p. 718.
66. "Can He Be Serious?" *National Review*, August 9, 1966, p. 757.
67. *Life* magazine ran an editorial swipe at "Senator Fulbright's elegant defeatism" in "Fulbright the Undecider," *Life*, May 13, 1966, 4. See also the hostile stance taken by the *Reporter*, February 24, 1966, 16. Representative of friendly notices was Alex Campbell, "Fulbright on Camera," *New Republic*, May 21, 1966, 19–22.
68. Richard Reston, "Report on Washington," *Atlantic*, October, 1966, 10–12.
69. J. William Fulbright, *The Arrogance Of Power* (New York: Vintage, 1966).
70. Fulbright's lectures were presented under the auspices of the Christian A. Herter Lecture Series. They were "The Higher Patriotism," delivered April 21, 1966, text in U.S. Senate *Congressional Record*, April 25, 1966, pp. 8869–74; "Revolutions Abroad," delivered April 27, text in U.S. Senate, *Congressional Record*, April 28, 1966, pp. 9325–30; "The Arrogance of Power," delivered May 5, text in U.S. Senate, *Congressional Record*, May 17, 1966, pp. 10805–10.
71. *The Arrogance Of Power*, p. 248.
72. Ibid., p. 164.
73. Ibid., p. 206.
74. Ibid.
75. Ibid., p. 255.
76. J. William Fulbright, *Prospects For The West* (Cambridge, Mass: Harvard University Press, 1963), p. 2.
77. *The Arrogance Of Power*, p. 174.
78. Ibid., p. 222.
79. Ibid., p. 162; compare with this line from *Old Myths and New Realities* (p. 143), ". . . the ultimate source of war and peace lies in human nature."
80. *The Arrogance Of Power*, p. 161.
81. Ibid., p. 5.
82. For a sharply critical review of Fulbright's efforts at psychological explanations of international behavior, see Henry Fairlie, "The Senator and World Power," *Encounter*, May 1968, 57–66.
83. The Arrogance of Power, p. 249.
84. On America's "Lockean consensus," see Louis Hartz, *The Liberal Tradition In America* (New York: Harcourt, Brace & World, 1955).
85. Fulbright, *Prospects For The West*, p. 112.
86. Ibid., p. 114.
87. Fulbright, *Old Myths And New Realities*, p. vii.
88. Ibid., p. vi.
89. Fulbright, *The Arrogance Of Power*, p. 44.
90. Ibid., p. 45.
91. Ibid., p. 54.
92. See *The Arrogance Of Power*, ch. 3; for a good contemporary assessment of Fulbright's turnaround, see Maurice J. Goldbloom, "The Fulbright Revolt," *Commentary*, September 1966, 63–69.

93. *The Arrogance Of Power*, p. 196.
94. Richard N. Goodwin, *Triumph Or Tragedy: Reflections on Vietnam* (New York: Vintage Books, 1966), p. 38.
95. *The Arrogance Of Power*, p. 196.
96. Ibid., p. 217.
97. Ibid., p. 186.
98. Ibid., p. 92.
99. Ibid., p. 96.
100. Ibid., pp. 80–81.
101. Ibid., p. 152.
102. Ibid., p. 81, pp. 201–2.
103. Ibid., p. 71.
104. Ibid.
105. Ibid., p. 83.
106. Ibid., p. 77.
107. Ibid., p. 78.
108. Ibid., p. 19–21.
109. Ibid., p. 20.
110. Ibid., p. 22.
111. Ibid., p. 28.
112. Ibid., p. 20, 131.
113. Ibid., p. 179.
114. Ibid., p. 180.
115. Ibid., p. 195.
116. Ibid., p. 186.
117. Ibid., p. 237.
118. Ibid., pp. 237–41.
119. Ibid., p. 171.
120. Ibid., p. 205.
121. Ibid., p. 204.

Chapter 6

1. See Roger D. Masters's book by that title. (New York: Knopf, 1967).
2. Henry Steele Commager, "How Not To Be A World Power," *New York Times Magazine*, March 12, 1967, p. 28.
3. Edmund Stillman and William Pfaff, *Power and Impotence: The Failure of America's Foreign Policy* (New York: Random House, 1966), p. 131.
4. Ronald Steel, *Pax Americana* (New York: Viking, 1967), pp. 15–16.
5. "The High Price of Power," *New Republic*, September 10, 1966, 5.
6. See Hans J., Morgenthau, "To Intervene or Not to Intervene," *Foreign Affairs* (April 1967), 434. See also William Pfaff, "Muddied American Messianism," *Commonweal*, March 22, 1968, 8–9.

7. Hans J. Morgenthau, *A New Foreign Policy for the United States* (New York: Praeger, 1969), pp. 16–17.
8. See Frank Church, "How Many Dominican Republics and Vietnams Can We Take On?" *New York Times Magazine,* November 28, 1965, p. 45.
9. Morgenthau, *A New Foreign Policy for the United States,* p. 3.
10. *Power and Impotence,* p. 62.
11. *Pax Americana,* p. 27.
12. Ibid; see also John Kenneth Galbraith, "Foreign Policy: The Stuck Whistle," *Atlantic,* February, 1965, esp. pp. 65–66.
13. Morgenthau, *A New Foreign Policy for the United States,* p. 27.
14. See his contribution to "Liberal Anti-Communism Revisited: A Symposium," *Commentary,* September, 1967, pp. 68–71; quote at p. 69.
15. *Pax Americana,* p. 6.
16. Theodore Draper, "The American Crisis: Vietnam, Cuba and the Dominican Republic," *Commentary,* January, 1967, 27.
17. See "Ideological Trap," *Commonweal,* May 19, 1967, 252–53.
18. Hans J. Morgenthau, "Globalism: Johnson's Moral Crusade," *New Republic,* July 3, 1965, 20.
19. See Morgenthau, "To Intervene or Not to Intervene," 434.
20. "Vietnam—Did U.S. Make a Mistake?" *Gallup Opinion Index,* April 1968, p. 14.
21. "Vietnam—'Hawks' 'Doves,' " *Gallup Opinion Index,* April 1968, p. 15.
22. "Vietnam," *Gallup Opinion Index,* October 1969, p. 14.
23. "Vietnam," *Gallup Opinion Index,* February 1973, p. 8.
24. "Impact of U.S. Involvement in Vietnam," *Gallup Opinion Index,* March, 1972, p. 13; see also John E. Mueller, "Trends in Popular Support for the Wars in Korea and Vietnam," *American Political Science Review,* 65 (June 1971), 358–75.
25. See David W. Levy, "The Debate Over Vietnam: One Perspective," *Yale Review* (Spring 1974), 333–46.
26. "The Limits of Commitment: A *Time*-Louis Harris Poll," *Time,* May 2, 1969, 16.
27. Ibid., 17.
28. See "Military Spending," *Gallup Opinion Index,* March 1973, p. 10; "National and Military Budget," *Gallup Opinion Index,* November, 1973, p. 16.
29. "Arab-Israeli Situation," *Gallup Opinion Index,* August, 1968, p. 20.
30. "Majority Would Reduce U.S. Troop Commitment to NATO," *Gallup Opinion Index,* November, 1973, pp. 17–20.
31. "Should U.S. Keep Troops in West Germany?" *Gallup Opinion Index,* November, 1968, p. 8.
32. "Public Would Have President Seek Congressional Approval Before Committing U.S. Forces Abroad," *Gallup Opinion Index,* December, 1973, pp. 10–13; quote at p. 10.
33. H. H. Wilson, "Starting at Fulton, Missouri," *Nation,* April 3, 1972, 438.
34. James A. Johnson, "The New Generation of Isolationists," *Foreign Affairs,* October 1970, 136.

35. Ibid., 141.
36. Graham Allison, "Cool It: The Foreign Policy of Young America," *Foreign Policy* (Winter 1970–71), 147.
37. Ibid.
38. "Isolationist Viewpoint Gains in Appeal," *Gallup Opinion Index*, March, 1969, p. 21, 22.
39. Ibid., p. 24.
40. As an example of the term's promiscuous uses, see the editorial entitled "Who Are the Isolationists?" *Nation*, September 12, 1966, 202–3.
41. "Isolationist Viewpoint Gains in Appeal," p. 21.
42. See "Impending Talks Have Lessened Fear of China," *Gallup Opinion Index*, October, 1971, pp. 5-6; compare with the apprehension found four years earlier: "Red China," *Gallup Opinion Index*, April, 1967, p. 22, and "Greatest Threat—Russia or China?", *Ibid.*, p. 23.
43. "The Limits of Commitment: A *Time*-Louis Harris Poll," p. 16.
44. Ibid.
45. Ibid., p. 17.
46. On limitationist critics as "critics of means," see Robert W. Tucker, "The American Outlook," in Robert E. Osgood et al., *America and the World: From the Truman Doctrine to Vietnam* (Baltimore: Johns Hopkins, 1970), esp. p. 74.
47. "Senator Fulbright on 'Meet the Press.' " Text in U.S. Senate, *Congressional Record*, January 23, 1967, p. 1223.
48. Ibid., p. 1224.
49. J. William Fulbright, "The War and Its Effects—I," U.S. Senate, *Congressional Record*, December 8, 1967, p. 35559.
50. Ibid.
51. The *New Republic*'s T.R.B. well captured the point: "It was Vietnam that turned Fulbright from a provoked dissenter to an opposition leader." "Senate Spectacular," *New Republic*, February 4, 1967, 6.
52. "Excerpts From Rusk Testimony on Vietnam and Exchanges With Senate Panel," *New York Times*, March 12, 1968, p. 16.
53. Ibid.
54. See John W. Finney, "Criticism of War Widens in Senate on Build-Up Issue," *New York Times*, March 8, 1968, p. 1.
55. "Fulbright's Solution: 'Honorable Compromise,' " *U.S. News and World Report*, February 5, 1968, 31.
56. Author's interview with J. William Fulbright, Washington, D.C., March 9, 1981.
57. See, for example, Haynes Johnson and Bernard M. Gwertzman, *Fulbright the Dissenter* (Garden City, N.Y.: Doubleday, 1968) pp. 241–42.
58. See David Sanford, "A Talk With Senator Fulbright," *New Republic*, March 9, 1968, 19–20.
59. James Fletcher, "The Politics of Emptiness," *National Review*, February 13, 1968, 133.

60. U.S. Senate, Foreign Relations Committee, "The Gulf of Tonkin, the 1964 Incidents," *Hearings*, 90th Cong., 2d Sess., February 20, 1968, p. 81.
61. U.S. Senate, *Congressional Record*, July 31, 1967, p. 20702.
62. Ibid.
63. "National Commitment," *Washington Post*, August 2, 1967.
64. "Fulbright's Dilemma," *Newsweek*, August 28, 1967, 19.
65. "Rethinking the Unthinkable," *Reporter*, September 21, 1967, p. 14.
66. U.S. Senate, *Congressional Record*, March 7, 1968, pp. 5644–45; see the lengthy floor debate following Fulbright's remarks at pp. 5646–59.
67. U.S. Senate, Foreign Relations Committee, "Foreign Assistance Act of 1968; Part I—Vietnam," *Hearings on S. 3091*, 90th Cong., 2d Sess., March 11, 12, 1968, p. 135.
68. U.S. Senate, Committee on Foreign Relations, "Changing American Attitudes Toward Foreign Policy," *Hearings*, 90th Cong., 1st Sess., February 20, 1967, p. 14.
69. U.S. Senate, Committee on Foreign Relations, "The Nature of Revolution," *Hearings*, 90th Cong., 2d Sess., February 19, 21, 26, and March 7, 1968, p. 123.
70. Text in U.S. Senate, *Congressional Record*, August 9, 1967. pp. 22126–29. The address was recast for publication as "The Great Society is a Sick Society," *New York Times Magazine*, August 20, 1967, pp. 30ff.
71. *Congressional Record*, August 9, 1967, p. 22127.
72. J. William Fulbright, "The United States and 'Responsibilities of Power,' " *New York Times*, January 27, 1968.
73. Ibid.
74. "The Price of Empire," p. 22128.
75. J. William Fulbright, "Beyond Coexistence," delivered May 30, 1967, Pacem in Terris, Geneva, Switzerland; text in U.S. Senate, *Congressional Record*, June 7, 1967, quote at p. 15018.
76. Ibid., p. 15017, 15018.
77. Ibid., p. 15018.
78. Ibid.

Chapter 7

1. See Benjamin I. Page, "Policy Voting and the Electoral Process," *American Political Science Review* 66 (September 1972), 979–95; Richard Brody, "Popular Control of Public Policy: A Normal Vote Analysis of the 1968 Election," *American Political Science Review* 66 (June 1972), 429–49.
2. On the public's mood, see, in addition to the poll data in chapter 6, Bruce Russett, "The Americans' Retreat from World Power," *Political Science Quarterly* 91 (Spring 1975), 1–21, and Bruce Russett and Miroslav Nincic,

"American Opinion on the Use of Military Force Abroad," *Political Science Quarterly* 91 (Fall 1976), 411–31.

3. Richard M. Nixon, *RN: The Memoirs of Richard Nixon* (New York: Grosset and Dunlap, 1978), p. 343.

4. See especially the data presented by Russett and Nincic, "The Americans' Retreat from World Power."

5. Nixon, p. 349.

6. Ibid., p. 343.

7. Typical of the magnification of Kissinger's role are Bruce Mazlish, *Kissinger: The European Mind in American Policy* (New York: Basic Books, 1976), pp. 306; Roger Morris, *Uncertain Greatness: Henry Kissinger and American Foreign Policy* (New York: Harper and Row, 1977), *passim:* Stephen R. Graubard, *Kissinger: Portrait of a Mind* (New York: Norton, 1973), pp. 272–73; David Landau, *Kissinger: The Uses of Power* (Boston: Houghton Mifflin, 1972), pp. 3–13.

8. Richard M. Nixon, "Asia After Viet Nam," *Foreign Affairs* 46 (October 1967), 111–25.

9. Ibid., p. 113.

10. Ibid., p. 114.

11. Ibid., pp. 112–13.

12. Ibid., p. 121.

13. For a partial text of Nixon's rambling discourse, see Tad Szulc, *The Illusion of Peace: Foreign Policy in the Nixon Years* (New York: Viking, 1978), pp. 125–27. Under the ground rules imposed, reporters could not name the "high administration official" conducting the briefing nor use direct quotations.

14. Ibid., p. 126.

15. Ibid., pp. 126–27.

16. Ibid., p. 127.

17. Text in *Department of State Bulletin*, November 24, 1969, p. 440.

18. Richard M. Nixon, *U.S. Foreign Policy for the 1970's: A New Strategy for Peace* (Washington, D.C.: Government Printing Office, February 18, 1970), p. 2.

19. Ibid., pp. 2–3.

20. Ibid., p. 6.

21. See Richard Nixon, *U.S. Foreign Policy for the 1970's: Building for Peace* (Washington: Government Printing Office, February 25, 1971), pp. 156–63; *idem, U.S. Foreign Policy for the 1970's: The Emerging Structure of Peace* (Washington: Government Printing Office, February 9, 1972), pp. 17–37; *idem, U.S. Foreign Policy for the 1970's: Shaping a Durable Peace* (Washington: Government Printing Office, May 3, 1973), pp. 16–39.

22. Henry Brandon, *The Retreat of American Power* (Garden City, N.Y.: Doubleday, 1973), p. 83.

23. Nixon, *R.N.*, p. 395.

24. Quoted in Brandon, p. 81.

25. Henry Kissinger, *White House Years* (Boston: Little, Brown, 1979), p. 225.
26. See, illustratively, Hans J. Morgenthau, "Mr. Nixon's Foreign Policy," *New Republic*, March 21, 1970, 23–25; *idem*, "Nixon and the World," *New Republic*, January 6, 1973, 17–20; Stanley Hoffmann, "Will the Balance Balance at Home?" *Foreign Policy* (Summer 1972), 60–86.
27. J. William Fulbright, *The Crippled Giant* (New York: Vintage Books, 1972). Fulbright today doubts that he will do further writing, either on contemporary affairs or, alas, his own memoirs.
28. Ibid., p. 242.
29. Ibid., pp. 270–72.
30. Ibid., p. 9.
31. Ibid., p. 10.
32. Ibid., p. 151.
33. Ibid., p. 157.
34. Ibid., p. 270.
35. Ibid., p. 272.
36. Ibid., p. 164.
37. Ibid., p. 165.
38. Ibid., p. 274.
39. Ibid., p. 154.
40. Ibid., p. 158.
41. Ibid., p. 277.
42. Ibid., p. 4.
43. Ibid., p. 7.
44. Ibid., p. 7.
45. Ibid.; see also p. 164.
46. Ibid., p. 13.
47. Ibid., p. 161.
48. Ibid., p. 274.
49. Ibid., p. 272.
50. Ibid., pp. 269–70.
51. Louis Hartz, *The Liberal Tradition in America* (New York: Harcourt, Brace and World, 1955); see also Bernard Bailyn, *The Ideological Origins of the American Revolution* (Cambridge: Harvard University Press, 1967), and Gordon Wood, *The Creation of the American Republic* (Chapel Hill: University of North Carolina Press, 1969).
52. Fulbright, *The Crippled Giant*, p. 158.
53. Ibid., p. 22.
54. On China, for example, see ibid., p. 52.
55. Ibid., p. 160.
56. Ibid., p. 94.
57. Ibid., p. 155.
58. Ibid., p. 99.
59. Ibid., p. 97.
60. Ibid., pp. 91–92.

61. Ibid., p. 135.
62. Ibid., p. 155.
63. Ibid., p. 277.
64. Ibid., p. 170.
65. Ibid., p. 274.
66. J. William Fulbright, "Accomplishment of World Peace"; text in U.S. Senate, *Congressional Record,* October 9, 1973, pp. S18830–34; quote at p. 18832.
67. Ibid.
68. Ibid.
69. Kenneth Crawford, "Nixon's 'Knaves'," *Newsweek,* June 23, 1969, p. 38; Robert B. Semple, Jr., "Nixon, Defending Policies, Hits 'New Isolationists'; Pledges A World Role," *New York Times,* June 5, 1969, p. 1.
70. See John W. Finney, "President's Speech Stirs Resentment in Congress," *New York Times,* June 5, 1969, p. 1; "Vietnam Has Forced Distortion of Our Foreign Policy," *U.S. News and World Report,* June 28, 1971, 25–26.
71. J. William Fulbright, "The Wars in Your Future," *Look,* December 2, 1969, p. 82.
72. "The National Broadcasting Co. Presents a Reply to President Nixon on the Subject of Southeast Asia," August 31, 1970; text in U.S. Senate, *Congressional Record,* September 1, 1970, pp. 30596–98; quote at p. 30596.
73. U.S. Senate, *Congressional Record,* April 2, 1970, p. 10156.
74. "Face the Nation," July 15, 1970; text in U.S. Senate, *Congressional Record,* July 6, 1970, pp. 22806–8; quotes at p. 22806, 22807.
75. Stanley Karnow, "The Kissinger-Fulbright Courtship," *New Republic,* December 29, 1973, 15.
76. Ibid., 16.
77. U.S. Senate, *Congressional Record,* August 6, 1971, p. 30298.
78. U.S. Senate, *Congressional Record,* September 21, 1973, p. S 17151.
79. U.S. Senate, Committee on Foreign Relations, *Hearings,* 93rd Cong., 2d Sess., "Detente," September 19, 1974, p. 262.
80. J. William Fulbright, "Getting Along With the Russians," Address to the American Bankers Association, July 11, 1973; text in U.S. Senate, *Congressional Record,* July 18, 1973, pp. S 13793–96, quote at p. 13794.
81. J. William Fulbright, "Normalizing Relations With the Soviet Union—Avenues and Obstacles," U.S. Senate, *Congressional Record,* June 26, 1974, pp. S 11597–98; quote at p. 11598.
82. Ibid., p. 11597.
83. Ibid.
84. Ibid., p. 11598.
85. J. William Fulbright, "American Foreign Policy in the 20th Century Under an 18th Century Constitution," *Cornell Law Quarterly,* 47 (Fall 1961), 1, 6.
86. J. William Fulbright, "The Legislator as Educator," *Foreign Affairs,* 57 (Spring 1979), 719–26. For a scholarly critique of that "stampede," see Thomas M. Franck and Edward Weisband, *Foreign Policy by Congress* (New York: Oxford University Press, 1979).

87. Daniel Yergin, "Fulbright's Last Frustration," *New York Times Magazine*, November 24, 1974, p. 88.
88. U.S. Senate, *Congressional Record*, February 3, 1972, p. 2512.
89. J. William Fulbright, "Summary of Activities of the Committee on Foreign Relations, 91st Congress," U.S. Senate, *Congressional Record*, December 30, 1970, p. 44015.
90. J. William Fulbright, "The Legislator: Congress and the War," address delivered at the University of South Florida, February 4, 1971; text in U.S. Senate, *Congressional Record*, February 5, 1971, pp. 1867–70, quote at p. 1868.
91. U.S. Senate, *Congressional Record*, June 19, 1969, p. 16615. A useful discussion is Charles J. Stevens, "The Use and Control of Executive Agreements: Recent Congressional Initiatives," *Orbis* (Winter 1977), 905–31.
92. Senate Resolution 85, U.S. Senate, *Congressional Record*, February 4, 1969, p. 2603.
93. See John W. Finney, "Senate Panel Asks U.S. Commitments Be Put to Congress," *New York Times*, March 13, 1969, p. 1.
94. See "Senate Moves to Restrict Foreign Commitments," *Congressional Quarterly Almanac 1969* (Washington, D.C.: Congressional Quarterly, 1970), p. 179.
95. Kenneth Crawford, "Neo-Isolationism," *Newsweek*, April 21, 1969, 40.
96. John W. Finney, "Curbs on Policy Feared By Nixon," *New York Times*, June 20, 1969, p. 19.
97. See John W. Finney, "Senate, 70 to 16, Calls For a Curb on Commitments," *New York Times*, June 26, 1969, p. 1.
98. U.S. Senate, *Congressional Record*, June 25, 1969, p. 17245.
99. U.S. Senate, *Congressional Record*, June 19, 1969, p. 16625.
100. An excellent monograph exists on the subject. See Naomi Lynn and Arthur McClure, *The Fulbright Premise* (Bucknell University Press, 1973).
101. Ibid., p. 138.
102. See Franck and Weisband, esp. chaps. 1 and 2.
103. U.S. Senate, *Congressional Record*, October 10, 1973, p. S 18985.
104. U.S. Senate, Committee on Foreign Relations, *Hearings*, 93d Cong., 1st Sess., "War Powers Legislation, 1973," April 11 and 12, 1973, p. 3.

Chapter 8

1. Clifton Daniel, "Fulbright Says U.S. May Be Facing Peril," *New York Times*, January 1, 1975, p. 3. The quote is from Daniel's interview with Fulbright on the Senator's last day in office.
2. Michael Barone, Grant Ujifusa, and Douglas Matthews, *The Almanac of American Politics: 1974* (Boston: Gambit, 1973), p. 39.

3. Ibid., p. 42; *idem, The Almanac of American Politics: 1972* (Boston: Gambit, 1972), p. 33.
4. Tom Braden, "A Place for the Fulbrights," reprinted in U.S. Senate, *Congressional Record*, June 21, 1974, p. S 11216.
5. "The Fall of Fulbright," *Arkansas Gazette*, May 30, 1974; reprinted in U.S. House of Representatives, *Congressional Record*, June 11, 1974, p. H 5046.
6. Andrew Kopkind, "The Speechmaker: Senator Fulbright as the Arkansas de Tocqueville," *New Republic*, October 2, 1965, 19.
7. Quoted in Daniel Yergin, "Fulbright's Last Frustration," *New York Times Magazine*, November 24, 1974, p. 14.
8. See, for example, J. William Fulbright, "If I Were a U.S. Senator Today," *Miami Herald*, August 9, 1981, p. 5E.
9. Author's interview with J. William Fulbright, Washington, D.C., March 9, 1981.
10. J. W. Fulbright, "Foreign Policy Advice," *New York Times*, April 6, 1980.

Bibliography

IN ADDITION TO my March 9, 1981, interview with Fulbright, the following sources are directly cited in the study.

I. Fulbright's Books, Articles, Speeches, and Public Comments

"Face the Nation—July 5, 1970." U.S. Congress. Senate. 91st Cong., 2d Sess. *Congressional Record*, July 6, 1970, pp. 22806–8.

"Fulbright, Advice and Dissent." CBS News Special Report. Broadcast on the CBS Television and Radio Network, February 1, 1966.

Fulbright, J. William. "Accomplishment of World Peace." U.S. Congress. Senate. 93d Cong., 1st Sess., *Congressional Record*, October 9, 1973, pp. S 18830–4.

———. "The American Character." U.S. Congress. Senate. 88th Cong., 1st Sess. *Congressional Record*, December 6, 1963, pp. 23726–8.

———. "American Foreign Policy in the 20th Century Under an 18th-Century Constitution." *Cornell Law Quarterly*, 47 (Fall 1961), 1–18.

———. "The Arrogance of Power." U.S. Congress. Senate. 89th Cong., 2d Sess. *Congressional Record*, May 17, 1966, pp. 10805–10.

———. The *Arrogance of Power*. New York: Vintage Books, 1966.

_____. "Beyond Coexistence." U.S. Congress. Senate. 90th Cong., 1st Sess. *Congressional Record*, June 7, 1967, pp. 15017–9.

_____. "Challenge To Our Complacency." *New York Times Magazine*, September 14, 1958, pp. 24ff.

_____. "The Cold War in American Life." U.S. Congress. Senate. 88th Cong., 2d Sess. *Congressional Record*, April 7, 1964, pp. 7093–7.

_____. "Congress and the Peace." *Journal of the National Education Association*, 32 (November 1943) 217–18.

_____. *The Crippled Giant.* New York: Vintage Books, 1972.

_____. "The Dangerous Apathy." U.S. Congress. Senate. 85th Cong., 2d Sess. *Congressional Record*, June 20, 1958, pp. 11844–8.

_____. "Dangerous Delusions: A Note on Senator Goldwater." *Saturday Review*, October 24, 1964, 24ff.

_____. "The Elite and the Electorate: Is Government by the People Possible?" *Challenges To Democracy: The Next Ten Years.* Ed. by Edward Reed. New York: Praeger, 1963.

_____. "For a Concert of Free Nations." *Foreign Affairs*, 40 (October 1961) 1–18.

_____. "Foreign Policy Advice." *New York Times*, April 6, 1980.

_____. "Getting Along With the Russians." U.S. Congress. Senate. 93d Cong., 1st Sess. *Congressional Record*, July 18, 1973, pp. S 13793–6.

_____. "The Great Society is a Sick Society." *New York Times Magazine*, August 20, 1967, pp. 30ff.

_____. "The Higher Patriotism." U.S. Congress. Senate. 89th Cong., 2d Sess. *Congressional Record*, April 25, 1966, pp. 8869–74.

_____. "If I Were a U.S. Senator Today." *Miami Herald*, August 9, 1981.

_____. "Law: The Basis of World Peace." *NEA Journal* (February 1946), 61–2.

_____. "The Legislator." *Vital Speeches*, May 15, 1946, pp. 468–72.

_____. "The Legislator as Educator." *Foreign Affairs*, 57 (Spring 1979), 719–26.

_____. "The Legislator: Congress and the War." 92d Cong., 1st Sess. *Congressional Record*, February 5, 1971, pp. 1867–70.

_____. "Let's Talk Sense About Cuba." *Saturday Evening Post*, May 16, 1964, 8ff.

_____. "The Most Significant and Important Activity I Have Been Privileged to Engage in During My Years in the Senate." *Annals of the American Academy of Political and Social Science*, 424 (March 1976), 1–5.

_____. "Normalizing Relations With the Soviet Union—Avenues and Obstacles." 93d Cong., 2d Sess. *Congressional Record*, June 26, 1974, pp. S 11597–8.

_____. "Old Myths and New Realities." U.S. Congress. Senate. 88th Cong., 2d Sess. *Congressional Record*, March 25, 1964, pp. 6227–32.

_____. *Old Myths and New Realities.* New York: Random House, 1964.

_____. "On the Brink of Disaster." U.S. Congress. Senate. 85th Cong., 2d Sess. *Congressional Record*, August 6, 1958, pp. 16317–20.

_____. "Power Adequate to Enforce Peace." *New York Times Magazine*, October 17, 1943, pp. 9, 38–39.

————. "The Price of Empire." U.S. Congress. Senate. 90th Cong., 1st Sess. *Congressional Record*, August 9, 1967, pp. 22126–9.

————. "Prospects For Peace With Freedom." U.S. Congress. Senate. 89th Cong., 1st Sess. *Congressional Record*, July 1, 1965, pp. 15460–1.

————. *Prospects For The West*. Cambridge, Mass.: Harvard University Press, 1963.

————. "Revolutions Abroad." U.S. Congress. Senate. 89th Cong., 2d Sess. *Congressional Record*, April 28, 1966, pp. 9325–30.

————. "The Situation in the Dominican Republic." U.S. Congress. Senate. 89th Cong., 1st Sess. *Congressional Record*, September 15, 1965, pp. 23855–61.

————. "Some Aspects of American Foreign Policy." U.S. Congress. Senate. 86th Cong., 2d Sess. *Congressional Record*, September 1, 1960, pp. 19207–9.

————. "Sovereignty and the Charter." *New Republic*, August 1945, 158–9.

————. "Summary of Activities of the Committee on Foreign Relations, 91st Congress." 91st Cong., 2d Sess. *Congressional Record*, December 30, 1970, p. 44015–7.

————. "Two Views of U.S. Foreign Policy." *Foreign Policy Bulletin*, April 15, 1956, pp. 116, 118.

————. "The United States and 'Responsibilities of Power.' " *New York Times*, January 27, 1968.

————. "The War and Its Effects—I." U.S. Congress. Senate. 90th Cong., 1st Sess. *Congressional Record*, December 8, 1967, pp. 35557–60.

————. "The War in Vietnam." U.S. Congress. Senate. 89th Cong., 1st Sess. *Congressional Record*, June 15, 1965, pp. 13656–8.

————. "The Wars in Your Future." *Look*, December 2, 1969, 82ff.

————. "We Must Negotiate Peace in Vietnam." *Saturday Evening Post*, April 9, 1966, 10–14.

————. "What Makes U.S. Foreign Policy?" *Reporter*, May 14, 1959, 18–21.

————. "Where Do We Stand?" U.S. Congress. Senate. 86th Cong., 2d Sess. *Congressional Record*, March 28, 1960, pp. 6715–17.

Meyer, Karl E., ed. *Fulbright of Arkansas: The Public Positions of a Private Thinker*. Washington, D.C.,: Robert B. Luce, 1963.

"The National Broadcasting Co. Presents a Reply to President Nixon on the Subject of Southeast Asia." Text in U.S. Congress. Senate. 91st Cong., 2d Sess. *Congressional Record*, August 31, 1970, pp. 30596–8.

"Senator Fulbright on 'Meet the Press.' " U.S. Congress. Senate. 90th Cong., 1st Sess. *Congressional Record*, January 23, 1967, pp. 1222–4.

U.S. Congress. House. Fulbright's Maiden Address and Subsequent Debate. 78th Congress, 1st Sess. *Congressional Record*, February 16, 1943, pp. 1011–2.

————. House. Fulbright Speech. 78th Congress, 1st Sess. *Congressional Record*, September 20, 1943, pp. 7659–60.

U.S. Congress. Senate. Prepared remarks by J. W. Fulbright. 79th Cong., 2d Sess. *Congressional Record*, February 19, 1946, p. A 1284.

———. Fulbright's Critique of Dulles. 84th Cong., 2d Sess. *Congressional Record*, February 27, 1956, p. 3369.

———. Fulbright's Colloquy with Senator Mansfield on Policy Toward the Third World. 84th Cong., 2d Sess. *Congressional Record*, April 15, 1956, p. 6501.

———. Fulbright's Senate Address on Mideast. 85th Cong., 1st Sess. *Congressional Record*, August 14, 1957, pp. 14701–10.

———. Prepared remarks by J. W. Fulbright. 85th Cong., 2d Sess. *Congressional Record*, August 21, 1958, pp. 18903–5.

———. 86th Cong., 2d Sess. *Congressional Record*, March 5, 1960, pp. 4555–72.

———. 88th Cong., 2d Sess. *Congressional Record*, March 25, 1964, pp. 6236–45.

———. Fulbright on the National Commitments Resolution. 91st Cong., 1st Sess. *Congressional Record*, June 19, 1969, pp. 16615–19.

———. Fulbright's Comments on Nixon's Trip to China. 92d Cong., 1st Sess. *Congressional Record*, August 6, 1971, p. 30298.

II. Public Documents

Dulles, John Foster. "The Evolution of Foreign Policy." *Department of State Bulletin*, January 25, 1954.

Dodd, Thomas. "A Reply to Senator Fulbright on the Dominican Republic." U.S. Congress. Senate. 89th Cong., 1st Sess. *Congressional Record*, September 16, 1965, pp. 24168–73.

Javits, Jacob. "Uneasiness in Germany." U.S. Congress. Senate. 88th Cong., 2d Sess. *Congressional Record*, April 25, 1964, pp. 9070–1.

———. "U.S. Foreign Policy and Chile," U.S. Congress. Senate. 88th Cong., 2d Sess. *Congressional Record*, April 22, 1964.

Nixon, Richard M. *U.S. Foreign Policy For the 1970's: A New Strategy For Peace*. Washington, D.C.: Government Printing Office, 1970.

———. *U.S. Foreign Policy for the 1970's: Building For Peace*. Washington, D.C.: Government Printing Office, 1971.

———. *U.S. Foreign Policy for the 1970's: The Emerging Structure of Peace*. Washington, D.C.: Government Printing Office, 1972.

———. *U.S. Foreign Policy for the 1970's: Shaping a Durable Peace*. Washington, D.C.: Government Printing Office, 1973.

Public Papers of the Presidents, Harry S. Truman, 1945. Washington, D.C.: Government Printing Office, 1961.

"Secretary Rusk's News Conference of March 27." *Department of State Bulletin*, April 13, 1964, pp. 570–6.

U.S. Congress. House. Debate and Vote on the "Fulbright Resolution." 78th Congress, 1st Sess. *Congressional Record*, September 21, 1943, pp. 7705–29.

U.S. Congress. Senate. *Military Situation in the Far East; Hearings Before the Committee on Armed Services and Committee on Foreign Relations.* 82nd Cong., 1st Sess., 1951.

————. Committee on Appropriations. *Hearings on the Supplemental Appropriation Bill of 1954.* 83d Cong., 1st Sess., 1953.

————. Committee on Foreign Relations. *What is Wrong With Our Foreign Policy. Hearings.* 86th Cong., 1st Sess., 1959.

————. Committee on Foreign Relations. *Executive Sessions of the Senate Foreign Relations Committee, Volume XI.* 86th Cong., 1st Sess., 1959.

————. Committee on Foreign Relations. *Supplemental Foreign Assistance, Fiscal Year 1966—Vietnam, Hearings on S. 2793.* 89th Cong., 2d Sess., 1966.

————. Committee on Foreign Relations. *Changing American Attitudes Toward Foreign Policy; Hearings.* 90th Cong., 1st Sess., 1967.

————. Committee on Foreign Relations. *Foreign Assistance Act of 1968; Part I—Vietnam; Hearings on S 3091.* 90th Cong., 2d Sess., 1968.

————. Committee on Foreign Relations. *The Gulf of Tonkin, The 1964 Incidents; Hearings.* 90th Cong., 2d Sess., 1968.

————. Committee on Foreign Relations. *The Nature of Revolution; Hearings.* 90th Cong., 2d Sess., 1968.

————. Debate on the National Commitments Resolution. 91st Cong., 1st Sess. *Congressional Record,* June 19, 20, 25, 1969, *passim.*

————. Committee of Foreign Relations. *War Powers Legislation, 1973; Hearings.* 93d Cong., 1st Sess., 1973.

————. Committee on Foreign Relations. *Hearings: Detente.* 93d Cong., 2d Sess., 1974.

————. Committees on Foreign Relations and Armed Services. *Southeast Asia Resolution—Joint Hearings.* 88th Cong., 2d Sess., 1964.

————. General Debate on Gulf of Tonkin Resolution. 88th Congress, 2d Sess. *Congressional Record,* August 5–8, 1964, pp. 18132–9, 18398–18416; 18422–30; 18442–71; 18668–9; 18672; 18714–6.

————. 89th Cong., 1st Sess. *Congressional Record,* September 15, 1965, pp. 23861–6.

————. General Debate on Dominican Incursion. 89th Cong., 1st Sess. *Congressional Record,* September 17, 20, 21, 30, October 7, 1965, pp. 24221–46; 24429–30; 24505–6; 24557–8; 25620–3; 26237–41.

————. 89th Cong., 1st Sess. *Congressional Record,* October 22, 1965, pp. 28372–28406.

————. General Debate on Vietnam. 89th Cong., 2d Sess. *Congressional Record,* March 1, 1966, pp. 4379–86.

————. General Debate on China. 89th Cong., 2d Sess. *Congressional Record,* May 3, 1966, pp. 9605–18.

————. General Debate on S. Res. 151. 90th Cong., 1st Sess. *Congressional Record,* July 31, 1967, pp. 20702–19.

————. General Debate on Vietnam. 90th Cong., 2d Sess. *Congressional Record,* March 7, 1968, pp. 5644–59.

157

———. General Debate on National Commitments Resolution. 91st Cong., 1st Sess. *Congressional Record,* February 4, June 19, 20, 26, 1969, pp. 2603–4; 16615–72; 17219–27.

———. General debate on Southeast Asia. 91st Cong., 2d Sess. *Congressional Record,* April 2, 1970, pp. 10150–7.

———. General debate on Foreign Policy. 92d Cong., 2d Sess. *Congressional Record,* February 3, 1972, pp. 2510–2.

———. General debate on detente. 93d Cong., 1st Sess. *Congressional Record,* September 21, 1973, pp. S 17151–72.

———. General debate of War Powers Resolution. 93d Cong., 1st Sess. *Congressional Record,* October 10, 1973, pp. 18984–19006.

U.S. Department of State. *Foreign Relations of the United States: 1946.* Vol. 6. Washington, D.C.: Government Printing Office, 1970.

III. Polls

"Arab-Israeli Situation." *Gallup Opinion Index,* August 1968, p. 20.

"Greatest Threat—Russia or China?" *Gallup Opinion Index,* April 1967, p. 23.

Harris, Louis. "Americans are 85 Pct. With Johnson on Ordering Vietnam Air Strikes." *Washington Post,* August 10, 1964.

———. "58 Pct. of Public Backs U.S. Course in Viet-Nam." *Washington Post,* December 21, 1964.

"Impact of U.S. Involvement in Vietnam." *Gallup Opinion Index,* March 1972, p. 13.

"Impending Talks Have Lessened Fear of China." *Gallup Opinion Index,* October 1971, pp. 5-6.

"Isolationist Viewpoint Gains in Appeal." *Gallup Opinion Index,* March 1969, pp. 21–24.

"The Limits of Commitment: A *Time*-Louis Harris Poll." *Time,* May 2, 1969, pp. 16–17.

"Majority Would Reduce U.S. Troop Commitment to NATO." *Gallup Opinion Index,* November 1973, pp. 17-20.

"Military Spending." *Gallup Opinion Index,* March 1973, p. 10.

"National and Military Budget." *Gallup Opinion Index,* November 1973, p. 16.

"Public Would Have President Seek Congressional Approval Before Committing U.S. Forces Abroad." *Gallup Opinion Index,* December 1973, pp. 10–13.

"Red China." *Gallup Opinion Index,* April 1967, p. 22.

"Should U.S. Keep Troops in West Germany?" *Gallup Opinion Index,* November 1968, p. 8.

"Vietnam." *Gallup Opinion Index,* October 1969, pp. 14–15.

"Vietnam." *Gallup Opinion Index,* February 1973, p. 8.

"Vietnam—Did U.S. Make a Mistake?" *Gallup Opinion Index,* April 1968, p. 14.

"Vietnam—'Hawks,' 'Doves.' " *Gallup Opinion Index,* April 1968, p. 15.

IV. Books, Articles, Newspapers

"The Absentee." *Newsweek,* January 3, 1966, 15–16.

Acheson, Dean. *Present at the Creation.* New York: W. W. Norton, 1969.

"Advice and Dissent." *Newsweek,* February 21, 1966, 30–31.

Allison, Graham. "Cool It: The Foreign Policy of Young America." *Foreign Policy,* 1 (Winter 1970–71), 144–60.

Almond, Gabriel. *The American People and Foreign Policy.* New York: Harcourt, Brace, 1950.

"Are Our Policies Turning Obsolete?" *Business Week,* April 4, 1964, 28.

"As Fulbright Sees U.S. Policy Abroad." *U.S. News and World Report,* February 15, 1959, 87.

Bailyn, Bernard. *The Ideological Origins of the American Revolution.* Cambridge: Harvard University Press, 1967.

Baker, Russell. "An Ozark 'Professor' Studies Wall Street." *New York Times,* March 6, 1955, p. 17.

———. "Green, 91, Quits as Senate Chief of Foreign Policy." *New York Times,* January 31, 1959, p. 1.

———. "Fulbright Calls for Calmness in Race to Match Gains by Reds." *New York Times,* June 30, 1961, p. 1.

———. "Goldwater Says Kennedy Drifts." *New York Times,* July 15, 1961, p. 12.

Barone, Michael, Ujifusa, Grant, and Matthews, Douglas. *The Almanac of American Politics: 1972.* Boston: Gambit, 1972.

———. *The Almanac of American Politics: 1974.* Boston: Gambit, 1973.

Bigart, Homer. "Fulbright Warns of 'Fatal' Course by U.S. in Vietnam." *New York Times,* April 29, 1966, p. 1.

Brandon, Henry. *The Retreat of American Power.* Garden City: Doubleday, 1973.

Brody, Richard. "Popular Control of Public Policy: A Normal Vote Analysis of the 1968 Election." *American Political Science Review,* 66 (June 1972), 429–49.

Brower, Brock. "The Roots of the Arkansas Questioner." *Life,* May 13, 1966, 92–94ff.

Brown, Seyom. *The Faces of Power.* New York: Columbia University Press, 1968.

Burns, James MacGregor. *Leadership.* New York: Harper and Row, 1978.

Campbell, Alex. "Fulbright on Camera." *New Republic,* May 21, 1966, 19–22.

"Can He Be Serious?" *National Review,* August 9, 1966, pp. 757–58.

Carr, E. H. *The Twenty Years' Crisis.* New York: Harper & Row, 1964.

Chamberlain, John. "These Days—Fulbright's Chancy Bet on History." *Washington Post,* September 25, 1965.

Childs, Marquis. "Tyranny of the Majority in the United States." *Washington Post,* September 27, 1965.

"Chinks in Fulbright's Armor." *Christian Century,* April 22, 1964, p. 509.

Church, Frank. "How Many Dominican Republics and Vietnams Can We Take On?" *New York Times Magazine,* November 28, 1965, pp. 45ff.

Claude, Inis L., Jr. *Power and International Relations.* New York: Random House, 1962.

Coffin, Tristram. *Senator Fulbright: Portrait of a Public Philosopher.* New York: E. P. Dutton, 1966.

Commager, Henry Steele. "How Not To Be A World Power." *New York Times Magazine,* March 12, 1967, pp. 28ff.

Cottam, Richard W. *Foreign Policy Motivation.* Pittsburgh: University of Pittsburgh Press, 1977.

Crawford, Kenneth. "Fulbright's Rightness." *Newsweek,* October 16, 1961, 32.

———. "Democratic Dialogue." *Newsweek,* April 13, 1964, 32.

———. "Replacement Needed." *Newsweek,* October 10, 1966, 44.

———. "Neo-Isolationism." *Newsweek,* April 21, 1969, 40.

———. "Nixon's 'Knaves.' " *Newsweek,* June 23, 1969, 38.

"Criticism and Praise For Dulles' Views." *U.S. News and World Report,* March 9, 1956, 111–13.

Daniel, Clifton. "Fulbright Says U.S. May Be Facing Peril." *New York Times,* January 1, 1975.

Davenport, Walter. "Just a Boy From the Ozarks." *Collier's,* February 10, 1945, 14ff.

"Debate and Disquiet." *Newsweek,* February 6, 1967, 35.

"The Dilettante." *Nation,* September 7, 1970, 166.

"The Disinvited Guest." *Time,* December 31, 1965, 14.

Divine, Robert A. "The Education of John F. Kennedy." in Frank J. Merli and Theodore A. Wilson, eds. *Makers of American Diplomacy.* New York: Charles Scribner's Sons, 1974.

———. *Eisenhower and the Cold War.* New York: Oxford University Press, 1981.

"Dominican Republic—Erratic Attack." *Time,* September 24, 1965, 44.

Draper, Theodore. "The American Crisis: Vietnam, Cuba and the Dominican Republic." *Commentary,* January, 1967, 27–47.

———. *The Dominican Revolt: A Case Study in American Policy.* New York: Viking, 1968.

Drury, Allen. "Fulbright Terms Foreign Policy 'Unwise' and Harmful to West." *New York Times,* December 15, 1956, p. 13.

Dulles, John Foster. "A Policy of Boldness." *Life,* May 10, 1952, 146–60.

Evans, Rowland, and Novak, Robert. "Inside Report; The Fulbright Furor." *Washington Post,* September 20, 1965.

"Excerpts From Rusk Testimony on Vietnam and Exchanges With Senate Panel." *New York Times,* March 12, 1968, p. 16.

"Exchange Over Airways." *New York Times,* February 17, 1943, p. 13.

"Exhaustive, Explicit and Enough." *Time,* February 25, 1966, 21–23.

Fairlie, Henry. "Old Myths and New Realities." *Reporter,* June 16, 1966, 19–21.

———. "The Senator and World Power." *Encounter,* May 1968, 57–66.

"The Fall of Fulbright." *Arkansas Gazette,* May 30, 1974.

Finney, John W. "Criticism of War Widens in Senate on Build-Up Issue." *New York Times,* March 8, 1968, p. 1.

————. "Senate Panel Asks U.S. Commitments Be Put to Congress." *New York Times*, March 13, 1969, p. 1.

————. "President's Speech Stirs Resentment in Congress." *New York Times*, June 5, 1969, p. 1.

————. "Curbs on Policy Feared By Nixon." *New York Times*, June 20, 1969, p. 19.

————."Senate, 70 to 16, Calls For a Curb on Commitments." *New York Times*, June 26, 1969, p. 1.

Fletcher, James. "The Politics of Emptiness." *National Review*, February 13, 1968, pp. 133–36, 151.

Franck, Thomas M., and Weisband, Edward. *Foreign Policy by Congress*. New York: Oxford University Press, 1979.

"Fulbright and Myths." *Commonweal*, April 17, 1964, 101–2.

"Fulbright Fears Isolationist Fight." *New York Times*, October 19, 1943, p. 8.

"Fulbright, Hatch Now Hit UNO Veto." *New York Times*, November 24, 1945, p. 5.

"Fulbright Hints U.S. Weighs Use of Troops in Asia." *New York Times*, May 5, 1961, p. 1.

"Fulbright: 'Mistaken Policies' Behind U.S. Troubles in World." *U.S. News and World Report*, August 15, 1958, 86.

"Fulbright on the Dominican Crisis." *New York Times*, September 18, 1965.

"Fulbright the Undecider." *Life*, May 13, 1966, 4.

"Fulbright's Dilemma." *Newsweek*, August 28, 1967, 18–19.

"Fulbright's Leadership." *New Republic*, May 4, 1959, 5–6.

"Fulbright's Progress." *Nation*, April 13, 1964, 357–58.

"Fulbright's Solution: 'Honorable Compromise.' " *U.S. News and World Report*, February 5, 1968, 31.

Gaddis, John Lewis. *The United States and the Origins of the Cold War*. New York: Columbia University Press, 1972.

Galbraith, John Kenneth. "Foreign Policy: The Stuck Whistle." *Atlantic*, February, 1965, 64–68.

————. "A Positive Approach To Foreign Aid." *Foreign Affairs* (April 1961), 444–57.

Gilbert, Felix. "Bicentennial Reflections." *Foreign Affairs*, 54 (July 1976), 635–44.

Gleijeses, Piero. *The Dominican Crises: The 1965 Constitutionalist Revolt and American Intervention*. Baltimore: Johns Hopkins University Press, 1979.

Goldbloom, Maurice J. "The Fulbright Revolt." *Commentary*, September 1966, 63–69.

Goodwin, Richard N. *Triumph or Tragedy: Reflections on Vietnam*. New York: Vintage Books, 1966.

Goshko, John M. "Supporters of U.S. Dominican Stance Lower Boom on Fulbright's Criticism." *Washington Post*, September 17, 1965.

Goulden, Joseph C. *Truth is the First Casualty: The Gulf of Tonkin Affair—Illusion and Reality*. Chicago: Rand, 1969.

Graubard, Stephen R. *Kissinger: Portrait of a Mind*. New York: W. W. Norton, 1973.

"Growing Foreign Policy Row: Two Top Democrats Urge Changes." *U.S. News and World Report*, April 6, 1964, 19.

Grundy, Kenneth W. "The Apprenticeship of J. William Fulbright." *Virginia Quarterly Review* (Summer 1967), 382–99.

Halberstam, David. *The Best and the Brightest*. New York: Random House, 1972.

Hale, William Harlan. "The Man From Arkansas Goes After Mr. Dulles." *Reporter*, April 18, 1957, 30–32.

Hamilton, Thomas J. "Plan To Sell War Stocks For Foreign Scholarships." *New York Times*, December 20, 1945, p. 1.

Hartz, Louis. *The Liberal Tradition in America*. New York: Harcourt, Brace & World, 1955.

"The High Price of Power." *New Republic*, September 10, 1966, 5–6.

Hoffmann, Stanley. "Will the Balance Balance at Home?" *Foreign Policy*, 7 (Summer 1972), 60–86.

Holsti, Ole R. "The Belief System and National Images: A Case Study." *Journal of Conflict Resolution*, 6 (1962), 244–52.

"House Group Backs World Peace." *New York Times*, June 16, 1943, pp. 1, 4.

"House Votes 360–29 For Collaboration in Peace After War." *New York Times*, September 22, 1943, p. 1.

Hyman, Sidney. "The Advice and Consent of J. William Fulbright." *Reporter*, September 17, 1959, 23–25.

———. "Fulbright, The Wedding of Arkansas and The World." *New Republic*, May 14, 1962, 19–26.

"Ideological Trap." *Commonweal*, May 19, 1967, 252–53.

Jervis, Robert. *Perception and Misperception in International Relations*. Princeton, N.J.: Princeton University Press, 1976.

Johnson, Haynes, and Gwertzman, Bernard M. *Fulbright the Dissenter*. Garden City, N.Y.: Doubleday, 1968.

Johnson, James A. "The New Generation of Isolationists." *Foreign Affairs*, 49 (October 1970), 136–46.

Johnson, Lyndon B. *The Vantage Point*. New York: Holt, Rinehart and Winston, 1971.

Johnson, Walter and Colligan, Francis J. *The Fulbright Program: A History*. Chicago: University of Chicago Press, 1965.

Jones, Joseph M. *The Fifteen Weeks*. New York: Viking, 1955.

Kaplan, Morton A. "Old Realities and New Myths." *World Politics*, 17 (January 1965), 334ff.

———. *System and Process in International Politics*. New York: Wiley, 1957.

Karnow, Stanley. "The Kissinger-Fulbright Courtship." *New Republic*, December 29, 1973, 15–18.

Kearns, Doris. *Lyndon Johnson and the American Dream*. New York: New American Library, 1976.

Kennan, George F. *Memoirs, 1925–1950*. Boston: Little, Brown, 1967.

————. "The Sources of Soviet Conduct." *Foreign Affairs,* 25 (July 1947), 466–82.

Kenworthy, E. W. "Fulbright Becomes a National Issue." *New York Times Magazine,* October 1, 1961, pp. 21ff.

————. "The Fulbright Idea of Foreign Policy." *New York Times Magazine,* May 10, 1959, pp. 10–11ff.

————. "President Requests Support of Congress." *New York Times,* August 6, 1964, p. 1.

————. "Fulbright Urges a Holding Action in Vietnam War." *New York Times,* June 16, 1965, p. 1.

————. "Fulbright: Dissenter." *New York Times,* October 31, 1965, sec. 4, p. 4.

————. "McNamara Balks at Public Inquiry." *New York Times,* February 5, 1966, p. 1.

————. "Fulbright Fears Conflict With China Over Vietnam." *New York Times,* February 8, 1966, p. 1.

————. "Rusk Says Peace of World is Issue in Vietnam War." *New York Times,* February 19, 1966, p. 1.

Kissinger, Henry A. "Domestic Structure and Foreign Policy." *Daedalus,* 95 (Spring 1966), 503–29.

————. *White House Years.* Boston: Little, Brown, 1979.

Kopkind, Andrew. "The Speechmaker." *New Republic,* October 2, 1965, 15–19.

Kraft, Joseph. "Inside and Outlook—Fulbright and His Critics." *Washington Post,* September 25, 1965.

Krock, Arthur, "In The Nation." *New York Times,* June 18, 1943, p. 20.

————. "In The Nation." *New York Times,* May 2, 1961, p. 36.

Landau, David. *Kissinger: The Uses of Power.* Boston: Houghton Mifflin, 1972.

Lawrence, W. H. "Kennedy Planning to Give Bowles Foreign Policy Job." *New York Times,* November 30, 1960, p. 1.

Leviero, Anthony. "Vandenburg Move Clarifies Aid Plan." *New York Times,* April 8, 1947, p. 5.

————. "Fulbright Offers Specific Charges Against McCarthy." *New York Times,* August 1, 1954, p. 1.

Levy, David W. "The Debate Over Vietnam: One Perspective." *Yale Review* (Spring 1974), 333–46.

Lippmann, Walter. *The Cold War: A Study in U.S. Foreign Policy.* New York: Harper, 1947.

————. "A Senator Speaks Out." *Newsweek,* April 13, 1964, 19.

————. "Soviet-American Relations." *Washington Post,* September 28, 1965.

Liska, George. *Quest For Equilibrium: America and the Balance of Power on Land and Sea.* Baltimore: Johns Hopkins University Press, 1977.

Lubasch, Arnold H. "Red PT Boats Fire at U.S. Destroyer on Vietnam Duty." *New York Times,* August 3, 1964, p. 1.

Lynn, Naomi and McClure, Arthur. *The Fulbright Premise.* Bucknell University Press, 1973.

McCarry, Charles. "Mourning Becomes Senator Fulbright." *Esquire,* June, 1970, 116–19, 178–79.

Masters, Roger D. *The Nation is Burdened.* New York: Knopf, 1967.

Mazlish, Bruce. *Kissinger: The European Mind in American Policy.* New York: Basic Books, 1976.

Morgenthau, Hans J. "Mr. Nixon's Foreign Policy." *New Republic*, March 21, 1970, 23–25.

———. *A New Foreign Policy For The United States.* New York: Praeger, 1969.

———. "Nixon and the World." *New Republic*, January 6, 1973, 17–20.

———. "Senator Fulbright's New Foreign Policy." *Commentary*, May 1964, 68–71.

———. "Globalism: Johnson's Moral Crusade." *New Republic*, July 3, 1965, 19–22.

———. "To Intervene or Not To Intervene." *Foreign Affairs*, 45 (April 1967), 425–36.

Morris, Roger. *Uncertain Greatness: Henry Kissinger and American Foreign Policy.* New York: Harper and Row, 1977.

Nathan, James A., and Oliver, James K. *United States Foreign Policy and World Order.* 2d ed. Boston: Little, Brown, 1981.

"National Commitment." *Washington Post*, August 2, 1967.

"New Age in the Senate." *New York Times*, January 31, 1959, p. 4.

"The New Realism." *Time*, February 18, 1966, 19–20.

Nixon, Richard M. "Asia After Viet Nam." *Foreign Affairs*, 46 (October 1967), 111–25.

———. *RN: The Memoirs of Richard Nixon.* New York: Grosset and Dunlap, 1978.

Oberdorfer, Don. "Common Noun Spelled f-u-l-b-r-i-g-h-t." *New York Times Magazine*, April 4, 1965, pp. 79–80ff.

"On the Subject of Arrogance." *Time*, May 13, 1966, p. 31.

Page, Benjamin I. "Policy Voting and the Electoral Process." *American Political Science Review*, 66 (September 1972), 979–95.

"Panic Button." *Washington Post*, September 17, 1965.

Pfaff, William. "Muddied American Messianism." *Commonweal*, March 22, 1968, 8–9.

"Planning for Peace Seen Gaining in U.S." *New York Times*, February 28, 1943, p. 33.

Polsby, Nelson. "Towards an Explanation of McCarthyism." *Political Studies*, 8 (October 1960), 250–71.

Polsby, Nelson, Gallaher, Miriam, and Rundquist, Barry. "The Growth of the Seniority System in the U.S. House of Representatives." *American Political Science Review*, 63 (September 1969), 787–807.

"Portrait of the Chairman." *Time*, February 18, 1966, 21–22.

"Post-War Pledge Put Up to Senate." *New York Times*, October 15, 1943, p. 1.

"President Favors A General Pledge." *New York Times*, October 30, 1943, p. 5.

Reed, Roy. "Fulbright, the Scholar in Foreign Affairs." *New York Times*, June 2, 1974, sec. 4, p. 3.

"The Reporter's Notes." *Reporter*, February 24, 1966, 16.

Reston, James. "Dulles and Fulbright—Feud or Truce?" *New York Times*, February 1, 1959, p. 10E.

Reston, Richard. "Report on Washington." *Atlantic*, October 16, 1966, 10–12.
"Rethinking the Unthinkable." *Reporter*, September 21, 1967, 14–16.
Robinson, James A., and Snyder, Richard C. "Decision-Making in International Politics." In *International Behavior: A Social-Psychological Analysis*. Ed. by Herbert C. Kelman. New York: Holt, Rinehart, and Winston, 1965.
Rogin, Michael Paul. *The Intellectuals and McCarthy*. Cambridge, Mass.: M.I.T. Press, 1967.
Rostow, Walt W. *The Stages of Economic Growth: A Non-Communist Manifesto*. London: Cambridge University Press, 1960.
Rovere, Richard. "Letter From Washington." *New Yorker*, April 11, 1964, 149–55.
_____. *Senator Joe McCarthy*. New York: Harcourt, Brace, 1959.
Russett, Bruce. "The Americans' Retreat From World Power." *Political Science Quarterly*, 91 (Spring 1975), 1–21.
_____, and Nincic, Miroslav. "American Opinion on the Use of American Force Abroad." *Political Science Quarterly*, 91 (Fall 1976), 411–31.
Sanford, David. "A Talk With Senator Fulbright." *New Republic*, March 9, 1968, 19–20.
Schlesinger, Arthur, Jr. "Liberal Anti-Communism Revisited: A Symposium." *Commentary*, September 1967, pp. 68–71.
_____. *A Thousand Days*. Boston: Houghton Mifflin, 1965.
Seib, Charles B., and Otten, Alan L. "Fulbright: Arkansas Paradox." *Harper's*, June 1956, 60–66.
Semple, Robert B., Jr. "Nixon, Defending Policies, Hits 'New Isolationists'; Pledges A World Role." *New York Times*, June 5, 1969, p. 1.
"Senate Moves to Restrict Foreign Commitments." *Congressional Quarterly Almanac, 1969*. Washington, D.C.: Congressional Quarterly, 1970.
"Senate Spectacular." *New Republic*, February 4, 1967, 6.
"Senate Votes 85 to 5 to Cooperate in Peace." *New York Times*, November 6, 1943, p. 1.
"Senator Fulbright Dissents." *Nation*, October 4, 1965, 177–78.
"Senator Fulbright's Wave of the Future." *Chicago Tribune*, September 17, 1965.
"Senators Draw Up A Post-War Pledge of Collaboration." *New York Times*, October 14, 1943, p. 1.
Sevareid, Eric. "Congress: Soul Searching in Order." *Washington Evening Star*, October 4, 1965.
_____. "Why Our Foreign Policy is Failing: An Exclusive Interview With Senator Fulbright." *Look*, May 3, 1966, 23–27.
Shannon, William V. "New Myths For Old." *Commonweal*, April 17, 1964, 102–3.
Sheehan, Neil. "The Covert War and Tonkin Gulf: February-August, 1964." *The Pentagon Papers as Published by the New York Times*. New York: Quadrangle Books, 1971.
"Should Fulbright Be Muzzled?" *National Review*, August 24, 1965, p. 718.
Smith, Beverly, Jr. "Egghead From the Ozarks." *Saturday Evening Post*, May 2, 1959, 31ff.

Snyder, Richard C., Bruck, H. W., and Sapin, Burton. *Foreign Policy Decision-Making.* New York: Free Press, 1963.

Sorenson, Theodore C. *Kennedy.* New York: Harper & Row, 1965.

"Sovereignty Gone, Fulbright Holds." *New York Times,* December 12, 1945, p. 6.

Steel, Ronald. *Pax Americana.* New York: Viking, 1967.

"Stemwinder." *Washington Post,* September 16, 1965.

Stevens, Charles J. "The Use and Control of Executive Agreements: Recent Congressional Initiatives." *Orbis* (Winter 1977), 905–31.

Stillman, Edmund, and Pfaff, William. *Power and Impotence: The Failure of America's Foreign Policy.* New York: Random House, 1966.

Szulc, Tad. *The Illusion of Peace: Foreign Policy in the Nixon Years.* New York: Viking, 1978.

"Texts of Fulbright and Truman Statements on Mideast Policy." *New York Times,* January 25, 1957, p. 6.

Trask, Daniel. "The Congress as Classroom: J. William Fulbright and the Crisis of American Power." In Frank J. Merli and Theodore A. Wilson, eds. *Makers of American Diplomacy.* New York: Charles Scribner's Sons, 1974.

Truman, Harry S. *Memoirs: Year of Decisions.* New York: Doubleday, 1955.

_____. *Memoirs: Years of Trial and Hope, 1946–1952.* Garden City, N.Y.: Doubleday, 1956.

Tucker, Robert W. "The American Outlook." *America and the World: From the Truman Doctrine to Vietnam.* Baltimore: Johns Hopkins Press, 1970.

Tweraser, Kurt. *Changing Patterns of Political Beliefs: The Foreign Policy Operational Codes of J. William Fulbright, 1943–1967.* Beverly Hills: Sage, 1974.

"The Ultimate Self-Interest." *Time,* January 22, 1965, 14–18.

"U.S. Policy: Old Myths, Mixed Voices." *Newsweek,* April 6, 1964, 17.

"Vandenberg Gives New Post-War Idea." *New York Times,* July 3, 1943, p. 6.

"Vietnam Has Forced Distortion of Our Foreign Policy." *U.S. News and World Report,* June 28, 1971, 25–26.

The Vietnam Hearings. New York: Vintage Books, 1966.

Walton, Richard J. *Cold War and Counterrevolution: The Foreign Policy of John F. Kennedy.* New York: Viking, 1972.

"War Not Crusade, Taft Tells Bar." *New York Times,* August 27, 1943, p. 2.

"We and They." *New Republic,* April 18, 1964, 3–4.

Weisband, Edward. *The Ideology of American Foreign Policy: A Paradigm of Lockian Liberalism.* Beverly Hills: Sage, 1973.

White, William S. "Dulles Assailed in Senate on View Soviet is Losing." *New York Times,* February 28, 1956, p. 1.

_____. "Dulles Faces Fire on Mideast Plan; House Unit For It." *New York Times,* January 25, 1957, p. 1.

_____. "Fulbright's Folly—An Irresponsible Speech." *Washington Post,* September 17, 1965.

"Who Are the Isolationists?" *Nation,* September 12, 1966, 202–3.

Wicker, Tom. "U.S. Planes Attack North Vietnam Bases; President Orders 'Limited' Retaliation After Communists; PT Boats Renew Raids." *New York Times*, August 5, 1964, p. 1.

Wilson, H. H. "Starting at Fulton, Missouri." *Nation*, April 3, 1972, 438–39.

Wood, Gordon. *The Creation of the American Republic*. Chapel Hill: University of North Carolina Press, 1969.

Yergin, Daniel. "Fulbright's Last Frustration." *New York Times Magazine*, November 24, 1974, pp. 14ff.

Index